contents

what is poor girl gourmet?

Well, the gourmet—or lover of good food—part came pretty easily. My mother was a scratch-baker, homemade-meals kind of woman—in fact, we still laugh about how my three siblings and I banded together to demand a never-before-experienced-in-our-household meal of TV dinners around the time I was twelve or thirteen. My first taste of junky baked goods came in second grade. I didn't even know what those yellow, frosting-filled cakes were before grade school. My mother saw to it that my childhood was full of wholesome food—and inexpensive food at that, for we were not wealthy by any stretch and there were many mouths to feed.

My mother was influenced, of course, by her mother. My grandmother was a fabulous cook, and owned an Italian restaurant for which she created all of the recipes. That my grandmother, who was not trained as a chef, had an Italian restaurant was a source of great, sometimes gloating, pride for me as a child. I'd like to think it was because I was duly impressed by her determination as a woman in the late 1960s opening a restaurant without any training, but something tells me it might have been more about free spaghetti and meatballs at that time. Now, it's most definitely about her being a home cook who followed her dream at a time when that wasn't the easiest path for her to take. Those early dining experiences at her restaurant impressed upon me the joy that sharing food with family and loved ones brings, as our entire family would often gather there on Sunday for a six- or seven-course dinner.

By the time I was an adult with a proper professional career—for thirteen years I produced promotional campaigns and graphic packages for television clients such as A&E, The CBS Evening News, Discovery Channel, History, and ESPN—my love of food was well established. Fortunate, then, that my income allowed me to travel and learn more about food—at home and abroad. My husband, JR, and I fell in love with Italy—not terribly surprising, given my Italian Nana's influence, of course—and it was there that I learned more and more about fresh, local foods, as each region of Italy has its own cuisine. Wild game and earthy truffles inland, the freshest of seafood at the coast, and cheeses unique to their own locale throughout the countryside. With good food comes good wine, and I do love me some wine. JR and I have been lucky enough to visit wineries in Italy and France—you should know that this is something that anyone can do: you simply need to contact the winery in advance and ask for a visit; many are happy to comply—and over the years, I have read up on wine when I very likely should have been reading up on television industry news. I don't consider myself an expert; I'm just a dedicated, and possibly too enthusiastic, fan.

As you might imagine, advertising spending directly impacts the television industry, so when the economy began to sour for

everyone else, its toll had already been felt in my world of television promotion. I had been a freelancer for most of those thirteen years, which meant that despite having no work, I could not collect unemployment benefits and so JR and I needed to plan out our spending carefully, including—and probably most importantly—food spending. While I was trucking along, making a good living in television, I routinely spent between $160 and $200 per week on groceries. For two people. I shopped at Whole Foods. I bought fancy cheeses, imported prosciutto, and generally anything that struck my fancy while I was in the store. I did not shop sales, and I often bought food that we did not need (I admit this in the event that the mere mention of fancy cheeses didn't expose me). I thought nothing of cooking up a standing rib roast on any given Sunday in the cooler weather— hey, rib roast goes well with football, you know—and lamb chops, osso buco, and Del-

monico steaks made regular appearances on our menu. I have an image of me—purely imaginary—with a loaded grocery cart, and I am grabbing just about any food I see, while dancing and singing, oblivious to the obscenity of my spending ways.

However, even in those heady days of willy-nilly food spending, I did embrace much of the food known as *cucina povera*, literally, the poor kitchen. *Cucina povera* arose from peasant cooking in Italy, though every culture has some version of this style of cooking, as it was historically a necessity for the majority of people. It also happened that the food I most enjoyed while traveling in Italy was the simple country cooking, and so I incorporated some of those dishes into my repertoire as well.

Thus, it was a short jump from luxury-food girl to this new food-shopping paradigm. I already had the tools for cooking good food on a budget, I simply hadn't employed them—nor had it been required of me—until my television work evaporated. Needing a creative outlet—sitting on my hands is just not my way—I took the sudden and mammoth gap in my work schedule as an opportunity to start a food blog—Poor Girl Gourmet—based on the way JR and I had started eating.

Over the years spent as this dancing, singing, cart-filling fool, I had developed a shopping routine, one that included shopping at Whole Foods, my local farm stand, and also at a favorite Italian specialty market. I didn't want to change this routine. It was important to me that food not become a source of stress, and that shopping not become depressing. I didn't want to chide myself as I walked those formerly gilded aisles. Food shopping still had to have some magic, because there is nothing more magical than taking raw ingredients and creating something that gives yourself and others pleasure. I also developed relationships with the people who work at those stores and stands. I love chatting with my favorite butchers at Whole Foods, or my artist and writer friend at the farm stand, or the folks at each department of the Italian specialty shop who all are so sweet and helpful.

So I kept shopping at my usual spots, but I adjusted my approach. I made a shopping list and stuck to it—no unnecessary items make it into my cart these days—and I may miss fancy cheeses, but now, when I do splurge for them, it is usually a special occasion and I enjoy them even more. We eliminated our fit-for-a-Renaissance-era-pope meat purchases, and we also greatly reduced the amount of meat we eat. On these pages, you will find a number of meat-free or low-meat dishes. I am a carnivore, and it would be an understatement to say

that JR is a big fan of meat—at one point he raised his own Black Angus cattle at our house—oh, and the property isn't quite big enough for cattle, by the way—so it was vitally important that these low- or no-meat dinners be delicious.

While it was important to me that I rein in my food spending—significantly—I didn't want my food values to be compromised. I don't want to eat junk, and so I had to figure that out as well. I rely heavily on Whole Foods 365 Everyday Value brand products. I find that they are less expensive than comparable store brand products at my regional grocery chain, and Whole Foods—they aren't paying me, by the way; this is just how I choose to shop on a budget—promotes food values that I also embrace. I do not want bovine growth hormone in my milk. I'd like not to eat genetically modified meats. I am a carnivore, yet I still want to know that the meat I'm buying comes from animals that are treated humanely. I prefer that the people producing my food are able to make a living. For this reason, I spread my produce shopping around, and frequent farmers markets and my favorite farm stand. That farm stand provides JR and me delicious produce, and it's generally less expensive than at Whole Foods. This is not to say that I do not buy produce at Whole Foods, because I do. I am just very cognizant of what's on sale, and plan accordingly.

The changes I've made to the way I shop are painless, and, more than that, they've reduced our weekly food bill by more than half. Now, I spend between $65 and $90 per week—and this is for all three meals, every day of the week. I'm sure that you, too, have your own techniques for how to save money on food spending. For me, the key is to cook at home. Even when I was doling out cash like it was going out of style, our meals were usually of restaurant quality for significantly less money. Wow. I just had a scare thinking about how ugly my food bill would have been if we ate out all the time. Yikes. Cooking is not difficult nor is it complex, and is most definitely not more expensive than purchasing prepared foods. There is more than one study out there in the world indicating that inexpensive prepared food—think of the freezer section of your grocery store—is bad for our health, that the chemicals and trans fats in these foods are increasing disease and obesity. My hope is that this book will help debunk the myth that fresh, healthful food is expensive or difficult to prepare. Fresh,

healthful options *are* available for less; you just need to shop smart and put a little effort into the making of food. It's easy. I'm telling you: If I do it, anyone can.

Now, speaking of inexpensive and good, that brings us to the pricing. Each of the meals on these pages serves at least four people for $15 or less. I am not a mathematician—in fact, I had to take a remedial math class during my freshman year of college— however, I have done my best to price each recipe on these pages down to the penny. I employ my own shopping strategies in the pricing, but in order to be absolutely certain that you aren't cursing me later for requiring you to clip coupons, buy meat only on sale (ahem, although, honestly, you should really *only* buy meat on sale unless that meat costs

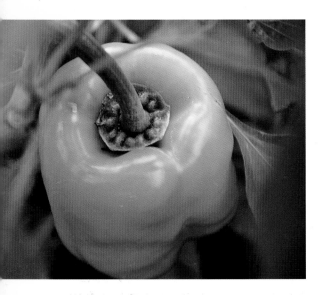

around a few bucks a pound), or make eight pounds of beans in your pressure cooker on Sunday and use them in every meal all week long, I have made sure of a few things.

For one, I kept the price of meat at the non-sale price, though I do *only* shop for what's on sale, unless it's something like the ground meat I use for my meatballs, which costs $3.79 per pound. I do use canned beans in addition to dried, though I do not think that we can live on beans alone.

I include the cost of every ingredient in the pricing here, save for salt and pepper. Remember, I am a big, huge fan of Whole Foods 365 Everyday Value items, so most of the pricing is based upon the cost of those products, especially pantry items.

In most cases, you can do better than the price estimates on these pages, but I firmly believe in under-promising and over-delivering, and I do not want you to think (and be annoyed) that these prices are

difficult to achieve. Quite to the contrary, in fact; and there is generally enough leeway between the meal price and our $15 limit that you'll still be under, even if the prices of a few ingredients vary slightly, as they are likely to do from my area to yours.

It's important, too, to have a number of tools at your disposal when trying to eat well for less, so I've included suggestions for alternate uses of sauces so that if you aren't in the mood for, let's say, chicken one night, you know that the honey-balsamic sauce will go well with pork. It's always good to have some mix-and-match options.

If you have the space, I do highly recommend growing your own food—any food at all, even just a lone potted herb on the windowsill—for it will cut down on your overall food bill. And by the mere mention of "windowsill," it should be obvious that you do have at least a wee bit of space upon which you can grow your own. If you have more space than a windowsill and can plant a kitchen garden, in addition to saving you money, it also allows you to keep your food free from pesticides. And then, there is nothing quite like having a still-warm tomato in your salad, or beans that were on the vine minutes before you're eating them.

I do hope you'll enjoy the recipes on these pages. They've done the trick at my house, and the transition from shopping fool to parsimonious gal—or Poor Girl Gourmet, as it were—has been painless. And most important, it has been delicious. For it would all be for naught if the food weren't good.

Buon appetito!

poor girl gourmet pointers

Tips to Help You Conserve Some Coin

To get us all on the proverbial same page as we work toward feeding four people for $15 or less, I want to share with you some of the ways that I endeavor to cut back on my food bill.

One of my primary goals when I realized that I had to rein in my spending was to be certain that creating meals and shopping didn't feel like punishment—I didn't want to have to radically change what I was doing in terms of where I shopped or the quality of what I was purchasing—so my recommendations here reflect that. I could not think of anything more depressing than to go to a store that didn't have good produce or meats in the name of saving money. I do not expect you or me—food lovers that we are—to subsist on beans and rice or MSG-rich packaged noodle meals.

Instead, I adapted my existing habits— shopping at my local farm stand, Italian market, and grocery stores where I enjoy the shopping experience, and employed one of the basic tenets of *cucina povera:* Use good, fresh ingredients, prepared with care and attention to detail, and your meals will never disappoint.

So let's get started on our low-budget, high-quality food adventure.

Learn to cook at home.

Okay, so there could be no more obvious bit of advice, could there be? But really, if you can make a good meal at home—and I intend to help you do that with the recipes in this book—you might find that restaurant meals can be a bit disappointing from time to time. Don't get me wrong, your favorite restaurant still rocks, but those random meals out "just because" are never as good as you hope, am I wrong? And home-cooked leftovers make for great workday lunches, further helping stretch your budget. Add to that, cooking is *easy*. Really. It is. I promise.

Do not waste food.

This also sounds obvious, I realize, and you are probably well aware of this yourself—we all routinely throw out food that has gone bad awaiting its use. When shopping, purchase only what you need, and if you have leftovers that freeze well, freeze them. If you have stale bread on your counter, make breadcrumbs or croutons. Store leftover wine in the refrigerator for use in sauces or stews. Compost vegetable and fruit scraps, or save vegetable scraps and freeze them to make Vegetable Scrap Stock (page 1). Consider what other purpose your leftovers could serve before tossing them in the waste bin.

Plan meals for a week.

Or even for the next three or four days. But do plan in advance. This will help you not to waste food, and to avoid buying what you do not need—which you know will then be wasted if it's not eaten before it spoils.

Shop sales.

This is a technique that my mother used consistently when I was a child and it helped her stretch her dollars while feeding four chowhound kids. Check store fliers or Web sites before making your grocery list for those pre-planned meals, and plan around what meat you can get for the least amount of money.

Have I mentioned, "Buy what you need"?

Once you've planned your meals for the week, make a shopping list, and stick to it. And, yes, sometimes I *do* have to talk myself down from that impulse purchase, but I do, and my bank account thanks me for it.

That said, buy in bulk.

Buy items that you know you will use frequently in bulk. If you know you will use twelve cans of crushed tomatoes in short order, buy them by the case, either at a wholesale club or even at your grocery store. Some grocery stores will discount a case of any one product. If you eat spaghetti all the time, and no other type of pasta will do, purchase a case and stow it away. You're going to use it anyway, so you might as well save some cash in the process. And do not be afraid to buy meat in bulk, or family packs, and freeze what you won't use. Just be sure that you use the frozen meat within a month

or two. Too much time in the freezer does not improve the flavor, my dear. But if your family loves chicken legs (or pork cutlets, or whole chicken, or ground meats, or sausage, or bacon, or pancetta . . . you get the idea) and you're getting a good price, by all means, stock up and freeze away.

Cut coupons.

But for the love of all that is good in this world, people, only for things that you actually *use*. It is just not a savings if you would never have spent the money in the first place. Truthfully, I am not much of a coupon clipper, but when I see a coupon that makes sense for me, I am all over that bad boy. I especially like coupons that offer a certain dollar amount off of the total purchase price, because you cannot go wrong with that. Those tend to be available around store grand openings, seasonally, and through mailings from stores with which you hold a customer loyalty card.

Shop in ethnic markets.

Or at least the ethnic aisle of your grocery store where items like beans, olives, and spices are sold at a lower price than their more mainstream brand name counterparts. If you need turmeric, why buy it for double (or more) in the baking section of the market when it's available in the ethnic aisle? Or, for me, the Italian market is a regular stop. I find higher-quality imported meats and cheeses there than I can find at my regional grocery store, and the prices are generally better than those of the regional grocery store. If you adore Indian, try to find an Indian market to source ingredients—they're buying more of those products because that's what their customers are after, so it stands to reason that they can sell them at a lower price than a grocery store that has a lower demand for the same product.

But supplement those imported goods by buying as much locally produced food as possible.

This means so many things, but starts with this general charge I lay unto you: Buy foods that were produced near where you live. This cuts down on shipping costs, and also benefits the environment by cutting back on fossil fuels used to transport goods long distances. Purchase foods at farmers markets—you know the foods are fresh, you might learn about a new food in the process, and you help support a local business. Buy from farm stands; the prices tend to be less expensive than the supermarket because the foods are produced on the premises. There we are again with those transportation costs. If the food doesn't leave the property, it's going to cost less—buying local is good for your community, good for the environment, and good for your wallet. Don't get me wrong, I still like Italian wines and cured meats and cheeses from overseas, as well as coffee—which doesn't grow in New England, where I live—but for produce and proteins that do grow nearby, it saves you and me money and strengthens our communities when we choose to purchase those locally raised items. Oh, and did I neglect to mention: Fresher tastes better? Well, then, now I have.

Right, so fresher tastes better. Buy in season.

Seasonal fruits and veggies are plentiful at that happy moment in time when it is *their* season. Hence, the cost is lower, and—get this—you are more likely to, *without even trying*, buy locally produced food. Another thing about purchasing foods during their natural season is that it gives you something to anticipate, to look forward to. You don't really want that pasty-tasting tomato in January, do you? No, you want the sweet, juicy, bursting-with-flavor, kissed-by-the-sun-that-shines-on-you August tomato. That's what you want. It's about quality as well as cost, our little mission is.

How much fresher can it get? Grow something yourself.

Even if you live in a fifth-floor walk-up, you can make room for a basil, thyme, or parsley plant. Or whatever herb is your very most favorite. While I am fortunate enough to have a garden at my house, I live in a cold climate. So to fend off the winter blues, I keep thyme and rosemary in my house all throughout the cold season. These are the two herbs I use most frequently, and not having to purchase them every other week saves me money and frustration. If you have a deck, porch, or landing, you can grow a tomato plant in a pot and enjoy your very own fresh, warm-from-the-sun tomatoes at harvest time. Okay, so you hate tomatoes. Fine. Select another vegetable that is a favorite—lettuce, beans, peppers, or peas—and plant that in your container garden.

Establish a relationship with your grocer/butcher/farmer/wine merchant.

Perhaps you're bashful, or a full-on introvert, but you are missing out if you don't form relationships with the people who produce or procure your comestibles. First, it's plain old good manners to be friendly to these folks. Second, you are sure to learn something from them because it is quite likely that you are not yourself a grocer, butcher, farmer, or wine merchant. These folks are experts in their field. A good butcher can help you decide just how many people you'll be able to serve with that chuck roast. A greengrocer or farmer will know what produce is at its peak and can let you know what crop will be available next. Not only that, the farmer probably has a serving suggestion or two for his or her crops. A wine salesperson will eventually get to know your taste and can help you find quaffing wines that will expand your knowledge of wine and help keep money in your bank account. There is no shame in being smart with your money, and these hard-working people know just where you're coming from when you're looking for the best value for your money.

Buy meat on the bone.

Have you ever looked at the price of boneless skinless chicken breast versus a whole chicken or even skin-on, bone-in chicken breasts? No? Well, I suggest you do. Trust me, for the cost savings, you most certainly can learn to bone and skin your own chicken breasts. Yes. Yes, you can. And when you seek out meat on the bone, you will find many a scrumptious cut—whether it be lamb, beef, pork, or chicken—that have the added benefit of not costing very much. And that is a good thing.

And while we're on that theme, buy less expensive cuts of meat.

I, too, used to love me a rack of lamb or a standing rib roast whenever I happened to be in the mood for it, but I've found that less expensive cuts of meat are equally—and sometimes more—tasty than those expensive cuts we all got used to when we were busy rolling around in money. Cuts like shanks, shoulder, and legs are inexpensive, and are easily dressed up for company or dressed down for comfort. While we're at it, do not dismiss the potential of the chicken—it is versatile and not at all boring. Particularly when you follow the next tip.

Use sauces to gussy things up.

There is no faster way to make a meal seem more fancy than to add a sauce. And while you may be sitting there thinking, "Egads— how many calories is *that* going to add?" rest assured, there are just as many possibilities for wine- or juice-based sauces as there are milk- and cream-based. I'll share recipes for both types and will be sure to let you know if the sauce will work well with another type of meat. A little bonus for you, my friend. For we like versatility and bonuses, yes, we do.

Now, how about a garnish, too?

Garnishes are also inexpensive ways to add flair to your dinners. Whether it's a dollop of sour cream, a drizzle of olive oil, a grating of cheese, or a sprinkling of herbs, garnishes take meals to a fancy-pantsy level. And for not much money per serving.

Hey, and sometimes, use less meat, or no meat at all.

Cutting food costs is aided if you reduce the quantity of meat you use as well as the frequency with which you eat it. Perhaps instead of meat all seven nights of the week, you have one night that is meat-free or nearly meat-free. And if you're going nearly meat-free, cured meats, like bacon, are a great addition to dishes that are composed mostly of vegetables; they pack a flavor punch that belies their sparing use.

Purchase vegetables in their whole state.

You already know that you pay a premium for pre-cut vegetables. If you have less time than money, that's all good, but if you are trying to conserve your financial resources, spend just a little extra time peeling and seeding that butternut squash, cutting that broccoli into florets, or peeling and trimming carrots.

Do not forsake your freezer.

When you find a great deal for meat on sale, go ahead and stock up, freezing meal-sized portions for future use. I nearly always have meal-sized stacks of pancetta in my freezer for a staving-off-the-temptation-of-takeout Pasta Carbonara (page 38). Likewise, many of the recipes on the following pages call for fresh herbs, but don't use an entire bunch of that herb. Have you noticed that some clever marketer came up with the idea of selling frozen packages of herbs at the grocery store? Do you see the lightbulb above your head? Simply take the unused portion of the herb, rinse it, dry it completely, and chop it as though you're preparing it for its next use, then freeze it in an airtight container until the next time you need it. Voilà—freshness and no waste. We love that, don't we?

Buy store brands.

But only store brands from a store you trust. My sister once purchased store brand salsa from a store that was convenient, but of which she wasn't terribly fond, and found it completely unappetizing. She had to go back out and purchase the name brand. But when it works, it really can save you money. I was an aficionado of an expensive imported Italian pasta back in the days when I was a shopping fool, but the cost got to be prohibitive once my income was scaled back. Whole Foods Market, a market that I trust, stocks a store brand pasta that is comparable to the fancy brand I used to buy, and for less than half the price. So choose wisely. If you shop at a store like Trader Joe's you are already purchasing store brands. And stores like Costco, BJ's Wholesale, Whole Foods Market, and regional chain supermarkets all offer store brands—if you love the store, you are likely to love the store brand flavor. And the store-brand savings.

Do not forget about those rewards cards.

Not only do you get a better price on many items week-to-week with grocery store rewards cards, some grocery stores even partner with gas stations to take a certain amount off of your next fill-up, provided you earn a certain number of points—by spending money at the grocery store. Is this a carrot that is being dangled? Yes, it is. But the trade-off is that you will save money on your grocery bill, and perhaps land an additional reward for your pocketbook. Who doesn't like that?

Pick your battles.

And by this, my friend, I mean do not be afraid to splurge if there is something you cannot live without. You cannot live by parsimony alone. No, you cannot. So if you love fancy chocolate, or Parmigiano-Reggiano, or some imported cheese, buy it. But do follow the next tip, won't you please?

Use expensive items sparingly.
As you can see, no one—certainly not me—is saying that you should never again purchase a fine imported olive oil, or cheese, or even a rare fungi that costs more than gold per ounce. Think of these as items to be used sparingly. You'll still be able to enjoy them, and won't have to purchase them as frequently as if you used them as a main ingredient.

Basic Techniques

Some techniques are going to be repeated in lots of recipes, so to make it easier for you and for me—all that repeating will wear us down, you know—I've explained a few here; others, you'll find peppered throughout the book.

Cleaning Leeks
Leeks are notorious for hiding dirt within their layers, the rings seemingly suctioning up soil as the leeks grow, so it is imperative that one always washes them well. We'll be using only the white and light green parts of leeks in the recipes in this book, and the way I clean these parts is by first cutting the leek crosswise into two- to three-inch lengths. I then cut those in half lengthwise, and place the cut pieces into a small mixing bowl full of cold water. I agitate the leeks in the water to expel the dirt, then change the water, and repeat that process until no more dirt appears in the bowl. Once that's all done, simply dry the leeks with a kitchen towel, then proceed with preparing them for the recipe.

Kneading
While some people may look at kneading dough as work, I truly, unabashedly love it. It is an amazing experience each and every time to bring dough from its nascent, rough stages to the smooth and silky dough we desire. I have taken shortcuts in the past, and I can assure you that it is well worth your while to knead for as long as the recipe requires.

I generally bring dough to the point of just coming together in the mixing bowl—I use a stand mixer, but dough can also be formed by hand or in a food processor—and then roll it out onto a lightly floured countertop to knead it by hand. Kneading is a lot like upper-body exercise, as you alternate folding the dough into itself from right hand to left hand—or left hand to right hand, depending upon how you look at it.

Place the dough on your countertop. Rub a little flour on your hands. Starting with whichever hand you prefer, pull a corner of the dough up from the countertop and push it back into the middle of the dough. Move the dough a quarter turn, and repeat the process, pushing and turning for the amount of time specified in the recipe. And in so doing, you are elongating the glutens within the dough, forming what I like to think of as silken threads of gluten that build the body of the bread or pasta.

There is nothing quite like a well-kneaded pasta dough—so supple that it can be rolled out thinly enough to remind you of a silk scarf—and likewise, a well-kneaded bread rewards you with bakery-worthy nooks and crannies. If that weren't enough, I find that kneading also helps soothe the mind—pushing out the stress as you form the silken gluten threads. So very Zen, really.

Pureeing Hot Liquids

Hot liquids do not like to be pureed in large quantities. Early on in my cooking endeavors, I was in a rush (note: I had not yet learned that cooking is not a race), and tried to puree a couple cups of corn chowder at once. Approximately three seconds after I started the blender, I was dripping with hot, pale yellow, partially blended chowder. All over my face, in my hair, on my clothing, and on the walls and ceiling—yes, ceiling—of my very tiny kitchen.

I would not wish this on anyone else, and so I must warn you: Be sure to let the hot liquid cool to lukewarm before starting the puree, and always work in small batches—one cup or less—when pureeing liquids that have been heated. For ease of execution on the return of the pureed soup to the saucepan, pour the little puree batches from the blender into a batter bowl with a spout and a handle while you work your way to the bottom of the saucepan.

Reserving Pasta Cooking Water

Many of the recipes in the Entrées chapter call for reserved pasta cooking water. It's used to add moisture to sauces, and the glutens transferred from the pasta to the cooking water help to thicken a sauce slightly.

It is best to do this in the sink so as to avoid water overflowing onto your countertop. Drain the pasta into a colander placed over a bowl (an 8-cup heatproof mixing bowl should do) to collect the cooking water, and then you can measure out the amount you need, until you feel comfortable judging the quantity without measuring.

A Rather Handy Egg Separating Gadget

There's no need to run out and purchase an egg separator—eggs happen to have one built in. It's known as the shell. You will need two bowls, however.

Simply crack the shell as close to the halfway point as possible, and, holding the broken egg over one bowl, transfer the yolk back and forth between the shell halves, allowing the egg white to fall into the now-designated-for-egg-whites bowl. Once all of the white has been removed from the yolk, place the yolk into its special yolk bowl. Save the whites for another use; they'll keep for two days in the refrigerator, or six months if frozen, or you can whip up a quick egg white and veggie scramble straightaway if you need a snack.

Toasting Nuts

Toasted nuts add textural and flavor interest to many dishes, and are extremely easy to make. Simply place the desired amount of whole, shelled nuts on a 9 by 13-inch rimmed baking sheet and bake them at 350°F until lightly browned, 10 to 12 minutes. Or you can use chopped nuts, and it will take about half the time. Remove them from the oven, allow the nuts to cool, and remove the loose skins by rubbing them between two kitchen towels—you don't have to go crazy trying to pick off every last bit of skin, by the way. Store them for no more than two weeks in an airtight container until you're ready to use them, lest they become soft, and you'll have them at the ready any time the toasted nut craving strikes.

Making Croutons

This is a great way to extend the life of bakery or homemade bread—particularly if you're taking the whole don't-waste-food directive to heart, as you should. Preheat the oven to 350°F. Cut the bread into 1-inch cubes. Toss the cubes with 1 to 2 tablespoons of extra virgin olive oil or more, depending upon the amount of leftover bread you have. Season them with kosher salt and freshly ground pepper and bake on a 9 by 13-inch rimmed baking sheet, turning the bread cubes over once, until they're golden brown, 12 to 15 minutes. I like to use croutons in soups such as Ribollita (page 16), and, of course, on salads

whenever the urge strikes. And, of course, you should seal these up in an airtight container where they'll keep for up to two weeks.

Making Breadcrumbs

Another good way to extend a bakery loaf's life is to make breadcrumbs of the remainder. Cut the bread into 1-inch cubes and allow to dry on a 9 by 13-inch rimmed baking sheet overnight. In a food processor or blender, chop the cubes until they become crumbs. I like mine a little more robust, so I stop when they've just become crumbs, but if you want them more finely ground, go ahead and keep processing until you have a texture you like. Like croutons, these bad boys belong in an airtight container where they will keep for two to three days, or up to six months in the freezer. The freezer is our friend, after all.

Roasting Garlic

One of the tricks of eating well for less money is to have an arsenal of low-cost, big-flavor ingredients, and roasted garlic is certainly one of those items. You can add roasted garlic to soup, stew, pasta, stir-fries, or any number of potato or rice dishes. It also makes for a wonderful condiment spread on fresh bread, or combine it with sour cream and thyme, parsley, or oregano for a tasty dip, or serve it as an accompaniment to goat cheese—I could go on and on, but you get the idea.

ROASTED GARLIC

1 head garlic, outer skin removed
1 teaspoon extra virgin olive oil
Kosher salt
Freshly ground black pepper

Preheat the oven to 375°F. Trim the top quarter inch of the garlic cloves off the head of garlic. Place the garlic on a piece of aluminum foil just large enough to wrap the bulb up snugly for baking. Bend the foil up around the garlic to create a rim of foil to catch any drips, then drizzle the olive oil over the cut side of the garlic head, and sprinkle with salt and pepper. Wrap the foil tightly around the head, and roast on the middle rack until the garlic is softened and has started to brown, about 45 minutes. Remove the garlic from the oven and allow it to cool for at least 5 minutes before removing the roasted cloves (if you're using them right away), or refrigerate it in its foil package for use within a week.

ESTIMATED COST FOR ONE HEAD OF ROASTED GARLIC: 54¢. One head of garlic costs 50¢. A teaspoon of olive oil will run us 4¢. There. That's it. And for 54¢, you have a secret flavor weapon at the ready for any use necessary. From the preceding list, you can see there is many a necessary use.

Alrighty, now that we're all well versed, let's get cooking!

soups and salads

VEGETABLE SCRAP STOCK

{ **Makes 8 cups, pretty much free** }

The three primary vegetables used as the base of many soups, stews, and sauces are carrots, celery, and onion. Conveniently, these are also the three primary vegetables used in stock—including meat stocks. Once you're cooking at home more often, you, my friend, will have scraps from peeling carrots, trimming celery, and removing layers from those onions. Each time you make a dish that calls for these ingredients, save the scraps. Rinse the carrots and celery before trimming and peeling, then save those carrot peels and trimmings, the celery tops and bottoms, and the outer rings of the onion—not the brown, papery onion skin, though. Save them in the freezer in a one-gallon-capacity plastic food storage bag (or other gallon-sized storage container), and when you have packed the bag full, make some stock. We're trying to keep our costs down, and we also want to be able to season whatever dish we're preparing as we like, so this recipe doesn't call for seasonings. However, if you do have a bunch of parsley, thyme, or sage that needs using up and you want that added flavor, by all means, toss it into the pot as well. By employing scraps for stock, you're being both thrifty and less wasteful. These are good things. Here's how it works:

1-gallon bag vegetable scraps

8 cups water, or enough to cover the scraps completely

1 Place the vegetable scraps into a large stockpot (at least 8-quart capacity) and cover them with water. Bring the contents of the pot to a simmer, then cover and continue the simmer for 2 to 3 hours. Let the stock cool, then strain the solids out. Save the stock in the freezer if you have no immediate plans for it, or in the refrigerator if you're going to be making soup in the next 2 to 3 days.

NOTE: If you are ambitious, you can also save meat bones from your delicious homemade meals (separately) in the freezer and make meat stocks as well. Just add the chicken carcass, or the turkey carcass (honestly, if the host of Thanksgiving is only going to toss it, it would be a shame not to make some stock; you can use it in place of chicken stock), or the pork, beef, or ham bones to the mix and simmer away. Same procedure. Free stock. Frugal you.

For the purpose of pricing the soups in this book, I base the vegetable, chicken, or beef stock cost on the Whole Foods 365 Everyday Value per-cup price. And I like their product. It's not salty, it tastes good, and it's convenient. But if we are to emulate our forebears who lived on less, we all need to know how to make stock at home. Particularly vegetable stock.

ROASTED FENNEL AND CARROT SOUP WITH HONEYED MASCARPONE

{ **Serves 6 to 8, $5.00 to $10.00** }

This recipe uses a possibly less-familiar vegetable—fennel. In my opinion, fennel is entirely undervalued. Its sweet, slightly licorice flavor becomes more pronounced when it is roasted, and it pairs beautifully with carrots in this soup. Your friends and relations will be pleasantly surprised with this introduction to fennel, if they are not already aficionados. The honeyed mascarpone is optional, but for me, it pushes this soup over the top deliciously, rendering it almost fancy, even—either way, it's a rather tasty dish.

¼ cup mascarpone (see Note)

2 medium fennel bulbs (approximately 2 pounds)

1½ pounds carrots (approximately 9 medium), peeled, cut into 2-inch lengths

6 tablespoons extra virgin olive oil, divided

Kosher salt

Freshly ground black pepper

1 medium leek, white and light green parts only, cleaned (see page xiv), coarsely chopped

1 teaspoon dried thyme, or 1 tablespoon fresh

4 cups plus 2 cups vegetable broth

¼ cup (more if you have a relentless sweet tooth) plus 2 tablespoons honey

1 Preheat the oven to 375°F. Take the mascarpone out of the refrigerator. You'll want it to come to room temperature so that it doesn't ice your lovely soup, and it's also easier to blend with the honey if it isn't cold.

2 Remove the fronds from the fennel bulb, cutting at an angle to preserve as much of the bulb as possible. Trim the very bottom of the bulb, and then cut lengthwise, from the top (where the fronds were) to the bottom, into wedges approximately 2 inches thick.

3 Toss the fennel and carrots in a large bowl with 3 tablespoons of the olive oil, coating well. Spread them in a single layer on a 10 by 15-inch rimmed baking sheet. Season with salt and pepper.

4 Roast the fennel and carrots until they are just beginning to brown, approximately 30 minutes, turning them over midway through the cooking time for even browning on both sides. Remove your roasted veggies from the oven and set aside.

5 Heat the remaining 3 tablespoons of olive oil in a medium saucepan or soup pot over medium heat. Add the leek, and sauté until it is softened, 3 to 5 minutes. Add the roasted fennel and carrots, and the thyme. Cook over medium heat for 2 to 3 minutes to combine the flavors. Add 4 cups of the vegetable broth, bring to a gentle simmer, and cook at the gentle simmer, covered, for 15 minutes. Remove from the heat and let it cool to lukewarm.

6 Now, you're quite likely hungry while you're making this, but do resist the temptation to move to the blending step immediately after removing the pot from the heat. You do need to allow it to cool so as to avoid your blender exploding all over the kitchen walls, counter, you, and your Golden Retriever (or Pug, Beagle, Rottweiler, Labradoodle, Maine Coon Cat, Cockatoo, what-have-you). For I have been there. And there is nothing that impedes cooking progress quite like a blender explosion followed by the subsequent washing of walls, pets, and self. To read more about how to avoid a mess when pureeing hot liquids, see page xv.

7 So, working in small, lukewarm batches, puree the fennel, carrots, leeks, and broth, adding room-temperature broth from the remaining 2 cups as needed to help thin the mixture. You'll need 1½ to 2 cups total of room-temperature broth during the pureeing process. Alternatively, you may use an immersion blender for this step, adding the room-temperature broth before starting to puree.

8 Transfer the pureed soup to a heatproof mixing bowl (at least 8-cup capacity) as you go. Once all of the soup has been pureed, return the puree to the soup pot/saucepan, and warm it to serving temperature over medium heat, stirring occasionally.

9 While the soup is coming back up to temperature, it's time to make the honeyed mascarpone. Combine the mascarpone and ¼ cup of the honey and blend well. If you'd like to adjust the sweetness down, simply add a touch more mascarpone, or, likewise, if you'd like it sweeter, add a bit more honey. Remember, you're eating this, so you have to like how it tastes, and I'm not going to be stopping by to be sure you used my exact ratios.

10 Now, to finish the soup. Add the remaining 2 tablespoons of honey, stirring well to combine, then add salt and pepper to taste. It is very important to salt sufficiently, as it highlights the flavors of the fennel and carrot, and contrasts nicely with the sweetness of the honeyed mascarpone.

11 Serve the soup forth with a dollop of honeyed mascarpone atop each bowl. Watch for even your die-hard meat-and-potatoes-loving friend or family member to look up, a bemused smile on his or her meat-loving, I-can't-believe-you're-serving-me-another-vegetarian-meal face, and say, "Wow." And then say, "That's pretty darned good. What's the name of this vegetable again?"

NOTE: Mascarpone is an Italian cream cheese available in Italian markets and in most supermarkets.

Seasonal Suggestion: Fennel is in season in the fall and winter, so it is least expensive to make the dish during that time.

ESTIMATED COST FOR FOUR: $8.94. The amount of fennel used costs just about $3.00 at $1.49 per pound. The carrots cost $1.20, at 5 pounds for $3.99. The olive oil for roasting is 36¢ for 3 tablespoons at $7.99 for 33.8 fluid ounces of oil, which is 67 tablespoons; likewise, the oil for sautéing costs the same. The leek should cost close to $1.00. The broth is $2.39 for 4 cups, using the Whole Foods store brand, so 6 cups will run us $3.59. The thyme costs 18¢. The honey for the soup is 50¢, while the honey for the honeyed mascarpone is $1.00. The mascarpone was $4.99 for 8 ¾ ounces, so 57¢ per ounce. Our 2 ounces of mascarpone is therefore $1.14. The soup alone costs $10.19 for 6 to 8 servings. We'll divide it by six to stay on the low end of servings and the high end of cost estimates, and using that approach, it costs $1.70 per serving, so $6.80 for four, plus $2.14 for the honeyed mascarpone, which brings us to a total of $8.94. And you have some leftovers for lunch—which, at $2.24 for a unique, healthful soup, is certainly better than any takeout by either price or goodness criteria.

Feeling flush with cash? Add a little bacon as a garnish and really wow the crowd for an additional $1.75, figuring that each slice of fancy (Black Forest or similar) bacon is about 1 ounce at $6.99 per pound.

PEA SOUP WITH MINT

{ Serves 4, $5.00 to $10.00 }

This is a dish that just screams out "Happy spring!" Ahhh, but the nice thing is that you can capture that joyous blooms-are-all-around-us feeling any time of year, as this lovely soup can be made with frozen peas whenever your heart desires. And I must be perfectly honest, I employ my fair share of frozen peas throughout the year. If mint isn't your favorite herb, feel free to substitute thyme, marjoram, or any herb you fancy, for that matter.

3 tablespoons extra virgin olive oil

1 medium leek, white and light green parts only, cleaned (see page xiv), coarsely chopped

1 medium shallot, finely chopped

3 tablespoons coarsely chopped fresh mint

2 pounds green peas, defrosted overnight in the refrigerator if using frozen

4 cups vegetable broth

Kosher salt

Freshly ground black pepper

Parmigiano-Reggiano, for serving (optional)

1 Heat the oil in a large saucepan over medium heat. Add the leek and shallot, and sauté until the leek has softened and the shallot is translucent, 3 to 5 minutes. Add the mint and peas, and stir to combine. Continue stirring for 3 to 5 minutes, rolling the peas on the bottom over the peas on the top. Add the vegetable broth and, yes, do that stirring thing once more—always with the stirring, we are—then bring the pot to a simmer over medium heat. This will take from 15 to 20 minutes. The key here is that you want to cook the peas well enough that the soup has a nice, smooth texture, as opposed to a grainy texture, which is what you would have upon your tongue should the peas be undercooked. Bringing the pea mixture up to a simmer at a medium heat, instead of getting all gung-ho on the starchy beads at a higher heat, allows us to keep the pretty green color that is the same shade as new

leaves unfurling on the springtime trees, and avoid that particular shade of green that we would prefer not to associate with our suppers. For we want a pretty soup in addition to a smooth soup, my friend, yes we do.

2 Once the pot has come to a simmer, remove it from the heat and allow the pea mixture to cool for 10 minutes. And remember, we are trying to achieve a pretty green, so don't go forgetting about the soup during its cooldown phase—as it will continue to cook and the pea color will become dull.

3 If you would prefer to use an immersion blender for the pureeing task, please do. Otherwise, at the 10-minute cooldown mark, get out your blender or food processor and begin pureeing the soup in small batches, for you have been warned about what can happen if you puree hot liquid in large quantities (see page xv), and so you know that your kitchen would soon be the color of spring, only in large, streaky, messy splotches, were you to puree too much hot pea-containing liquid at once. Pour your small batches of puree into an 8-cup (or larger) mixing bowl as they are finished.

4 Once you have completed the small-batch pureeing, return the soup to the pot and reheat it to your desired serving temperature. Add salt and pepper to taste, shave a ribbon or two of Parmigiano-Reggiano over the bowl if you so desire, and serve it forth. Springtime in a cup. Or bowl, as it were, but available just about anytime.

NOTE: If you are making this with fresh peas and are also able to locate pea tendrils—the new growth and leaves of pea plants—they would make a pretty garnish for this soup, adding to the springtime appeal.

If you grow mint yourself, be certain to keep it in a container lest you have a lawn made of mint two years from now. Not that it wouldn't smell pretty, but nothing else will live where the mint marks its space.

ESTIMATED COST FOR FOUR: $7.98. The olive oil is 36¢. The leek should be in the $1.00 range, the shallot in the 25¢ range. The mint is half of a container that costs $1.99, so $1.00 for this usage. The peas cost $1.49 per 1-pound bag, so $2.98. The vegetable broth costs $2.39 for a 4-cup box, but you should be making Vegetable Scrap Stock (page 1), should you not? Ahhh, but in case you have not, I will include the $2.39 for you.

If you'd like to shave Parmigiano-Reggiano onto your soup, that will add approximately 60¢ per person, bringing our total to $10.38.

SPICY CARROT GINGER SOUP

{ **Serves 4, $5.00 to $10.00** }

I do not normally love carrot soup—I generally find it a bit too bland for my liking, and so I decided that if one were to appear in the pages of this book, it would need some jazzing up. I had a surplus batch of Roasted Carrots with Thyme (page 92) that needed to be consumed—for I do despise food waste—and I just happened to have some lime hanging around in the refrigerator. It was just a few short mental steps that brought me to the idea of using that lime and adding ginger for a spicy soup. And now I cannot ever again say that I do not love carrot soup, for this one is quite deserving of affection.

3 tablespoons extra virgin olive oil

1 medium leek, white and light green parts only, cleaned (see page xiv), coarsely chopped

1 tablespoon freshly grated ginger

⅛ teaspoon crushed red pepper flakes

2 pounds Roasted Carrots with Thyme (page 92), without butter

4 cups vegetable broth

The zest and juice of 1 lime

Kosher salt

Freshly ground black pepper

1 Heat the olive oil in a large saucepan over medium heat. Add the leek and sauté until softened and aromatic—yes, you will be able to smell the aroma of the leek—3 to 5 minutes. Add the ginger and crushed red pepper flakes, stirring to combine. Cook for 1 minute to meld the flavors. Add the carrots and broth, and bring the pot to a simmer over medium heat, 8 to 10 minutes. Cover the pot and simmer gently for 20 minutes. Remove the pot from the heat and let it cool to lukewarm to avoid a hot liquid pureeing disaster (see page xv).

2 Once the carrot mixture is lukewarm, puree it in small batches in a blender or food processor until smooth. You could also use an immersion blender for this step if you prefer. Transfer the pureed batches

to a large heatproof bowl, 8-cup capacity at the minimum, and then return the entire stunningly gorgeous orange puree back to the large saucepan. Bring the contents back to your desired serving temperature, and add the lime zest and juice. Stir well to combine the flavors, add salt and pepper to taste, and serve it forth. If they like spice, don't be surprised if your family informs you that this is the best carrot soup ever.

What the Heck Is a Simmer?

You'll notice that this book—and many, many other cookbooks—asks that various concoctions be simmered. A simmer is simply cooking a liquid at a point just below a boil. Instead of the vigorous, constant stream of rolling bubbles that constitute a boil, you want a steady, gentle bubbling happening in various locations around your cooking vessel.

ESTIMATED COST FOR FOUR: $6.45. The Roasted Carrots with Thyme cost $2.05 without the butter. The olive oil for sautéing the base of our soup is 36¢. The leek will cost around $1.00. I always purchase a small piece of ginger, lest a larger piece rot in my refrigerator awaiting other use, and you may be surprised to know that I usually spend 11¢ or 12¢ on an approximately 1-inch cube of ginger root, which is all you need for this soup. The crushed red pepper flakes are estimated at 3¢. A lone lime will cost you 50¢, though you know and I know that you can do better than that. However, I like to estimate up so that you and I may both be pleasantly surprised. The vegetable broth cost $2.39 for a 4-cup container, though you may want to consider the Vegetable Scrap Stock (page 1) as a cost-saving alternative. After all, you're already using the veggies from which the scraps derive in other dishes.

If you are feeling fancy, you may want to add a tablespoon of sour cream to each of your family's bowls, for an added cost of 8¢ each at $2.19 for 30 tablespoons.

CHICKEN ORZO SOUP

{ **Serves 8, $5.00 to $10.00** }

That "good for colds" thing may just be an old wives' tale, but this soup always works to make JR and me feel better when we're under the weather. As you know from reading all about the process in the Vegetable Scrap Stock recipe (page 1), making your own stock is both easy and economical. This recipe calls for you to make your own chicken stock, and the texture of the chicken in the final product is well worth the effort. Not to mention that having a steaming pot on the stove might even help your sinuses out. Either way, this dish is sure to make you and your loved ones feel better. If you'd prefer to make the soup with a rotisserie chicken and purchased stock, or the chicken stock variation of Vegetable Scrap Stock (page 2), that's all good; however, the simmering to make the stock results in chicken that pulls apart from itself, which is the texture that we're after.

Chicken Stock

10 sprigs parsley

12 sprigs thyme

3 sprigs sage

1 (3- to 4-pound) whole chicken, cut into 6 pieces (legs, wings, breasts)

1 medium yellow onion, unpeeled, halved crosswise

1 head garlic, unpeeled, halved crosswise

2 medium carrots, unpeeled, washed, quartered crosswise

2 celery stalks, well washed, with leafy tops still on, quartered crosswise

2 tablespoons whole black peppercorns

16 cups cold water

1 Tie a piece of kitchen twine around the herbs to make it easier to remove them when the stock is finished. Place the chicken, onion, garlic, carrots, celery, peppercorns, and herb bundle into a large stockpot (at least 8-quart capacity). Pour in the water to cover all the ingredients. If you have to add more water to make sure everything's covered, do so. Bring to a simmer over medium heat, then cover and continue simmering gently for 2 hours. Remove the pot from the heat and allow the stock to cool for about an hour. Transfer the chicken to a plate—I find tongs work best for this activity— and then strain the chicken stock through a fine-mesh colander into a 16-cup (or larger) heatproof container to remove all the solids. If you do not have such a large heatproof

container, you may simply work in batches until all of the stock has been strained. Allow the chicken to cool enough that you are comfortably able to handle it before removing the meat from the bones. When it comes time to remove the chicken from the bones, simply pull off the skin, discard it, and pull the chicken meat off the bones, being careful to remove and trash any small bones. Then, pull the chicken meat apart into spoon-manageable pieces; the meat will shred slightly as you do, which is just the effect we're looking for.

2 Reserve 12 cups of stock for the chicken soup. Pour the remaining 4 cups of stock into an airtight container and refrigerate or freeze it for future use.

ESTIMATED COST FOR FOUR: $7.32. The whole chicken should cost no more than $1.69 per pound, though you should be on the lookout for 99¢ per pound chicken on sale. On the high side, 4 pounds at $1.69 per pound is $6.76. The onion for the stock is 33¢ at 65¢ per pound. One head of garlic is 50¢, two medium carrots, estimating that two carrots equal ⅓ pound at the most and cost $3.99 for 5 pounds, is 27¢. Two stalks of celery are 40¢ or so. The fresh herbs are no more than a third each of bunches that should all be in the $1.99 range, so we'll add in $1.99 for those. The additional carrots for the soup are approximately 1 pound, which costs us 80¢, the celery is around $1.20, the sweet corn is $1.29 for a bag that contains 3⅓ cups, so that's 39¢; the orzo is no more than half of a box of pasta, and it costs $1.99 for a 1-pound box, so $1.00 for 8 ounces. However, orzo can also be available for anywhere from 99¢ to $1.39. The thyme should be the remaining 99¢ worth, given that you've purchased fresh thyme to make the stock and have used only half of it for that purpose. That totals $14.63 for eight servings, hence, $7.32 for four, or $1.83 per serving. And then you don't have to make dinner the next night or two nights from now, or a month from now if you choose to freeze the leftovers, and that, in addition to its possible curative powers, ought to be enough incentive to set a pot to simmer on your stove.

Soup

12 cups homemade chicken stock

Cooked meat from the stock chicken

6 medium carrots, peeled, cut crosswise into ¼-inch pieces

6 celery stalks, cut crosswise into ¼-inch pieces

1 cup frozen sweet corn

8 ounces (½ of a 1-pound box) orzo or other small pasta

1 teaspoon dried thyme, or 1 tablespoon fresh

Kosher salt

Freshly ground black pepper

1 Pour the stock into a large stockpot (at least 6-quart capacity) set over medium heat and add the chicken, carrots, celery, corn, and orzo. Simmer, stirring occasionally, until the orzo is cooked through, 15 to 20 minutes. Stir in the thyme, and add salt and pepper to taste. Of course, you can also add any other vegetables you'd like to the mix, and if you hate thyme, then do feel free to use an herb that you prefer. Serve it forth, and watch the box of tissues become obsolete almost before your eyes.

ROASTED BUTTERNUT SQUASH SOUP

{ **Serves 4, $5.00 to $10.00** }

I am extremely fortunate in that my farmer neighbors grow butternut squash and sell it in their front yard for a song. And while I am unable to carry a tune, I benefit just the same, as I am able to purchase 3 to 4 pounds of butternut squash for the same amount it would cost for one pound at the grocery store. Even at the going grocery store rate, this is an inexpensive and delicious use of one of fall's best flavors. Okay, in *my* opinion, one of fall's best flavors.

Roasted Squash

1 (4-pound) butternut squash, peeled, seeded, cut into 1-inch cubes

¼ cup extra virgin olive oil

Kosher salt

Soup

3 tablespoons extra virgin olive oil

1 leek, white and light green parts only, cleaned (see page xiv), coarsely chopped

1 teaspoon dried thyme, or 1 tablespoon fresh, plus additional fresh thyme, for garnish

3 cups plus 1 cup chicken broth

1 head roasted garlic (page xvii; see Note)

Freshly ground black pepper

¼ cup crème fraîche or sour cream, for garnish

1. Preheat the oven to 375°F. In a large bowl, toss the butternut squash with ¼ cup of olive oil. Spread the squash in a single layer on a 10 by 15-inch rimmed baking sheet.

2. Roast the butternut squash for 15 minutes and then salt it. Continue roasting until the squash is soft and beginning to brown, another 25 to 30 minutes.

3. Remove the squash from the oven. In a large saucepan, heat the remaining 3 tablespoons of olive oil over medium-high heat. Add the leek and sauté until it's softened, 3 to 5 minutes, stirring frequently. Stir in the thyme, and cook for 1 minute. Now add the butternut squash, and stir in 3 cups of the chicken broth. The remaining cup of broth is to be used while you puree, to thin the mixture as needed (and avoid burning

out your blender's motor). If you are using an immersion blender for the puree stage, go ahead and add all of the broth at once. Reduce the heat to medium, bring the soup to a gentle simmer, and let it simmer for 20 minutes to meld the flavors. Remove the garlic cloves from their skins and add the cloves to the soup. Remove the soup from the heat and let it cool to lukewarm.

4 Working in small batches, puree the soup in a blender, being extremely careful, for if you are not, it can be quite messy as we've discussed (see page xv for the full story). Return the puree to the saucepan and heat to your desired serving temperature. Add salt and pepper to taste.

5 Ladle the soup into bowls, top each with 1 tablespoon of crème fraîche or sour cream, and serve it forth.

NOTE: If you don't have a full head of roasted garlic at the ready, it's handy to make it while you're roasting the squash.

ESTIMATED COST FOR FOUR: $8.91. Four pounds of butternut squash will cost $3.16 at 79¢ per pound. The roasted garlic is 54¢, the olive oil for this dish is 84¢. The leek will cost around $1.00, the chicken broth cost $2.19 for a 4-cup container of Whole Foods 365 Everyday Value brand, and the thyme is 18¢. The crème fraîche is $3.99 for 8 ounces, we'll figure that each tablespoon is about ½ ounce, so that's $1.00 for the garnish for all four bowls of soup.

If you wanted to gussy this up even further, you could add a topping of Caramelized Onions (page 110) and a piece of bacon per person for an added cost of $2.76 for the onions and $1.75 for the bacon, figuring that each slice of a fancy bacon such as Black Forest is one ounce at $6.99 per pound. All of this gussying up brings our total to $13.42.

HEARTY PASTA FAGIOLI WITH KALE

{ **Serves 8, $5.00 to $10.00** }

Quick Meal

I use this soup to take the chill out of the air on those first, breezy autumn days, sometimes accompanied by garlic toast, or even half of a grilled cheese sandwich, cut on the diagonal, of course. It all reminds me of the return to school, the smell of fallen leaves, and the first wearing of my favorite sweater. Even better: This soup could not be easier to make. While I've specified canned tomatoes so that you can make it once the leaves have all been raked, and well into the winter, you are welcome to use fresh tomato puree in place of the canned.

3 tablespoons extra virgin olive oil

1 medium yellow onion, coarsely chopped

2 cloves garlic, coarsely chopped

1 teaspoon dried thyme, or 1 tablespoon fresh

⅛ teaspoon crushed red pepper flakes

4 cups vegetable broth, plus more to thin the soup as needed

1 (28-ounce) can fire-roasted crushed tomatoes such as Muir Glen, or regular crushed tomatoes

3 celery stalks, sliced in half lengthwise, then sliced crosswise into ¼-inch pieces

4 large kale leaves, stemmed, washed well, coarsely chopped

1 (15-ounce) can cannellini beans, including liquid

1 cup diminutive pasta, such as orzo, ditalini, or pastina

Kosher salt

Freshly ground black pepper

1 Heat the olive oil in a medium stockpot over medium heat. Add the onion and garlic and cook until the onion is translucent, 3 to 5 minutes. Add the thyme and crushed red pepper flakes, stir, and cook for 1 minute, then add the broth and the tomatoes, and stir once more to combine.

2 Stir in the celery and kale, then the beans and their liquid, and then the pasta. Cook over medium heat until the pasta is cooked through, 20 to 25 minutes. Add salt and pepper to taste. Pour in a bit more broth if the soup becomes too thick—you probably will need more if you have the soup as leftovers, as the pasta will absorb liquid while it sits.

ESTIMATED COST FOR FOUR: $5.09. The olive oil costs 36¢, the onion 33¢. The garlic is estimated at 10¢ for 2 cloves from a 50¢ head of garlic. The thyme is 18¢, and the crushed red pepper flakes are 3¢. The tomatoes were $2.99, though I have to tell you that I never buy them when they are not on sale, and when they are on sale, they cost $2.00. The vegetable broth should be Vegetable Scrap Stock (page 1), but for the purpose of our estimating here, we use the Whole Foods 365 Everyday Value brand at $2.39 for 4 cups. The celery is around 60¢ for 3 ribs out of a bunch that costs $1.99. The kale was $2.49 for the bunch; this recipe uses less than half a bunch, but we'll still call it $1.25. The beans are 99¢ for one can. The pasta is about half of a 1-pound box that costs $1.99, so $1.00 for that. The soup costs $10.27 for eight hearty servings, or just over $1.29 per serving.

Add a few toasted slices of bread brushed with olive oil and rubbed with garlic for a spicy and satisfying accompaniment, at an additional cost of approximately $1.99, figuring that a bakery loaf of country bread can be had for $3.39. You won't need more than half of that, though, and I highly recommend that you shop the bakery's day-old rack as it is prudent and a nice loaf of bread will then cost you half of its regular price. A drizzle of everyday olive oil is no more than 24¢, and the one clove of garlic from a 50¢ head is 5¢.

RIBOLLITA

{ Serves 8, $5.00 to $10.00 }

Ribollita is a soup that arises from the tradition of *cucina povera*, or the poor kitchen—also known as peasant cooking. Many of the dishes of *cucina povera* were designed to utilize leftovers, hence, Panzanella (page 28) was conceived of as a way to use the previous day's bread rather than have it go to waste. Ribollita was often made from another leftover soup—usually Minestrone—and its name translates to "reboiled." The soup would literally be recooked and then served over what? Yes, that's right. Leftover bread. It is fortuitous for us that those resourceful Italian cooks, who had no choice but to use every last bit of food in their houses, happened also to have fantastic taste. These foods tend to be very tasty despite their humble ingredients, and in many cases, they are also quite substantial.

There is one step at the end of the Ribollita process that, while seemingly an "extra," is actually vitally important to the garlicky goodness of the soup. If you don't love garlic, well, then, I suppose it *is* an extra. But if you, like me, are enamored of garlic, it is mandatory. Now, let us make the garlicky Ribollita.

1½ cups dry cannellini beans or Great Northern beans (approximately ½ pound)

5 tablespoons extra virgin olive oil

1 medium yellow onion, coarsely chopped

1 carrot, peeled, trimmed, coarsely chopped

1 celery stalk, coarsely chopped

1 clove garlic, finely chopped; plus 2 cloves, finely chopped; plus 1 large clove, peeled and halved

1 tablespoon finely chopped rosemary

¼ teaspoon crushed red pepper flakes

8 cups water

1 (15-ounce) can fire-roasted crushed tomatoes such as Muir Glen, or regular crushed tomatoes

1 bunch cavolo nero (also known as dinosaur kale; approximately ¾ pound), or 1 small head Savoy cabbage, washed, stemmed, chopped into ½-inch pieces

1 teaspoon dried thyme, or 1 tablespoon fresh

Kosher salt

Freshly ground black pepper

1 slice crusty bread per serving (or leftover bakery bread dried to crouton consistency)

1 The night before you plan to make the Ribollita, rinse the dried beans well, sifting through for pebbles. As beans are from the earth, they sometimes carry bits of earth with them to the grocery store. Once the rinsing water runs clear, place them in a large bowl and cover with cold water. The beans will expand to approximately double their dry size, so resist the temptation to soak them in a small bowl, lest you awake to find beans spilling over the bowl edge and cluttering your countertop. Not a very desirable first event of the day, I'm sure you'd agree.

2 To make the Ribollita, drain the beans and set them aside. Heat 3 tablespoons of oil in a large stockpot over medium heat. Add the onion, carrot, celery, and 1 finely chopped garlic clove, then cook until the onion is translucent and all of the vegetables are softened, 8 to 10 minutes. Add the rosemary and crushed red pepper flakes and stir to combine. Add the beans and stir to coat with the oil. Add the water and the tomatoes, and bring to a simmer. Cover, and cook for 1½ to 2 hours, or until the beans are cooked through, meaning you are easily able to bite into one.

3 Allow the soup to cool to lukewarm. If you have any questions about pureeing hot liquid, please see page xv, where you can read all about my pureeing mishap in order to spare you the same.

4 Now that the soup has cooled, use a slotted spoon to remove the beans—at least half, and more than half if you like a thicker soup—to a bowl. There should also be some liquid (as mentioned in the previous paragraph) in the bowl, and even some of the vegetables. You can't be sorting out celery and carrot pieces prior to pureeing; that would be infuriatingly tedious work. If you are using an immersion blender, you still want to remove the beans in order to puree them. Working in batches, puree the beans and then return them to the stockpot. Once all of the beans you've chosen to puree have been returned to the stockpot, reheat (not reboil, just reheat—but conceptually, you are free to think of it as reboiling if it helps you better connect with your inner practitioner of *cucina povera*) the soup. Add the cavolo nero at this point and cook it through, 20 to 25 minutes. Preheat the oven to 350°F.

5 Toward the end of the cavolo nero cooking time, you have two more tasks. First, heat 1 tablespoon of the remaining oil in a small pan over medium heat and add the thyme and the 2 cloves of finely chopped garlic; cook quickly, 2 to 3 minutes, until the garlic is good and fragrant. Add the garlicky-thyme mixture to the pot, and give it a good stir. This thyme-garlic sauté is the not-extra extra step. You must do it. Trust me. Now, taste the soup and add salt and pepper as you desire. I find that Ribollita requires a bit of salt to highlight its flavor.

6 It's also time to dry out the bread. Essentially, you are making croutons of it, so place the slices of bread on a baking sheet. Drizzle the remaining tablespoon of olive oil onto both sides of the bread. They do not have to be doused in oil; a drizzle really will be fine. Bake in the oven until each side is lightly browned, 5 to 7 minutes per side. Remove the bread from the oven and, using tongs to hold the bread as it will be hot, rub the cut side of the remaining garlic clove over one side of the bread. If you love, love, love garlic, go ahead and rub both sides of the bread. Your eyes may sting from the heat of the garlic when you bite into your crouton, but, hey, you love garlic, so you already know this to be the case.

7 Place a slice of bread at the bottom of a soup bowl, ladle out some recooked bean and vegetable soup to submerge your crouton, and then serve it forth, not feeling at all like a peasant, but like a very thrifty modern-day cook who just whipped up a very satisfying, tasty, and garlicky *zuppa*.

ESTIMATED COST FOR FOUR: $6.25. The beans cost $1.50 for a half-pound bag at my local farmers market, though they are available for approximately 85¢ in the bulk or dried bean section of your local grocery store. The olive oil costs 36¢. The onion should weigh about ½ pound, and therefore costs 33¢. The carrot should be about one-sixth of a pound, at a cost of 80¢ per pound, which we'll count as 14¢. One celery stalk is approximately 20¢. The garlic is added in at 5¢ for one clove. The rosemary would be less than half of a bunch costing $1.99, but we'll call it $1.00 just the same. The crushed red pepper flakes are 6¢. Water is free from the tap, though some of you may debate that given that you do get a water bill from your municipality. The 15-ounce can of fire-roasted tomatoes is $2.19, but you should be looking for this to be on sale and stock up when that time comes. The kale costs $2.49. The oil for the garlic and thyme mixture costs 12¢, the thyme 18¢, and the garlic 10¢. The bread should be no more than half of a bakery loaf costing $3.39, so that's $1.70, and the oil and clove of garlic for the toast are 12¢ and 5¢ respectively. The cost for the soup alone is $8.72, and, as there are 8 servings, the garlic toast will ultimately use up both halves of the loaf of bread and double the olive oil and garlic, for a total of $3.73. The whole lot of it costs $12.45, or $1.56 per serving.

If you so desire, drizzle a little extra virgin olive oil over top of the soup, and, heck, for good measure, you could even shave some Parmigiano-Reggiano onto the soup before serving, figuring that each shaving would be approximately ½ ounce. That would add 60¢ per person, and a drizzle of olive oil is likely to be less than a tablespoon across four bowls, so that adds another 12¢ to the tally for an additional $2.52 for four.

Cooking Split Chicken Breast

Throughout this chapter, there will be many a call for cooked split chicken breasts. In order to keep from boring you at the turn of every page, I thought it a good idea to give an overview of cooking those bone-in, skin-on chicken breast halves so that when the call for "1 whole cooked chicken breast" arises, you will be ready. Generally speaking, two bone-in, skin-on chicken breast halves—known as split chicken breast in butcher parlance—will weigh around 1¾ pounds.

Preheat the oven to 375°F. Place the chicken breast in a small roasting dish and season it with salt and pepper. Roast until the skin is crisp and golden brown, and when the meat is pierced, the juices run clear, 40 to 45 minutes.

Allow the chicken to cool slightly, then remove the skin from the chicken—discard it, or delight some crispy-skin-crazed family member with the offering—and remove the chicken breast from the bones. Slice the meat crosswise into 1-inch pieces, or, if you feel comfortable doing it and the chicken has cooled sufficiently that you will not burn yourself, use your fingers to pull the meat apart. Use these chicken pieces wherever that "1 whole cooked chicken breast" is called for, unless, of course, you happen to have leftover chicken that needs using up.

ESTIMATED COST FOR ONE WHOLE COOKED CHICKEN BREAST: $3.48. I buy the no-added hormones, GMO-free, prepackaged split chicken breasts at Whole Foods. In the prepackaged case, they cost $1.99 per pound. This is still less than the $4.99 per pound for Whole Foods' prepackaged boneless, skinless chicken breast, as those usually run one pound or more, so I choose this more parsimonious option.

CHICKEN, SAUSAGE, AND KALE SOUP

{ **Serves 4 to 6, $10.00 to $15.00** }

This soup was originally conceived of to use up leftover cooked chicken. Not being 100 percent sure whether you have that luxury at your house, here on these pages, this recipe is designed so that you can cook up one whole bone-in, skin-on chicken breast as described on page 19. Why? Because short of leftover chicken breast from a whole roasted bird, this is your least expensive option for fresh chicken breast. And you wouldn't be reading this if inexpensive were not your goal. Oh, but wait. There's more. It's also quite savory and satisfying. What more could we ask for?

1 whole cooked chicken breast, cut crosswise into 1-inch strips (page 19)

¼ cup extra virgin olive oil

1 medium yellow onion, coarsely chopped

1 medium carrot, peeled, trimmed, coarsely chopped

1 celery stalk, trimmed, coarsely chopped

2 cloves garlic, finely chopped

1 teaspoon dried thyme, or 1 tablespoon fresh

⅛ teaspoon crushed red pepper flakes

2 (6-inch) links sweet Italian sausage (approximately ½ pound), casings removed, meat cut into ½-inch pieces

4 cups chicken broth

1 (15-ounce) can cannellini beans, including liquid

1 bunch kale (approximately ¾ pound), washed, stemmed, coarsely chopped

Kosher salt

Freshly ground black pepper

1 While the chicken roasts, prepare the other ingredients.

2 Heat the olive oil in a large stockpot—at least 6-quart capacity, as the kale starts off as quite a gargantuan pile—over medium heat. Add the onion, carrot, celery, and garlic and sauté—you are in the soffritto phase of this soup now—until the whole lot is softened and has blended together such that the color is leaning toward orange, 10 to 15 minutes. Add the thyme and crushed red pepper flakes, then add the sausage—you should have in the neighborhood of 24 pieces of ½-inch sausage from the two links, in the event that you are curious—cooking until the sausage is lightly browned, 3 to 5 minutes. Add the broth, the beans with their liquid, and the kale.

3 Add the chicken pieces to the pot, cover, and simmer, stirring occasionally, until the massive pile of kale is fully incorporated into the soup, 20 to 25 minutes. Add salt and pepper to taste, and serve it forth.

ESTIMATED COST FOR FOUR: $13.13. The chicken is roughly $3.50. The olive oil costs 48¢. The onion will weigh around ½ pound, and at 65¢ per pound, that's 33¢. The carrot will weigh about ⅙ pound, so at $3.99 for 5 pounds, that's 14¢. The celery is one stalk from ten (okay, so you and I know that celery sometimes has as many as twenty stalks, but in the interest of rounding up, we'll call it ten) for $1.99, so that's 20¢. The garlic costs around 10¢. The thyme costs 18¢ and the crushed red pepper flakes cost 3¢. The sausage costs $4.99 per pound at regular price, though I never—and I mean *never*—purchase it at regular price, I buy it on sale for $2.99 per pound and freeze it in handy single dinner–size packages until I need it—but, in keeping with rounding up, we'll call our two links $2.50. The broth costs $2.19 for 4 cups, the beans 99¢. The kale costs $2.49 for the bunch, and that's for organic at the grocery store, or local and not necessarily organic, but still quite good just the same, from the local farm stand or farmers market. At our grand total of $13.13, four servings cost $3.28 each, and at 6 servings, the cost drops to $2.19 per serving.

ORZO, SUN-DRIED TOMATO, AND WALNUT SALAD WITH FETA

{ **Serves 4, $10.00 to $15.00** }

"Oh, wow. I just got a bite of the bacon. You didn't tell me there was bacon in this," JR managed to blurt out through a mouthful of orzo, walnuts, and sun-dried tomatoes the very first time I made this salad. "There isn't any bacon in it, honey, it's got to be the toastiness from the walnuts making you think there's bacon in it." Then there was silence. Followed by, "Wow! How about the oregano, huh?" After further taste testing—for scientific purposes, of course—it seems that there is a quality in the sun-dried tomatoes that also whispers "I'm bacon, I'm bacon, I'm bacon" to one's taste buds. But no. There is no bacon. There is only you, orzo, walnuts, sun-dried tomatoes, oregano, and a bit of feta. Oh, and deliciousness. There is deliciousness as well in this meat-free, any-time-of-year, pasta salad.

1 pound orzo pasta

½ cup extra virgin olive oil, plus more for drizzling

½ cup finely chopped sun-dried tomatoes, not packed in oil (look in the bulk section or in the canned tomato aisle)

1 cup toasted walnuts (page xv), very coarsely chopped

½ cup feta cheese crumbles

¼ cup coarsely chopped fresh oregano leaves (see Note)

Kosher salt

Freshly ground black pepper

1 large head romaine lettuce or the lettuce of your choosing

1 Cook the orzo in a large pot of boiling, salted water according to the manufacturer's directions, until the pasta is firm to the bite but cooked through, also known as al dente, and mentioned many, many times as such on these pages. (I will bore you with it by the time you are a third of the way through the Entrées chapter.) Strain the orzo and rinse immediately with cold water to prevent it from adhering to itself, which it will do if left unrinsed for too long. If this should happen to you, just run it under cold water and it will once more separate nicely.

2 Transfer the orzo to a large serving bowl and stir in the olive oil. Add the tomatoes, walnuts, feta, and oregano, and stir well to combine. Add salt and pepper to taste.

3 Arrange a bed of lettuce on each of four plates. Spoon the orzo salad atop the lettuce, drizzle a bit of extra virgin olive oil on the exposed lettuce leaves if you're feeling so inclined, and serve it forth—warm, at room temperature, or chilled, it's equally delicious. And, without the lettuce, this is a quick and convenient dish to take to a party.

NOTE: If you are unable to find fresh oregano, go ahead and substitute fresh parsley, but the very next time you see fresh oregano for sale, grab it and get thee to your kitchen to make this dish.

ESTIMATED COST FOR FOUR: $10.44. The orzo costs no more than $1.99, but, as I will so frequently harp upon, you must be on the lookout for pasta on sale for a lone dollar per box. It's foolish not to buy it then, for you know you will use it, and it will not go bad in the pantry awaiting use. The olive oil was 96¢. The sun-dried tomatoes were $7.99 per pound, and the quantity used was 2 ounces, so that's $1.00. The walnuts were $8.69 for a bag containing 4 cups, and so we add $2.17 to the tally. The feta was $3.99 for 6 ounces. We used 2 ounces, so that adds another $1.33. The oregano—if it does not grow wild around your garden as a result of you planting it and allowing it to go to seed in your first year of gardening—would be around half of a bunch from the grocery store costing $1.99, so we'll call that $1.00. The head of lettuce should be no more than $1.99.

If you were feeling as though you had some money to burn, you could add some pork tenderloin to this salad, figuring on using about ½ pound for four servings, at a cost of $10.99 per pound; so, an additional $5.50, which rightly pushes this into the Splurge category, as no one is giving away pork tenderloin. Or you could use that leftover chicken you can't quite decide what to do with and avoid food waste as we are wont to do.

SUMMER ROMAINE AND CORN SALAD WITH CHICKEN

{ **Serves 4, $10.00 to $15.00** }

This recipe is perfect for a summer day, particularly if you have leftover chicken and Pan-Sautéed Corn and Tomatoes (page 98) on hand. Although the recipe calls for chicken, you could just as easily substitute seafood, shellfish, or steak, and still have quite a scrumptious concoction on your hands. Or on your plate, to be more accurate.

1 large head romaine lettuce, trimmed, washed, cut crosswise into 1-inch wide ribbons

1 whole cooked chicken breast, cut crosswise into 1-inch strips (page 19)

3 cups Pan-Sautéed Corn and Tomatoes (page 98), chilled or at room temperature

½ cup Lime Corn Cream Dressing (page 25)

Kosher salt

Freshly ground black pepper

1 Distribute the lettuce evenly across four plates. Now be just as fair with the chicken, as you give each of the four of you an equal amount, arranging it nicely over the lettuce. While you're at it, give everyone ¾ cup of the Pan-Sautéed Corn and Tomatoes. Now share a couple tablespoons of the Lime Corn Cream Dressing with each of your dining partners, season with salt and pepper, and serve it forth.

ESTIMATED COST FOR FOUR: $11.97. One head of romaine should cost no more than $1.99 during the summer months when corn, tomatoes, and basil are at their peak. The chicken should be around 1¾ pounds from a bone-in, skin-on split breast, which costs $1.99 per pound, so that adds $3.50 to our tally. Our portions of the corn and tomato dish cost $5.80. The Lime Corn Cream Dressing costs 68¢ for ½ cup.

LIME CORN CREAM DRESSING

{ **Makes 2 cups, $5.00 or less** }

This dressing is so versatile, I felt it needed its own page. Within the pages of this book are two options for salads that make use of this dressing—one in this chapter and the other in the Splurges chapter (page 175), but this dressing would be fantastic as a dipping sauce for barbecued chicken wings or fish cakes, too.

1 cup fresh (2 medium ears) or frozen corn kernels

1 cup sour cream

The zest and juice of 1 lime

⅛ teaspoon kosher salt

Freshly ground black pepper

1 If you are using corn kernels fresh off the cob, it's quite easy to shave them. Simply shuck the ears of their husks and silks, leaving the stem intact. That's your handle to hold the ear of corn steady while you cut. Place the ear of corn tip-downward in a large bowl, using the stem to hold it steady. Using a serrated knife, start at the top and cut downward, keeping the knife as close as possible to the cob. You may have some random bits of silk in the mix; pick them out if they bother you. Work around the ear until all of the kernels have been shaved off, and away we go. Cook the kernels in a large pot of boiling, salted water, 1 to 2 minutes until golden. Drain in a colander, rinse them with cold water, and cool for 5 minutes. Or, you may store them away for use within a day or two in an airtight container within the confines of your refrigerator.

2 Puree the corn, sour cream, lime zest, lime juice, and salt in a blender or food processor until smooth. Add pepper to taste.

ESTIMATED COST FOR TWO CUPS OF DRESSING: $2.70. The corn could come either from two medium-size fresh ears at 55¢ per ear or from a 1-pound bag of frozen corn, we'll use the higher cost of fresh, $1.10. The sour cream costs $2.19 for 32 tablespoons, so our use here cost $1.10, and the lime was 50¢.

BLUE CHEESE WEDGE SALAD WITH GRILLED SIRLOIN TIPS

{ **Serves 4, $10.00 to $15.00** }

The iceberg lettuce wedge salad with blue cheese dressing is a steak house classic, and when you add grilled, marinated sirloin tips, it's an all-in-one meal that's perfect for a hot summer night. The blue cheese dressing would also be fabulous paired with chicken wings, grilled chicken legs doused with barbecue sauce (page 79), or, as I like to make use of whatever bit of dressing is left behind, as a dip for fresh-from-the-garden veggies like zucchini and carrots.

1 pound sirloin tips, ¾ inch to 1 inch thick

Kosher salt

Freshly ground black pepper

¼ cup Worcestershire sauce

¼ cup low-sodium soy sauce

2 cloves garlic, crushed

1 head iceberg lettuce, stem and any frowzy-looking outer leaves removed

1 medium tomato (approximately ½ pound)

Blue Cheese Dressing (recipe follows)

1 Season the sirloin tips with salt and pepper. Place them in a shallow bowl or one-gallon-capacity plastic food storage bag. Add the Worcestershire and soy sauces, and toss in the crushed garlic. Haven't we crushed garlic before? Well, the easiest way to do this is to take the cloves, unpeeled, place them on your cutting surface, and then, using the side of a knife or the back of a serving spoon, smoosh down upon the clove. The skin will peel off easily, and you will have released the essential oils that we are after for this marinade. Cover or seal your container, and refrigerate for at least 1 hour, and up to 24 hours.

2 At the appointed wedge-salad-making time, preheat the grill and cook your sirloin tips over medium heat to the desired doneness (7 to 9 minutes for medium). Allow the meat to rest for 5 minutes, then transfer to a cutting surface and cut crosswise into ¼-inch strips. Discard the remaining marinade.

3 While the meat is cooking, cut the head of lettuce lengthwise (top to bottom), into quarters. Likewise, you can slice your tomatoes the same way, lengthwise (down through the core rather than across it) into 8 as-equal-as-possible wedges. This would also be a fine time to make the dressing.

4 On each of four plates, place one iceberg quarter and two of the tomato wedges. Place one-quarter of the sirloin tip slices on each plate, drizzle a couple tablespoons—or more—of dressing across each plate, season with salt and pepper, and serve it forth.

Blue Cheese Dressing

¼ **cup mayonnaise**

½ **cup sour cream**

The juice of 1 lemon

1 tablespoon Worcestershire sauce

¼ **cup blue cheese crumbles**

1 In a medium bowl, combine the mayonnaise, sour cream, lemon juice, and Worcestershire sauce, and mix until you have a well-amalgamated dressing—no chunks of mayo floating around, no meaty-colored puddles of Worcestershire. Stir in the blue cheese crumbles, and, just to be sure it's good, sneak a taste with a piece of carrot or celery before serving.

ESTIMATED COST FOR FOUR: $14.66. The sirloin costs $7.99 per pound. We're using a pound here, and I always let the butcher know it's okay to be under the 1 pound mark, as no one will notice a missing tenth of an ounce. We are using 5 tablespoons of Worcestershire in the entire recipe. At $2.79 for 19 tablespoons, that's 74¢. Soy sauce is $3.29 for 30 tablespoons, and therefore costs 11¢ per tablespoon. We're using 4 tablespoons, so that's 44¢. The two cloves of garlic run us about 10¢. Mayonnaise costs $3.99 for 64 tablespoons. We are using 4 tablespoons, so that's 25¢. Sour cream costs $2.19 for 16 ounces and yields 32 tablespoons. We are using 8 tablespoons, so that costs 55¢. One lemon costs 50¢, and the crumbled blue cheese costs $3.99 for 6 ounces. We used about 1 ounce, so that's 67¢. The head of iceberg lettuce costs $1.79, and the tomato should cost no more than $3.25 per pound, so at ½ pound, that's $1.63.

If you are someone who is offended by the mere mention of iceberg lettuce—though I challenge you to try this and not find yourself smitten—this salad is equally as wonderful with romaine. Going the romaine route will add 20¢ to the tally as it is typically priced at $1.99/head. Likewise, you could substitute leftover chicken for the beef—skipping the Worcestershire marinade, of course—and enjoy a slightly less expensive variation on the wedge, as chicken can easily be found for less than $7.99 per pound.

PANZANELLA (ITALIAN BREAD AND TOMATO SALAD)

{ **Serves 4, $5.00 to $10.00** }

You're puttering about your kitchen. It's hot out. You don't feel like making dinner. Only you must. You have some tomatoes. You have some day-old bread. You pretty much have a meal. A no-cook, refreshing summertime meal, at that.

½ pound day-old country bread, such as ciabatta (or bread that has been allowed to sit out for a few hours to dry somewhat), cut into ½-inch cubes

2 large tomatoes (approximately 1 pound), cut into 8 wedges each

1 medium shallot, finely chopped

¼ pound ricotta salata (a salted, aged ricotta), cut into ¼-inch cubes, or feta cheese crumbles

¼ cup chopped fresh basil

¼ cup chopped fresh mint

Kosher salt

Freshly ground black pepper

¼ cup extra virgin olive oil

¼ cup white wine vinegar

1 Combine the bread, tomatoes, shallot, cheese, basil, and mint in a large bowl. Stir to combine, and add salt and pepper to taste. Now step away from the bowl for a half-hour or so to allow the tomatoes to release their juices into the salad. This might be a good time to catch up on that reading you've been meaning to do. Heck, maybe there are even a few recipes in this book you've been meaning to read over. Why don't you just go ahead and do that. Before you know it, it will be time to mix the olive oil and white wine vinegar together until the mixture thickens somewhat, and then it'll be time to pour that dressing over your dinner. Next thing you know, you'll be doling out bread salad to the whole family, just like that. So easy, yet so satisfying. Oh, and what do you know? So inexpensive.

ESTIMATED COST FOR FOUR: $8.33. The bread should really be from the day-old rack to begin with, so it should cost no more than $1.99 for 1 pound—you'll notice that bread usually has a weight associated with it, and many times, a country loaf is right around a pound. We're using a half-pound here, so that's $1.00. Even if you used fresh bakery bread, the tally will only rise by about 70¢. The tomatoes should be height-of-summer ripe, which happens to be when they are least expensive and locally grown, so our pound should cost around $3.25 at the most. The shallot should cost 25¢ or so. The ricotta salata is $3.99 per pound and we used a quarter of that, so we'll add another dollar to the tally. The basil and mint wish that you would grow them in pots or in the garden yourself, but if you bought them, they would each be about half of a bunch that costs $1.99, so $2.00 includes both basil and mint. The olive oil is 48¢; and with us using 4 tablespoons, the white wine vinegar is just over 35¢ at $2.99 for 34 tablespoons.

HARVEST SALAD WITH HONEY-BALSAMIC DRESSING

{ **Serves 4, $10.00 to $15.00** }

In the early autumn, winter squash is starting to become available at the farmers market or farm stand, but it just doesn't seem cool enough for soup. So when you aren't quite ready for soup just yet, this salad is a wonderful way to incorporate some of the early harvest bounty into your dinner plans. The skin of the acorn squash is edible, so be sure to wash the squash well before slicing it up for roasting, and if you aren't able to locate whole hazelnuts easily, you could substitute a half-cup package of chopped hazelnuts instead—you'll find those in the baking aisle, or toasted pecans would also do the trick—though, really, they are worth the effort; JR considers whole toasted hazelnuts a dessert.

Squash

1 (1¾- to 2-pound) whole acorn squash

¼ cup extra virgin olive oil

3 tablespoons packed brown sugar

Kosher salt

Freshly ground black pepper

Honey-Balsamic Dressing

¼ cup plus 2 tablespoons extra virgin olive oil

¼ cup honey

2 tablespoons Dijon mustard

2 tablespoons balsamic vinegar

Kosher salt

Freshly ground black pepper

Salad

3 cups (5 ounces) mixed baby greens or spring mix

½ cup toasted hazelnuts (page xvi)

¼ cup dried cranberries

4 slices bacon (approximately ¼ pound), cooked to desired crispness and crumbled

¼ cup Gorgonzola crumbles

1 Preheat the oven to 375°F. Cut the acorn squash in half lengthwise. It's easiest to do this by placing it top down—where the stem once lived—onto your cutting surface, and cutting straight through the pointed end down to the cutting surface. Once the squash is halved, remove the seeds and discard them, and then cut each half crosswise into ½-inch-wide slices, such that you have a lovely ripple effect from the ridges of the squash. Place the cut squash into a large mixing bowl.

2 In a small mixing bowl, combine the olive oil and brown sugar, and blend well. Pour over the squash, making sure to coat all of it. Season with salt and pepper.

3 Transfer the coated squash to a 9 by 13-inch rimmed baking sheet. Scrape any remaining oil and sugar from the bowl onto the squash as well. Bake, turning each piece over midway through the cooking time, until the edges of the squash are browning and the skin is easily pierced with a fork—as in, you could easily chew it if it weren't so darned hot—40 to 45 minutes. Remove from the oven and set aside to cool for 5 to 10 minutes.

4 While the squash cooks, combine the olive oil, honey, mustard, and balsamic vinegar for the dressing. Mix well to blend the dressing completely, and season with salt and pepper.

5 Place one-quarter of the mixed greens on each of four plates. Top each with one-quarter of the squash. Decorate each plate with 2 tablespoons of toasted hazelnuts, 1 tablespoon of dried cranberries, one-quarter of the bacon crumbles, and 1 tablespoon of the Gorgonzola crumbles. I normally advocate dressing on the side, but in this case, I think you should drizzle a tablespoon or two over each plate, as it adds to the aesthetically pleasing nature of this dish, then bring the remaining dressing to the table in the event more is desired. Serve this extremely attractive salad forth—I happen to love the colors of autumn, and this has got all of that going on—and celebrate the last warm days of the year.

ESTIMATED COST FOR FOUR: $13.25. The acorn squash should be purchased during—ahem—the harvest season, when it is least expensive. In my area, that means it costs 79¢ per pound, so 2 pounds will cost us $1.60. The olive oil for roasting costs 48¢, the brown sugar is 4¢ per tablespoon, so that adds 12¢ to the tally. The olive oil for the dressing costs 72¢, the honey costs $1.00, the mustard costs 32¢, and the balsamic costs around 49¢, coming as it does from a 16.9-ounce bottle that costs $7.99 for 33 tablespoons. The lettuce mix costs $3.99. The hazelnuts cost $6.99 for 2¼ cups, so that adds $1.55 to our total. The dried cranberries cost 48¢ for ½ cup, the bacon costs $1.75 for ¼ pound, and the Gorgonzola costs 75¢.

Green Tomatoes and Garden Chairs

JR had lived at the house we share now for just about ten years before my toothbrush and I showed up, and when I did, there was already a full complement of Black Angus cattle—seven, in fact, far too many for our property—living here. JR did keep a garden before I unpacked my bags, but I wanted something a little larger, a little more ambitious than his normal wee garden.

I stood by the chicken coop, watching him till the soil with his tractor that first year. Oh, yes. I wanted something quite grand, I did. My only previous experience gardening had come the year earlier—at my live-alone apartment—and that garden hadn't been a terribly successful endeavor.

The apartment house—an antique Colonial with sloping floors and bowed walls—was where I began cooking in earnest, making my first dinner for JR, one that caused him to repeatedly tell his friends, "She makes cream of mushroom soup from scratch." I created elaborate meals, fancy sandwiches to take along to the beach, fresh lemonade, stews, cakes; many of these dishes are still in my repertoire today. And I started a garden. During the second week of June. In New England.

An elderly man who lived in the building came out to assess my progress.

"What's that you're planting?" he asked.

"Oh, these are tomatoes," I cheerfully replied.

Now, if you don't garden, you might not know that tomato plants are easily recognizable as such. The gentleman had to ask because I was planting seed. During the second week of June. He sighed softly, took a moment to determine how, precisely, to let me down, and said, "I believe that you want to start tomato seeds a bit earlier."

Brushing the hair out of my eyes as I stood up, and not yet deterred, I replied, "Oh. Okay. Like how much earlier?"

"Like March."

Needless to say, there was no tomato harvest that year, not even the late harvest that, in reply to the kindly neighbor's counsel, I speculated we might get.

It is likely quite obvious to you then, that I had no gardening experience from my youth, either. The house where I grew up had far too small a yard for a garden. Add to that, nary a green thing would grow in the back of the house, so hardpan was the soil at our city center home—small city, but city nonetheless. Undeterred in her quest for fresh vegetables, my mother hosted a vegetable co-op in the garage of our two-family home.

On Saturdays, friends and neighbors would descend upon our home, my mother, clipboard in hand, reviewing checked boxes that constituted each order. Then, chirping out a command, food was quickly gathered and stashed in repurposed banana or iceberg lettuce boxes, and transported to each co-oper's car. Fresh food was a priority; we just didn't grow it ourselves.

Yet, not even a year after my failed tomato-growing attempt, I stood watching JR prepare a 60-foot by 20-foot garden for me, tilling the fertile and loamy soil that the resident cattle had so graciously amended (or that JR had so graciously amended) with their manure. I planted with abandon. I had no idea about yields or growth habits, and so I planted six mint plants, six oregano—six! Each! Hello, mint and oregano are *weeds!*—more peppers than two humans could ever consume, and, of course, tomatoes. I planted everything in one day—and I do mean *everything*—the entire garden full to the gills on that Memorial Day. And though

I was joking when I staged a collapse into the lawn, strewing my planting gear, empty nursery pots, and seed packets all around my facedown prone body—oh, by the way, this isn't a very funny joke as your loved one might think you've actually collapsed—I was exhausted. Gardening was *hard*, I'd decided.

Nonetheless, I continued gardening year after year, and my garden evolved from its first year form. Eventually, I had to dig up an entire 10-foot by 20-foot section that had become a well-knit carpet of oregano, taking much of the gorgeous manure-nurtured soil with it. We eventually installed a split rail fence. And by "we," I mean JR. Digging by hand into the rocky New England soil to install my pretty fence. Do you see a trend here? I have a whim, and JR pays. There was a year or two when the garden went fallow—neither of us having the time to deal with it, and hanging our heads in shame when visitors would ask to see it, so overgrown and unappealing had it become.

whim about raised beds, and someone else might have executed them. We started with four, vowing to reclaim the remainder of the garden in stages. Two of the four original beds are perennial beds—one full of bushy, waving fronds of asparagus; lavender, sage, thyme, and volunteer dill and cilantro in the other. The dill and cilantro are now considered perennial, for they show up each year whether I plant them or not. Gardening became much easier, more manageable. I no longer rush to plant everything in one day. Instead, I take my time, pacing myself so as not to overwhelm, planting cold-weather crops in the early spring, seeding a few rows of radishes and carrots in the early morning when I have a moment, gradually installing the seed starts into their beds—the idea of doing it all at once seems so absurd to me now, a killjoy for what is, undoubtedly, one of my most gratifying pursuits.

Two larger raised beds have been added since the original four, and our weathered and beaten Adirondack chairs, which JR made long before I moved in, are tucked into the back of the garden, near a large rock—one might call it a boulder—a rock that couldn't be moved by one lone man, and that now anchors the flower garden.

In these chairs, we sit each night and discuss that day's events. I get up and attend to my zucchini plants—or perhaps it's more accurate to say that I'm attending to my squash-bug-killing obsession—then do a little weeding, and settle back to enjoy a glass of wine, the view, and JR's company before making dinner. Occasionally, we'll sit a little longer, or return to the garden after dinner to watch the nightly show of fireflies along

Our neighbors are very talented gardeners, with some of the most creative gardening executions I've seen—a train garden, complete with a tiny train on tiny tracks chugging along past tiny trees; a garden border formed of neatly trimmed boxwood in the shape of a knot; a surfeit of rare plants. After I visit them, I always wonder when or if my yard will ever look so nice. After having had one of my "oops, that was my *outside* voice" moments and saying about as much to my neighbor, she replied, "Well, it *has* evolved a lot over 32 years." That's the thing about gardening—it's a constant evolution, the back-and-forth play between you and nature.

JR and I reclaimed our garden a few years ago. Someone might have had a the tree line beyond our garden and the abutting hay field.

The tomato bed is situated in front of my chair this year. We rotate our tomato crop each year, so this will not always be the case, and next year, it will likely be where the beets, carrots, radishes, and lettuce are currently living—at the far end of the garden. JR fashioned a tomato support for all eight tomato plants from the stalks of our neighbor's runaway bamboo—this was his idea, not my flight of fancy—and it's rather handsome—even our pro-level gardener neighbors are impressed. We'll enjoy hundreds of tomatoes—all heirloom, but for the Roma tomatoes for sauce, including the endangered Trophy Tomato, which was developed not far from our house, in Newport, Rhode Island, circa 1870. Just a bit younger than our house, this tomato is.

Once the cooler weather comes, whatever green tomatoes are left on the vine, I will transform into a chutney (page 36) that started as a friend's shared piccalilli recipe given to me that first year of the tractor-plowed garden—as it would have been unnecessary for the apartment garden—and one that I've modified into a chutney (much to our friend's chagrin, for he is a piccalilli purist).

GREEN TOMATO CHUTNEY

{ **Makes approximately 12 cups** }

This chutney may be preserved if it isn't to be eaten in the near future. If that's your plan, please see the bit on canning (page 131) in order to be sure that all canning implements and jars are property sterilized and such. This chutney goes well with pork and chicken; if you'd prefer to make a piccalilli instead, simply eliminate the apple, raisins, and nutmeg, and piccalilli purity has been restored.

12 cups sliced green tomatoes (½-inch, crosswise; approximately 12 medium)

¼ cup kosher salt, divided

3 large Vidalia onions, coarsely chopped

4 medium Granny Smith apples, peeled, cored, coarsely chopped

¼ cup golden raisins

¼ cup raisins

½ teaspoon crushed red pepper flakes

¾ teaspoon cayenne pepper

¾ teaspoon ground allspice

¾ teaspoon ground cloves

¾ teaspoon ground nutmeg

¾ teaspoon cinnamon

1½ cups granulated sugar

2 cups apple cider vinegar

1 Layer the green tomatoes in a large colander or steamer basket, sprinkling each layer with approximately ½ teaspoon of the salt in order to draw out moisture from them. Let the tomatoes sit for one hour, then rinse, and place in a large (at least 8-quart capacity), nonreactive (stainless steel) stockpot.

2 Add the onions, apples, and raisins to the stockpot, and stir to combine. Add the crushed red pepper flakes, cayenne pepper, allspice, cloves, nutmeg, cinnamon, sugar, and vinegar, and bring to a boil over medium-high heat.

3 Decrease the heat and simmer uncovered, stirring occasionally, until the tomatoes have broken down and the chutney is reduced by half, approximately 2 hours. Cool the chutney slightly before you spoon it into airtight containers—you will need multiples—and store in the refrigerator for up to a month.

entrées

PASTA CARBONARA

{ **Serves 4, $5.00 to $10.00** }

Quick Meal

As I have espoused the low-meat meal as a way to rein in that food spending of ours, I thought it apropos to start the entrée chapter with a low-meat meal, in this case, the delicious, silken, eggy dish that is Pasta Carbonara. This is the sort of dish that every cook should hold dear in his or her repertoire. It comes together with ease, and it is infinitely satisfying for so simple a preparation. It is also a great year-round staple dish that can easily solve that *to-take-out-or-not-to-take-out* dilemma, because even when it looks as though you have "nothing" in the house fit for consumption, you likely have these ingredients hanging around. And they are magic together. Go on, try this dish, and tell me you're not convinced.

1 pound linguine

8 tablespoons (1 stick) salted sweet cream butter, melted

3 large eggs, beaten lightly

½ cup grated Pecorino Romano cheese

Kosher salt

Freshly ground black pepper

¼ pound pancetta, cooked to desired doneness and crumbled

1 Cook the linguine in a large stockpot until it's al dente (follow the manufacturer's instructions). Drain the linguine, reserving ½ cup of the cooking water (for the best way to do this, see page xv), and return the pasta to the pot. Working off of the heat—so, not on the burner upon which you were just cooking, but on another heatproof surface— stir the melted butter into the pasta. I find a pasta fork works well for this task.

2 In a separate small mixing bowl, we are going to temper the eggs with the reserved pasta water, much as one does when making a custard. We are doing this to create a smooth sauce and to avoid the horror of scrambled eggs in what should be a creamy pasta dish. Gradually pour the pasta water into the eggs in a steady stream,

continuously whisking the eggs as you do. This gradual introduction of the hot liquid will raise the temperature of the eggs, keeping them from scrambling as they would if they were suddenly exposed to heat.

3 Now add the egg mixture to the pasta, stirring constantly as you do. Stir in the cheese, and salt and pepper to taste. That's it. You're done. Now take a pasta forkful—or two or three—dole it out onto a plate, and proceed similarly with the remaining three plates. Top the whole lot with the crumbled pancetta and eat at once. After your plate has been cleaned of every last morsel, marvel at how incredibly easy and delicious Pasta Carbonara is and, for only a very brief moment, have a fleeting thought of how you didn't feel deprived having but an ounce of meat.

NOTE: This is a good base dish from which to venture, adding peas or asparagus in the spring, chopped tomatoes in the summer, or any other vegetable that strikes your fancy when it's in season.

ESTIMATED COST FOR FOUR: $6.04. The pasta was $1.99 for a 1-pound box. You and I both know that you can find pasta on sale for half that price, but as we don't want anyone to be disappointed with their own personal final tally, we'll use that larger figure for our purposes here. The butter is one stick from a pack of four costing $2.79, so we round up and call that 70¢. The eggs should cost no more than 26¢ each, so that's 78¢. The Pecorino Romano cheese costs $7.99 per pound, and ½ cup is approximately 1 ounce, so that's 50¢. The pancetta costs $8.29 per pound, so a quarter pound would factor in at about $2.07.

If you'd like to cut the cost back even further, bacon can be substituted in place of the pancetta for an additional savings of approximately 32¢, with one pound of the fancy Black Forest bacon retailing for $6.99.

PEA PUREE LASAGNETTE

{ **Serves 4, $5.00 to $10.00** }

Quick Meal

As you know, part of eating for less involves eating meat less frequently or in smaller quantities. I realize that this may be an unpopular approach for carnivores, but one way to overcome complaint is to use a small amount of cured meat, such as bacon or pancetta, to garnish dishes. That way you get a fix of meat flavor without spending piles of money. Because if we have piles of money, we want to conserve them. And if we don't, well, we haven't a pile to spend.

This recipe is an assemblage of other items that can be prepared quickly, and as such, it comes together swiftly. Note that you'll be using an entire 16-ounce bag of frozen peas and an entire medium shallot in the preparation, though they are divided up for separate treatment. While it may look as though there are many steps, this is, in fact, a very convenient, nearly meat-free meal for a weeknight. And if you are not a carnivore, skip the bacon. It's still scrumptious without it.

1 cup plus 2⅓ cups frozen peas

1 medium shallot, finely chopped

1 teaspoon dried thyme, or 3 teaspoons fresh, divided

1 cup fresh ricotta (see Note)

Kosher salt

Freshly ground black pepper

6 wide lasagna noodles

2 tablespoons plus 3 tablespoons extra virgin olive oil

2 tablespoons unsalted butter, cut into pieces

2 tablespoons grated Pecorino Romano cheese

4 slices bacon, cooked to desired doneness and crumbled

¼ cup (4 tablespoons) crème fraîche or sour cream

1 Preheat the oven to 350°F. To make the pea puree, cook 1 cup of the peas, half of the shallot, and half of the thyme in ¼ cup water in a small saucepan over medium heat until heated through, 3 to 5 minutes. Remove from the heat and set aside to cool slightly, 5 to 7 minutes.

2 Once the pea mixture has cooled, add it, liquid and all, to a blender or food processor and puree. Alternatively, you could mash the mixture. In either case, it will resemble homemade baby food, and this is quite all right. Desirable, in fact.

3 Transfer the puree to a medium bowl and add the ricotta. Mix them well, until you have a pale green blend. Add salt and pepper to taste. Set aside. The puree may be made a day in advance and refrigerated in an airtight container if you so desire.

4 In a large pot of boiling, salted water, cook the lasagna noodles according to the manufacturer's directions until al dente. Rinse well with cold water to prevent the noodles from sticking to one another or to themselves. Set them aside.

5 Grease a 10 by 15-inch rimmed baking sheet with 2 tablespoons of the olive oil to prevent the finished lasagnette's bottom layer from gluing itself in place. Lay two sheets of pasta on the bottom of the pan the long way. Spread one-quarter of the pea puree on each. Cover each of these with another sheet of lasagna and spread the remaining pea puree evenly on both. Top with a third layer of pasta and evenly distribute 1 tablespoon of the butter pieces along the top noodle of each lasagnette stack. Sprinkle 1 tablespoon of cheese over each stack, season with salt and pepper, and bake until the lasagnette is lightly browned

and bubbling— indicating hotness as it does, 25 to 30 minutes. Remove the lasagnette from the oven and let it stand for 5 minutes so that it doesn't fall apart while you cut it. Do resist the temptation to cut before cooling as you will have a mess of light green filling and slippery lasagna noodles sloshing about as you attempt to serve them forth.

6 While the lasagnette cooks, cook the remaining peas, for they will grace the top of the lasagnette when all is completed. Heat the remaining 3 tablespoons of olive oil in a small saucepan over medium heat. Add the remaining half of the shallot and cook until translucent, 2 to 3 minutes. Add the peas and the remaining thyme to the pan, and cook until the peas are heated through, 5 to 7 minutes. Keep the topping peas warm until the lasagnette is ready to serve.

7 Top each lasagnette with one-quarter of the pea mixture. Sprinkle crumbled bacon onto each plate and then gild the lily by adding a dollop—by which I mean a tablespoon—of crème fraîche or sour cream if you so desire, and serve the brightly colored stacks forth to the delight, even, of the carnivores.

NOTE: It is most definitely worth the effort to locate fresh ricotta rather than shelf-stable-for-months ricotta.

Seasonal Tip: This would be a wonderful use of locally grown peas when they become available in the spring, though, as you can see, I make it using frozen peas, and therefore am able to enjoy it any time the pea puree craving strikes.

ESTIMATED COST FOR FOUR: $8.98. The peas cost $1.49 per bag. The ricotta was $5.99 for one pound, we used ½ pound, so that's $3.00. The shallot costs right around 25¢. The thyme runs us around 18¢. The lasagna noodles were $2.69 for a box with 18 sheets of pasta. You'll use 6 sheets for this meal, so that's 90¢. The olive oil for the entire dish is 60¢, and the butter is 18¢. The Pecorino Romano costs $7.99 per pound, and at ¼ ounce for 2 tablespoons, that adds 13¢ to the tally. The bacon was $6.99 for one pound, and we're using four slices, which are roughly one ounce each for a total of $1.75. The crème fraîche was $3.99 for 8 ounces, so using ½ ounce per serving, that's 50¢.

Go meat-free for a savings of $1.75 in bacon expense, and if you aren't feeling the crème fraîche love, go without to save an additional 50¢. Sans bacon and crème fraîche, the lasagnette costs $6.73 for four.

KALE LASAGNE WITH WALNUT PESTO

{ Serves 4, $5.00 to $10.00 }

I am a big fan of cavolo nero, or dinosaur kale, but this could be made with any leafy greens—spinach would be scrumptious; Swiss chard, succulent; and beet greens, delectable. "Bodacious," which would continue the alliteration, is a word of which I am not terribly fond, and so, "delectable" are the beet greens. This is a multistep recipe, so if you wanted to get a jump on the prep work, you could certainly make the walnut pesto and cook the greens a day ahead of time and refrigerate them until you're ready to make the béchamel sauce and assemble the lasagne.

Walnut Pesto

½ cup (2 ounces) walnuts

½ cup packed parsley leaves

¼ cup grated Pecorino Romano cheese

¼ cup extra virgin olive oil

Kosher salt

Freshly ground black pepper

Kale

2 bunches cavolo nero (also called dinosaur kale)

¼ cup extra virgin olive oil

1 medium shallot, finely chopped

Kosher salt

Freshly ground black pepper

Béchamel Sauce

5 tablespoons unsalted butter

7 tablespoons all-purpose flour

5 cups whole milk

⅛ teaspoon grated nutmeg

Kosher salt

Freshly ground black pepper

For Assembling

9 lasagna noodles, cooked al dente

¾ cup grated Pecorino Romano cheese, divided in thirds

1   The traditional way to make pesto is with a mortar and pestle. It's okay to exhale now. Even I don't do this, so I will not ask it of you. A good work-around for making pesto quickly without turning it into an actual paste is to use a mini food processor or food processor, and pulse each ingredient separately until it is coarsely ground. I process the walnuts before the parsley in order to avoid ending up with liquid parsley in the processor, which would add moisture to the pesto, for we don't want that. Once the walnuts and parsley are pulsed to a coarse texture—around the size of tiny pebbles for the walnuts—combine them with the cheese in a small bowl, add the olive oil, stirring to combine, then add salt and pepper to taste.

2   It is important that the kale be rinsed well—it is a broad leaf that grows near the dirt and as such, can pick up dirt—then dried, and finely chopped. You can chop the kale into strips if you like, but you may find yourself fighting clumps of kale while eating. Best to try for fork-manageable pieces of kale—say, 1-inch squares—in the preparation stage than at the dinner table.

3   Heat the olive oil in a large skillet or sauté pan over medium heat. Add the shallot and cook until translucent, 2 to 3 minutes. Add the kale and sauté until all of it is softened, turning it frequently to be sure that the pieces on the bottom do not burn, 5 to 7 minutes. Add salt and pepper to taste.

4 To make the béchamel sauce, create a roux by melting the butter in a large saucepan over medium heat, then whisking in the flour (keep the whisk moving constantly) until they are combined. Continue to cook your roux until it is a light golden brown, 3 to 5 minutes. Add the milk slowly, whisking continuously as it is added.

5 Once the milk is added to the roux, cook over medium heat until the sauce is thick, with a consistency similar to that of pancake batter, 10 to 12 minutes; whisk it constantly and be careful that the sauce does not scald on the bottom of the pan. Remove the pan from the heat, stir in the grated nutmeg, and add salt and pepper to taste.

6 Preheat the oven to 350°F. Line a 10 by 15-inch rimmed baking sheet with aluminum foil, and take out your lasagne pan or large casserole dish.

7 Now, you are ready for lasagne assembly. Spread enough béchamel sauce over the bottom of the lasagne pan

to just cover it. Place 3 lasagna noodles atop the béchamel. Cover with half of the cooked kale mixture. Top the kale mixture with one-third of the remaining béchamel sauce, then sprinkle with ¼ cup of Pecorino Romano. Repeat for the second layer, and then top with the last 3 lasagna noodles.

8 Mix the walnut pesto with the remaining béchamel sauce, and spread the mixture over the top layer of noodles. Sprinkle the last ¼ cup of Pecorino Romano over the assembled lasagne. Place the pan on your foil-lined baking sheet, and bake until the lasagne is browned on top and the sauce is bubbling on the sides, 40 to 45 minutes. Remove the lasagne from the oven and allow it to cool for 10 minutes before cutting into this gooey kale masterpiece. Serve it forth, and remind yourself that even though you are ingesting a huge amount of butter, milk, and cheese, there has to be some benefit from the leafy greens.

ESTIMATED COST FOR FOUR: $9.24. One-half cup of walnuts is $1.08. The parsley is an entire purchased bunch that costs $1.99. Ahem. Do you not have a parsley plant yet? Please, at least tell me you have a basil plant or pot of thyme. The Pecorino Romano for the pesto costs an additional 25¢. The olive oil for the pesto costs 48¢. The kale was $2.49 per bunch, and we used two bunches, so that's $4.98. The shallot/olive oil sauté will add 48¢ in olive oil and 25¢ in shallot to the tally. The béchamel sauce consists of 5 cups of milk for $1.25, butter at 44¢ for 5 tablespoons (out of 32 tablespoons for $2.79), a little more than 11¢ in flour, with flour costing $4.49 for a 5-pound bag that yields us seventy six ¼ cups of flour, and 5¢ in nutmeg. The lasagna noodles are half of a box that cost $1.99—it isn't as important that they be wide noodles as in the Pea Puree Lasagnette, so we're able to purchase a less expensive variety. Nine noodles therefore cost $1.00. We used $1.50 in grated Pecorino Romano, tossing around ½ cup over each of the three layers of lasagne. So for a total cost of $13.86, or $2.31 per serving, we have 6 servings of scrumptious greens-filled lasagne. Love that! Now who gets to take the leftovers for lunch?

GARLICKY TOMATOES AND OLIVES WITH WHOLE-WHEAT SPAGHETTI

{ **Serves 4, $5.00 to $10.00** }

Quick Meal

For years I have made a very simple fresh tomato sauce with tomatoes from my garden. Once the weather warms up, I find myself randomly craving that sauce—while brewing my coffee, while doing laundry—there is something about vine-ripened tomatoes that inspires epicurean daydreams. To gussy that basic sauce up just a touch, into the mix go some briny Kalamata olives and feta cheese, along with a fair amount of parsley for color and additional summertime flavor.

13.25 ounces whole-wheat spaghetti

3 tablespoons extra virgin olive oil

2 cloves garlic, finely chopped

2 medium tomatoes (approximately 1 pound), seeded, coarsely chopped

½ cup pitted Kalamata olives, coarsely chopped

½ cup packed parsley leaves, coarsely chopped

Kosher salt

Freshly ground black pepper

¼ cup feta cheese crumbles

1 Cook the spaghetti in a large pot of boiling, salted water according to the manufacturer's directions. You are looking to be on the al dente side of those directions. We do not want a soggy, mushy mess here, my friend.

2 While the spaghetti cooks, heat the oil in a large sauté pan over medium heat. Add the garlic and sauté for 1 minute. Add the tomatoes and olives and sauté until the tomatoes are softened and heated through, 3 to 5 minutes.

3 Drain the spaghetti, reserving 1 cup of its cooking water (see page xv). Add the pasta to the sauté pan with the tomatoes and olives, then pour in the pasta cooking water, and give it all a good stir to combine. Add the parsley, stirring once more. Add salt and pepper to taste. Serve a little taste of summer forth, topping each person's plate with 1 tablespoon of feta cheese crumbles.

ESTIMATED COST FOR FOUR: $8.86. The whole-wheat spaghetti costs $1.49 for 13.25 ounces. The olive oil costs 36¢ and the garlic 10¢. The tomatoes should cost no more than $3.25 per pound. The olives cost $7.99 per pound, and ½ cup is approximately 2 ounces, so that adds $1.00 to the tally. The feta is $3.99 for 6 ounces, ¼ cup is 1 ounce; therefore the cheese costs us 67¢. The parsley would be an entire package of parsley from the grocery store costing $1.99. Or you could buy a plant for $3.00 or so and take from it what you will all throughout the year.

PASTA WITH RICOTTA AND PRUNES

{ **Serves 4, $5.00 to $10.00** }

Quick Meal

I realize that you might be reading this and thinking, "Why would I enjoy prunes in my pasta?" I understand your skepticism. However, this is a delicious, healthful, and surprisingly quick recipe—it takes about 40 minutes to prepare, accounting for the time necessary to bring the water to a boil. As is often the case for me, this dish is inspired by an Italian preparation; in this case, a dinner I had during a vacation in Italy. I had never before considered prunes in a savory dish, but once I tasted it, I knew I had to make this at home.

Despite his initial reservations—I seem to recall a face being made in the direction of my plate at that restaurant in Italy, in fact—JR ate all of the pasta, even the prunes, and is now a full-on, prunes-in-your-pasta convert. "They kind of taste like meat," he says, between happy, meat-free bites.

1 pound medium-length, thick pasta, such as gemelli

3 tablespoons extra virgin olive oil

1 medium leek, white and green parts only, cleaned (see page xiv) finely chopped

12 ounces pitted prunes, quartered

½ cup fresh ricotta, plus an additional ¼ cup for serving

Kosher salt

Freshly ground black pepper

1 Cook the pasta in a large pot of boiling, salted water according to the manufacturer's instructions, until the pasta is al dente.

2 In a large skillet or sauté pan, heat the olive oil over medium heat and add the leek. Cook the leek until softened, 3 to 5 minutes. Add the prunes and cook until the prunes are softened and heated through, 5 to 7 minutes, and the pasta is ready to be added to the leek-and-prune pan.

3 Drain the pasta, reserving about 1 cup of the cooking water (see page xv). Add the cooked pasta and the pasta cooking water to the skillet. Stir to combine and simmer for 1 minute. Add ½ cup of the fresh ricotta and stir until it has melted. Add salt and pepper to taste. Remove from the heat and serve it forth. Top each serving with a tablespoon or so of fresh ricotta and additional pepper if desired.

ESTIMATED COST FOR FOUR: $8.75. The gemelli costs $1.39 for the 1-pound box. The olive oil is 12¢ per tablespoon, so that's 36¢. The leek should cost no more than $1.00. The prunes cost $3.99 for 16 ounces; we're using 12 ounces, so that's $3.00. The ricotta is your other big-ticket item at $5.99 for 16 ounces. You're using 8 ounces, so that's $3.00.

TOMATO TART

{ **Serves 4, $5.00 to $10.00** }

If, for some unfathomable reason, you haven't yet made the Savory Pie Crust (page 134), let this tomato tart be the motivation to get into the kitchen and do so. This is a wonderful do-ahead dish, and, as it takes advantage of vine-ripened summer tomatoes, also happens to make for an easy warm-weather meal with a simple salad of mixed greens.

1 Savory Pie Crust (page 134), egg wash omitted (see Note)

1 pound tomatoes (approximately 2 medium), cored, cut lengthwise into ¼-inch thick slices, seeds removed

1 tablespoon extra virgin olive oil

Kosher salt

Freshly ground black pepper

¼ cup grated Pecorino Romano cheese

2 ounces goat cheese, cut into ½-inch pieces as best as you are able

2 slices bacon, cooked to desired doneness and coarsely crumbled

8 fresh basil leaves, roughly torn

1 Set one oven rack in the customary middle position, and another rack one notch below the middle. Preheat the oven to 400°F. Place a 9-inch tart pan with a removable bottom on a 10 by 15-inch rimmed baking sheet to prevent that removable bottom from having its way with you. If the tart pan is not nonstick, grease it lightly, using the wrapper from the stick of butter that you used for the dough.

2 In order to make the transfer of dough to tart pan go smoothly, when I roll out dough for pie crust, I roll it out on a piece of reusable silicone parchment paper that is lightly—very lightly—dusted with flour. This same process will work with plastic wrap or disposable parchment paper, and saves you from having to fold the dough over your rolling pin—or worse, having to peel the dough off of the counter—to transfer it to the pan. So, roll half of the dough out into a 12-inch circle that is ¼ inch thick. To transfer it to the pan (which is now sitting on a rimmed baking sheet and should be very

near to you), simply pick up the parchment and slowly flip it over so the crust is facing down and centered over the pan. Lower the dough into the pan now, and gently peel back the parchment. Tuck the dough into the tart pan, folding a small amount of dough back over itself into the pan to form a crust edge. It is also important to know that if your dough round isn't perfect, this is the time to go ahead and patch any areas that require patching, simply using a dab of water to adhere the patch to the rest of the dough. This is particularly handy if your crust edges come up a tad short during the final fold-over. Remember, no need to get frustrated, there's always a work-around, and it's going to be delicious, patch or no patch.

3 Refrigerate your crust for 30 minutes to prevent it shrinking up on you during baking.

4 In order to achieve a crispy bottom crust, the likes of which will make you wonder why you even bother with frozen crust varieties, you must first bake the crust without its fillings, a process known as blind baking. It's quite easy, takes but a half an hour, and is worth the doing, for you will be amazed—amazed, I say—at the finished product. Remove the crust from the refrigerator, pierce the bottom of the crust all over with a fork, then cover it completely (edges, too) with aluminum foil, shiny side down, and pour in 1 cup of dried beans, distributing them evenly.

No need for fancy pie weights—inexpensive dried beans will do the trick to keep our crust free from buckling while we blind bake it. Bake for 20 minutes.

5 Keep the heat at 400°F, remove the tart shell from the oven, carefully—we don't want any burns, now—remove the foil and beans from the shell, and set them aside to cool, as those beans are now your fancy pie weights. Return the shell to the oven until it's golden brown, 5 to 10 minutes.

6 While the crust is blind baking away, toss the sliced tomatoes with the olive oil and season them with salt and pepper. Place them in a small baking dish or roasting pan and roast them on that rack we placed one notch down from the middle rack (where the crust is baking) for 15 minutes. Remove from the oven and set aside.

7 Keep the heat at 400°F. Remove the pie shell from the oven. Sprinkle the Pecorino Romano over the crust as evenly as you are able. Using a slotted spoon or tongs, remove the roasted tomatoes from their pan, leaving the accumulated juices behind, and arrange them in a single layer over the crust, tucking them into place as necessary. Place the goat cheese chunks on the tomato slices,

creating a lovely goat cheese and tomato kaleidoscope pattern as you do. Top that kaleidoscope with bacon crumbles, and return the whole lot to the oven. Bake until the goat cheese is lightly browned, 30 to 35 minutes. Now sprinkle torn basil leaves over the top of the tart. Allow to cool for 5 minutes before removing the tart from its pan—using oven mitts to do so, as that pan is still hot a mere 5 minutes out of a 400°F oven—and transfer to a cutting surface. Slice into 8 more-or-less-equal wedges, and, if the summer heat has really gotten to you, tell everyone to help themselves, they can find utensils in the drawer. They won't mind, so crispy is the crust, so sweet are the tomatoes.

NOTE: The pie crust recipe will make two crusts, and you will only use one of them here. If you aren't inclined to make another tart a day or two later, simply wrap the other half of the dough airtight and freeze it for future use. Oh, and there will be a future use.

> Once you're done with the bean pie weights, simply let them cool, store them in an airtight container, and bust out with them the next time you make this tart, or any bottom-crust-requiring dish.

ESTIMATED COST FOR FOUR: $8.51. The crust costs $1.02 as made in the Savory Pie Crust recipe, less the egg wash. The olive oil costs 12¢. Tomatoes should cost no more than $3.25 per pound. One-quarter cup of Pecorino Romano costs us 25¢. A 4-ounce log of goat cheese costs $3.99, we are using half, so that's $2.00. The bacon will be about 2 ounces, so at $6.99 per pound, that's 87¢. The basil consists of the leaves off of just one stalk of basil, but we'll go ahead and throw a dollar in for them. Even though you and I both know that's being more than generous.

HOUSE-MADE EGG PASTA

{ Serves 6 to 8, $5.00 or less }

The next time you are at a restaurant that touts "house-made pasta" on their menu, you just go ahead and say to your tablemates—and perhaps loudly enough for those at neighboring tables to hear you as well—"I make house-made pasta, *too*, you know." And it could not be easier. Really. You can use this recipe to fashion the Butternut Squash Ravioli (page 55), but any meal is elevated with the addition of house-made pasta. Even if you serve it solely with melted butter and grated cheese, it is a culinary marvel; perhaps you could use Harvey Marrs' Homemade Butter (page 147). Or top with Untraditional Bolognese Sauce (page 58) for a special Saturday night dinner-in treat. In any case, be sure to tell your tablemates that—you know—you made it *yourself.*

3 to 3½ cups Italian "00" flour (see Note)
1 tablespoon extra virgin olive oil
1 teaspoon kosher salt
5 to 6 large eggs

1 In a mixing bowl, combine 3 cups of the flour, the oil, salt, and 4 of the eggs. Mix to combine. If the dough is not coming together, meaning that there is still a quantity of loose flour in your mixing bowl, add another egg. There is a bit of a yin-yang thing in pasta making, as you will see. If the dough is still not coming together, add another egg. Then, if the dough is too sticky, add flour by the tablespoon until you have a cohesive dough that does not adhere to your fingers each time you touch it. Knead the dough, either by machine (using the flat beater attachment and medium-low speed) or by hand, until it is silken and smooth, 8 to 10 minutes. The importance of kneading for this length of time cannot be overemphasized. I

have made many a batch of perfectly good pasta that I kneaded for less than 10 minutes. But I have made spectacular pasta—the texture so silky and lovely—when I take the time to give it the full 10-minute treatment. Think of it as exercise. Exercise that results in food. Wow, could there be anything better? From exercise, I mean.

2 When you are done kneading the dough, form it into a ball and let it rest on your countertop, covered completely in plastic wrap, for 30 minutes, allowing its strands of glutens to relax.

3 After the pasta dough has sufficiently rested, roll it out into thin sheets for noodles. If you prefer another cut that is not a noodle, feel free to go ahead and make that. However, I am giving guidance on noodle making here. Using a sharp knife or pastry cutter, cut the ball of dough into 4 equal wedges. You will be working with one wedge at a time to keep the pasta supple. Be sure to cover the dough you aren't actively using with plastic wrap to prevent it from drying out. You may use either a rolling pin, a manual pasta machine, or a mechanized pasta machine to roll out the dough to your desired thickness. At my house, I use the pasta-roller attachment for the stand mixer. First, I roughly shape the dough

into a thick rectangle to ensure a close-to-uniform finished sheet. Next, I use my hands to flatten it out slightly before rolling. Then, I roll it out twice on the first setting, twice on the second, twice on the third, twice on the fourth, and once on the fifth, until it is the approximate thickness of one to two sheets of paper. That thickness is what I consider ideal for lasagna sheets, noodles of varying widths (spaghetti, fettuccine, tagliatelle, you get the idea), and ravioli.

4 If not continuing on to make ravioli, cut the pasta into ribbons the width of which are at your whim. Boil them in salted water until cooked through, 3 to 5 minutes.

NOTE: Italian "00" flour is a finely ground, high-gluten specialty flour for pasta and pizza dough; if you can't find it, go ahead and substitute unbleached all-purpose flour.

This is more pasta than four people can eat at one sitting; however, you can air dry leftovers for future use on a pasta drying rack, or, if you do cook all of the noodles, you can refrigerate them and reheat them in warm water for another meal in the next day or two. You may also freeze what you don't use, even prior to rolling it out. If you do, simply defrost it completely before attempting any rolling out.

ESTIMATED COST FOR THE BATCH OF PASTA, WEIGHING IN AT 1 3/4 POUNDS: $2.63. To feed four, we'll cut this total in half, and call it $1.32. The pasta flour costs $2.59 for just over 7 1/2 cups. We used 3 1/2 cups, so that's $1.21. The eggs should cost no more than 26¢ each, and we used 5, so that's $1.30. The olive oil costs 12¢.

BUTTERNUT SQUASH RAVIOLI IN A MAPLE-CREAM SAUCE

{ **Serves 6 to 8, $10.00 to $15.00** }

This dish is a perennial restaurant favorite. It is a favorite in my house, too, in no small part because it starts with House-Made Egg Pasta (page 53), and is easy to replicate at home. Add to that, the contrast of the maple against the bacon garnish ratchets the flavor up a level or two, and so expect to blow the minds of your loved ones with this one, you restaurant-chef-style home cook, you. They'll be asking for encore stagings of this meal all autumn long. This sauce comes together in less than 15 minutes; and because we like sauces that serve multiple purposes, you should know that it would also be good with pork or roasted chicken, so don't miss the opportunity to use it elsewhere. That's part of the fun, after all.

Filling

2 pounds butternut squash, peeled, seeded, cut into 1-inch cubes

2 tablespoons extra virgin olive oil

½ cup fresh ricotta

¼ cup grated Pecorino Romano cheese

1 teaspoon dried thyme, or 1 tablespoon fresh

Kosher salt

Freshly ground black pepper

1¾ pounds House-Made Egg Pasta (page 53), rolled out into 4 by 12-inch sheets

Maple-Cream Sauce

4 tablespoons unsalted butter

1 medium shallot, finely chopped

2 cups light cream

2 tablespoons maple syrup

½ teaspoon dried thyme, or 1½ teaspoons fresh

Kosher salt

Freshly ground black pepper

1 slice bacon per person being served, cooked to desired crispness and crumbled

1 Preheat the oven to 375°F.

2 To make the filling, toss the squash with the olive oil. Place the squash on a 9 by 13-inch rimmed baking sheet and bake until soft and some browning has occurred, approximately 30 minutes. This step may be done a day in advance; allow the squash to cool, then transfer it to an airtight container and refrigerate until ready to use.

3 Mash the squash with a potato masher or wooden spoon in a medium mixing bowl, then add the ricotta, Pecorino Romano, and thyme, mixing well. Add salt and pepper to taste and set aside.

4 For each ravioli, you need two 3½- to 4-inch squares of pasta, which you can make by cutting your pasta sheets with a knife, or by using a ravioli-cutting tool, which strongly resembles a cookie cutter, only in the shape of a ravioli. However, the least wasteful way to go is to cut the pasta with a knife into roughly uniform squares. It's okay if there is some additional pasta overhanging, it just adds to the homemade charm—and the fresh pasta deliciousness—if your squares lack perfect uniformity.

5 Before you begin to fill the ravioli, it is important to know that in order to seal them, you will need to use the wetting-the-dough technique, and so it goes like this: get a small bowl, like a cereal bowl, and fill it partway with warm water. Dip your index finger into the bowl to wet slightly. Run your finger around the edge of the pasta square to moisten it lightly—the pasta does not need to take a bath during this process—wetting your finger as needed to moisten all edges of both squares.

6 Now, place a tablespoon of filling into the middle of the pasta square designated as the bottom square. Take another square, and line up the left edges of the square. Gently press the moistened edges together to seal them up. Working clockwise around the edges, seal the rest of the edges together. At this point, you may need to use your fingers or a small spoon to tuck the filling back into the ravioli so that you can successfully close the right and bottom sides. Before you seal the bottom edge, be

sure to gently expel any air from the inside of the ravioli. *Voilà!* You've made a ravioli by hand, adding to your handmade and house-made triumphs.

7 Now place the finished ravioli on a baking sheet that is lined with plastic wrap or parchment paper dusted with flour and repeat until you have constructed 40 to 44 ravioli. If you aren't serving until the next night—or later—place the baking sheet containing them in the freezer for at least an hour, but up to 2 to 3 hours, and then transfer the frozen ravioli to a freezer-safe container or large plastic food storage bag.

8 In a large saucepan, bring salted water to a boil, and meanwhile, prepare to make the sauce. Just before the pasta water is at the boil, melt the butter in a large sauté pan over medium heat. Add the shallot, and cook until it's translucent, approximately 2 minutes. Pour in the cream, and simmer for 1

minute to meld flavors. Add the maple syrup, stirring to combine, then add the thyme, and cook the sauce over medium heat, stirring occasionally until the ravioli are done, 7 to 10 minutes. The ravioli should be entirely pasta colored when fully cooked. If you can see the color of the squash through the pasta, they aren't quite done. Add the cooked ravioli to the sauté pan and simmer in the sauce for 1 to 2 minutes, spooning the sauce to coat the ravioli. Add salt and pepper to taste.

9 Transfer 7 to 8 ravioli to each of four plates, then top with crumbled bacon, and serve them forth.

Seasonal Tip: As you probably know, butternut squash is in season during the fall and winter. It is at its least expensive at this time, and it is silly to purchase it out of season as it costs about three times its in-season rate. Silly, I say.

ESTIMATED COST FOR FOUR: $12.14. The olive oil for roasting the butternut was 24¢. The butternut squash itself was 79¢ per pound, for we only buy it when it is in season, and therefore, two pounds cost $1.60. The ricotta costs $5.99 for 1 pound, so ½ cup costs us $3.00. The Pecorino Romano was ½ ounce at $7.99 per pound, so that costs us 25¢. The thyme costs 18¢. The House-Made Egg Pasta runs us $2.63. It is $7.90 for the ravioli alone, and you will end up with 40 to 44 ravioli. Remember, ravioli are filling, so it is unlikely that you and yours will eat 10 to 11 ravioli each. Eight is a good high-side estimate for "all one can eat," in fact. So the ravioli cost 20¢ each, and you are more likely to serve no more than 32 out. That cost is $6.40. The butter for the sauce costs 36¢, the shallot costs 25¢ or so. The light cream was $2.69. The maple syrup costs $18.99 for a quart, so that's 60¢ for our 2 tablespoons at just less than 30¢ per tablespoon. The thyme for the sauce is 9¢, and the bacon is approximately ¼ pound at $6.99 per pound, so that adds $1.75 to the tally. The sauce is therefore $5.74. I wouldn't expect leftovers of the sauce. However, you will have enough leftover ravioli to make a lunch for a few people or a dinner for a couple, all for the grand total of $13.64.

If you don't have the time or the desire to make ravioli by hand, there is the option of using frozen butternut squash ravioli, which I found at $9.99 for 14 ounces; it brings the total for four to $15.73 and greatly reduces the preparation time of this dish. Though you will notice that that is over our $15 limit, and I *do* recommend making your own ravioli at least once in your lifetime.

UNTRADITIONAL BOLOGNESE SAUCE

{ Serves 6 to 8, $5.00 to $10.00 }

Any Italian, especially one from the region of Emilia-Romagna—the home of Bologna and therefore Bolognese sauce—would say, "This woman is *pazza* (crazy)—this sauce is not anything like Bolognese sauce! Blasphemy!" Granted, they would surely say it entirely in Italian, but for the purpose of setting a scene here, I hope you'll forgive the poetic use of *pazza*. The addition of tomato to the sauce is what keeps it from being considered a true Bolognese, and Italians do take their food rules and regulations rather seriously. As they should.

Regardless of its untraditional status, this is one of my most favorite comfort foods, and as such, has a place at our table nearly every other week in the cold, crisp, or rainy weather. Which is to say, nine of twelve months here at our New England home. Serve it over ribbons of House-Made Egg Pasta (page 53), or tagliatelle or pappardelle from your local Italian market. And if you haven't had a chance to make your own pasta or stop at the Italian market, regular old linguine will work just fine.

Two days from now, you can make baked ziti with any leftover sauce and some mozzarella cheese, or you can freeze it up for another time. And it will warm your belly and your heart each time.

Soffritto

2 tablespoons extra virgin olive oil

1 medium yellow onion, finely chopped

2 medium carrots, peeled, trimmed, finely chopped

2 celery stalks, finely chopped

4 cloves garlic, peeled and crushed with the blunt side of a knife or back of a spoon

Sauce

1 teaspoon dried thyme, or 1 tablespoon fresh

Freshly ground black pepper

1 tablespoon anchovy paste (see Note)

2 tablespoons tomato paste

1 pound ground meat, preferably a blend of pork, veal, and beef, but all beef would work as well, or ground turkey

1 cup dry red wine (table wine, not sweet wine)

1 cup milk (not skim)

1 (28-ounce) can fire-roasted crushed tomatoes such as Muir Glen, or regular crushed tomatoes

Kosher salt

Freshly ground black pepper

Parmigiano-Reggiano cheese, for serving

Extra virgin olive oil, for serving

1 To make the soffritto, warm the oil in a large saucepan over medium-low heat, and then add the onion, carrots, celery, and garlic, and cook until they are all nearly the same color. This part of the process takes a while, from 10 to 15 minutes, because the intent is to cook the vegetables extremely slowly to release their flavors and to meld them together. Be patient—it's worth it (as is the way with much in life that requires a wait). With the exception of the bus while you stand outside in a wind-whipped snowstorm, of course.

2 Once the soffritto is well amalgamated, add the thyme, then add pepper to taste and stir well. Add the anchovy paste (and do not turn up your nose at it, it is here to bring your sauce depth of flavor, and no one, not even you, will know it's there when you serve it forth) and tomato paste, and stir to combine.

3 Increase the heat to medium-high. Add the ground meat, breaking it up with a wooden spoon and pushing it down to the bottom of the pan, turning it over itself frequently to ensure that it cooks evenly. Once the meat is cooked through, pour in the wine, stirring to combine, then the milk, which also must be stirred in to combine. Or incorporate. Or unify, mix, merge, or marry—whichever synonym you prefer.

4 Now, if you want to keep it real, or at least closer to real, you can stop here and just let the sauce simmer for about 20 minutes to let the flavors meld together. Or, you can be completely unorthodox and do what I do. Add those darned tomatoes. An authentic Bolognese sauce does not have

any tomato save for the tomato paste, so the redness of the sauce comes from that very tomato paste, and also from the wine.

5 Once the tomatoes are incorporated, simmer the sauce gently on medium heat for 20 minutes, add salt and pepper to taste, and serve over pasta. Shave a little pricey Parmigiano-Reggiano over the top—we must splurge from time to time, after all—and perhaps drizzle a little extra virgin olive oil, and ecco, "behold," in Italian, there you have it.

NOTE: Anchovy paste is available in the Italian section of the market, or near the canned tomatoes or jarred tomato sauce.

Soffritto

Soffritto is the base of many a sauce and stew in Italian cooking—as well as in other cooking traditions. It traditionally consists of carrots, celery, onion, and pancetta or guanciale—pig's jowl—but for our cost-cutting purposes here, I have omitted the meat. Soffritto requires patience—the flavors of the vegetables need to blend together in order to provide the dish its complexity. So when you see the call for soffritto, know that you will spend at least 10 minutes cooking over medium-low heat, and you will be rewarded for your efforts with abundant flavor. Do not rush it—cooking is not a race—and you'll find that it's all easier to manage when you take your time.

ESTIMATED COST FOR FOUR: $5.85. The olive oil is 24¢, the onion weighs around ½ pound at 65¢ per pound, that's 33¢. The carrots are approximately one-third of a pound at 80¢ per pound, so that's 27¢. The celery we call 20¢ per stalk at $1.99 for 10 or more stalks in a bunch, so that's 40¢. The garlic is 20¢, figuring 10 cloves per 50¢ head of garlic. The thyme is around 18¢. The anchovy paste costs $1.99 for 4 tablespoons, so that's 50¢. The tomato paste is $2.19 for just over 5 tablespoons, so that's 88¢. The meat cost $3.79 per pound. The dry red wine should be from the very least expensive bottle you can find that is meant to actually be drunk by humans. So Two-Buck Chuck, or some similarly inexpensive wine, not to exceed $5.00 for 750ml. At $5.00, one-third of the bottle—which is roughly equivalent to 1 cup—is $1.67. The milk is 1 cup from 8 costing $1.99, and that adds 25¢ to the total. The tomatoes cost $2.99 per can, though I recommend you stock up on them while they are on sale, as you will most certainly use them while the winter wears on. Our total, then, is $11.70, which we will divide in half for serving 4 people once. If you were to serve this with one pound of House-Made Egg Pasta—an ample amount for four people—the total would be $7.35. And were you to use store-bought pasta—there is no shame in that, my friend—the total would be $7.84.

MOM'S MEATBALLS AND NOT MY NANA'S RED SAUCE

{ **Serves 4 with leftover meatballs, $10.00 to $15.00** }

My grandmother owned a red sauce Italian restaurant when I was growing up—a good old-fashioned Italian-American restaurant with those rough translations from southern Italian cuisine to the mid-twentieth-century American idea of Italian food. And I loved it. To judge from the crowds in her restaurant, I was not alone.

Nowadays, my preference is for regional Italian cuisine, but I am still comforted by the taste of chicken parm, the occasional meatball, and, of course, red sauce, though the version I make at home is chunkier than my Nana's. My meatballs are an interpretation of my mother's meatballs, which are—and I don't say this lightly—the world's best meatballs: super-moist and chock-full of soft Italian bread. I do apologize for taking away props from your mother's and Nana's meatballs, but you'll have to make these and then tell me you're not convinced. Serve them atop pasta, or keep them for some other meatballish use, such as a calzone using the Calzone Dough (page 138). Any leftover meatballs and sauce will freeze well if they aren't polished off within the week.

2 tablespoons extra virgin olive oil, plus more for oiling the baking sheet

1 medium yellow onion, finely chopped

2 cloves garlic, finely chopped

1 pound ground meat (see Note)

5 to 6 slices white Italian bread (see Note)

½ cup milk (not skim)

3 tablespoons dried oregano

½ cup freshly grated Pecorino Romano cheese

2 large eggs

Freshly ground black pepper

Kosher salt

1 Heat the oil in a skillet over medium heat; add the onion and garlic and sauté until the onion is just translucent, 3 to 5 minutes, being careful not to burn the garlic. Remove from the heat and set aside to cool.

2 Preheat the oven to 350°F.

3 In a large mixing bowl, press the ground meat around the bottom of the bowl making a flat little plateau for the bread to lie upon. Lay 2 to 3 pieces of bread on top (as many as you are able, given the size of your mixing bowl) and drizzle milk over the bread until the bread is soaked through. It may take less than ½ cup. Mash the soaked bread into the meat with a fork or your hands. Don't be afraid to get dirty. That's part of the fun. Maybe play some Pavarotti loudly and let your kids mash the meat up with their hands (washing those hands before and after, of course). Repeat with 2 to 3 additional pieces of bread.

4 Next add the oregano and Pecorino Romano and mix them into the meat mixture with a fork or your hands. Add the onion and garlic, combining well, then add the 2 eggs, one at a time, mixing well after each addition. (The eggs are the big secret. The extra egg renders the finished meatballs extremely moist.) Season with pepper—we're holding off on salting until the very end of the cooking process. You will have a very wet mixture on your hands. This is what you want, trust me, though you do want to be sure that the eggs are completely incorporated into the meat mixture before moving on.

5 Lightly oil a 10 by 15-inch rimmed baking sheet. We don't fry meatballs at my house. We bake the bad boys.

6 Using your hands, form the mixture into rounds that fit comfortably in your palms. They'll be between 2 and 3 ounces—a perfect serving size—or half a serving size, depending upon how you look at it. Place them in rows of three across the baking sheet—you should have 12 or so meatballs when all is done.

7 Bake the meatballs until they are lightly browned, 35 to 40 minutes. Allow the meatballs to cool on the baking sheet for 5 to 7 minutes. And while the meatballs are in the oven, get to work on the sauce.

NOTE: Mom uses beef in her meatballs. I use a blend of pork, veal, and beef. Go ahead and use turkey if you don't do red meat. As for the bread, you want a soft bread for this, so supermarket varieties are fine. This is old-school Italian-American after all.

not my nana's
red sauce

Soffritto

3 tablespoons extra virgin olive oil

1 medium yellow onion, finely chopped

1 celery stalk, finely chopped

1 medium carrot, very finely chopped or grated using a box grater

2 whole cloves garlic, peeled and crushed with the blunt side of a knife or back of a spoon

Sauce

1 teaspoon dried thyme, or 1 tablespoon fresh

2 tablespoons dried oregano, or ¼ cup fresh, coarsely chopped

1 tablespoon anchovy paste

2 tablespoons tomato paste

1 (28-ounce) can fire-roasted crushed tomatoes such as Muir Glen, or regular crushed tomatoes (see Note)

Kosher salt

Freshly ground black pepper

1 Heat the oil in a large saucepan over medium-low heat. Add the onion, celery, carrot, and garlic and cook slowly to meld the flavors as you know to patiently do, 10 to 15 minutes.

2 Once your soffritto is sufficiently orange-y (this is the color it most resembles when cooked down), add the thyme and oregano, and stir to combine. Next, add the anchovy paste and tomato paste. Stir to combine.

3 Add the tomatoes, stir well, and let the sauce simmer for about 20 minutes over medium heat. Add salt and pepper to taste. Sprinkle a bit of salt over the top of the meatballs and drop them into the sauce for a couple of minutes (not all of them, though—you aren't making enough sauce for 12 meatballs unless you double the recipe). Dole it all out over whatever *maccheroni* (that's Italian for macaroni) you choose, though I recommend spaghetti for this classic. Top your mountain of meatballs, sauce, and pasta with some additional grated Pecorino Romano, set it down on a red and white checkered tablecloth in your dining room, crank up the Pavarotti, and there you are in an Italian restaurant circa 1978. *Buon appetito!*

NOTE: If you are only able to find the type of tomatoes with basil already in the mix, don't worry your pretty little head about it, just go ahead and use them.

Seasonal Tip: I make this meal most frequently during the winter when canned tomatoes make more sense for my wallet than trucked-in hot-house tomatoes, and when a meaty dish helps to stave off the cold weather.

ESTIMATED COST FOR FOUR FOR BOTH MEATBALLS AND SAUCE: $10.82. Add a 1-pound box of pasta at $1.99 for the box—I should note that this is more than the recommended serving size for four, so no one in your house will be going hungry at this meal—and the total for the entire meal is $12.81 with pasta. The meatballs consist of the following: The olive oil is 24¢, the onion is ½ pound at 65¢ per pound, so, rounding up, that's 33¢. The garlic is 10¢. One pound of ground meat costs $3.79. The milk is 12.5¢ (½ cup at $1.99 for 8 cups), the bread was $2.29 for 18 or so slices, and you are using 6 slices, so 76¢. The eggs are also 52¢, and the Pecorino Romano is $7.99 per pound. The ½-cup costs us 50¢. The oregano is in the $1.00 range. Hence, the meatballs cost $7.37, and we'll get twelve 2-ouncers out of this batch, so that's roughly 62¢ per meatball. The lighter eaters in your home will only eat one meatball, but for the sake of rounding up, we'll call it two meatballs per serving to calculate our cost for four and that brings our meatball total for four to $4.96.

The tomato sauce costs $5.86. The olive oil is 36¢. The onion is another half-pounder, and that's 33¢. The carrot is around 14¢. The celery is 20¢. The garlic cloves are around 10¢ from a 50¢ head of garlic. The thyme and oregano were 18¢ each. The anchovy paste is 50¢ and the tomato paste is 88¢. The fire-roasted tomatoes were $2.99, though we buy those on sale for less, however, to avoid dismay, we use the higher price here.

HONEY-BALSAMIC CHICKEN THIGHS

{ **Serves 4, $5.00 or less** }

JR and I keep bees. Well, more accurately, JR keeps bees and I keep a safe distance away—generally indoors—while he tends to them. It is not fear that keeps me indoors, it's that I lack the *très à la mode* beekeeping suit that really is necessary when one opens up a hive packed with worker bees scrambling over one another to accomplish their to-do lists. Worker bees who now wonder why they see sky and your face—covered though it is in protective netting—staring down at them. And, like all curious beings, they will investigate. This is why I remain inside.

In exchange for his infrequent assistance—bees do not need all that much human help, we've found—they supply us with honey from their foraging of the alfalfa field abutting our property and the flowers and herbs in our garden. I'm not advocating setting up for home beekeeping straightaway—some people are a bit freaked out by hives and you might frighten visitors, though honeybees care not about humans so long as the humans don't threaten them. As I am not expecting you to harvest your own honey, you are free to use any purchased honey of your choosing for this dish.

The honey helps to tame the piquant bite of the balsamic vinegar, and together, they elevate the chicken thigh to considerable heights. So says me. Pair these with the Roasted Beets with Caramelized Beet Greens and Orange-Walnut Pesto (page 101), and think pleasant thoughts of natural sweeteners, as beet sugar was also historically used as such. Though beets are not nearly as active as bees. The Basic Polenta with Gorgonzola (page 118) also works well with these thighs.

4 bone-in, skin-on chicken thighs, approximately 1 ½ pounds total weight

Kosher salt

Freshly ground black pepper

Honey-Balsamic Glaze

2 tablespoons extra virgin olive oil

¼ cup honey

2 tablespoons balsamic vinegar

1 large clove garlic, minced

NOTE: You might imagine that this glaze would also be quite good on chicken wings, chicken legs, or Perfect Roasted Chicken (page 69) instead of the spicy orange sauce; or drizzled over pork chops, ribs, or even a tenderloin—purchased on sale, of course. If you are inclined to use this on a larger meat surface area than the thighs, simply increase the honey to ½ cup and the balsamic vinegar to ¼ cup, keeping the oil and garlic quantity the same. Simmer as instructed, let stand to thicken as instructed, and use it at will.

POOR GIRL GOURMET TIP: A little bit of oil helps to slick the path of honey, so I measure the oil in a liquid cup measure first, pour it into the pan or bowl where its use is required, then add the honey to the cup measure. The coating of oil allows the honey to slide out of the cup measure with no hassle whatsoever. And we are fond of no hassle, no doubt.

ESTIMATED COST FOR FOUR: $4.96. The chicken thighs can be had for as little as 99¢ per pound, or as much as $2.19 per pound, but I buy mine on sale for $1.69 per pound. However, for the purposes of our math here, we will use the nonsale price, despite the fact that I strongly recommend you not buy a single ounce of meat that is not on sale. For our 1½ pounds of chicken thighs at $2.19 per pound, the total is $3.29. The olive oil is 24¢, the balsamic is 19¢ per tablespoon, so therefore we add 38¢ to the tally. The garlic is approximately 5¢, and the honey—if not from your own personal hive—is $3.99 for 16 tablespoons, and that adds another $1.00.

1 Preheat the oven to 375°F.

2 Place the chicken thighs, skin side up, in a small roasting pan. Season the thighs with salt and pepper. Bake the thighs until the skin is crispy and the juices run clear when the thighs are pierced with a fork, 40 to 45 minutes.

3 While the chicken roasts, combine the olive oil, honey, vinegar, and garlic. Bring to a simmer over medium heat and simmer gently, stirring occasionally, until the sauce is thickened slightly, 5 to 7 minutes. Remove from the heat, add salt and pepper to taste, and let stand for 5 minutes to allow for the proverbial thickening upon standing.

4 Once the chicken is done, baste each thigh with the glaze and serve them forth.

CHICKEN IN CIDER GRAVY

{ Serves 4 to 6, $10.00 to $15.00 }

This is a variation of a chicken in white wine gravy recipe that I make when I have half a bottle of white wine hanging around. I developed this version to use the cider that was about to ferment in my refrigerator in place of the white wine, and added mustard. I think this is an improvement on the white wine version of the recipe, and the gravy would also be fantastic with pork shanks or pork shoulder. JR and I often enjoy this dish with Buttery Mashed Potatoes (page 121). Or you could serve this with Smashed Sugar-Roasted Sweet Potatoes (page 116).

If you want to increase the amount of chicken in this dish, you can add a couple additional drumsticks and thighs using the same amount of liquid. That would allow you to create a potpie worth of company with the Savory Pie Crust (page 134) a night or two later with very little effort.

1 (3- to 4-pound) whole chicken, pieced into thighs, drumsticks, wings, and breasts (see Note)

Kosher salt

Freshly ground black pepper

About ¼ cup extra virgin olive oil

1 medium yellow onion, finely chopped

1 medium carrot, finely chopped, plus 6 medium carrots (approximately 1 pound), peeled, sliced on the diagonal

1 celery stalk, finely chopped

1 teaspoon dried thyme, or 1 tablespoon fresh

2 tablespoons Dijon mustard

3 tablespoons unbleached all-purpose flour

1½ cups apple cider

2 cups chicken broth

1 Season the chicken pieces with salt and pepper.

2 You'll need enough oil to coat the bottom of a Dutch oven. Use a smidge more than ¼ cup if necessary. Heat the oil in a Dutch oven or other large, heavy pot with a tight-fitting lid over medium-high heat until the oil becomes shiny. Working in small batches, 3 to 4 chicken pieces each, add the chicken, skin side down, and brown until the skin is crisp. Remove the chicken from the pan and place it on a plate. There should still be enough oil to coat the bottom of the pan. If not, add enough to do so.

3 Reduce the heat to medium-low and add the onion, carrot, and celery. Cook over medium-low heat until the onion is translucent and the carrots and celery are softened, 10 to 15 minutes. Stir in the thyme and mustard. Cook for 1 to 2 minutes, then sprinkle the flour evenly over the vegetables in the pan and cook until no raw flour is evident, 2 to 3 minutes. Pour in the cider, scraping up any browned bits from the bottom of the pan, then add the broth and simmer, uncovered, for 1 to 2 minutes.

4 Place the sliced carrots and the chicken, skin side up, into the pot. The chicken should be in one layer with only the skin above the liquid. Bring the liquid back to a gentle simmer, cover, and cook until the chicken meat falls off the bone—meaning no knife, peeps—approximately 1 hour 15 minutes, being careful throughout not to let the liquid come to a boil. Add salt and pepper to taste, and serve it forth.

NOTE: Ask your butcher to cut the chicken for you if you aren't comfortable doing it yourself.

ESTIMATED COST FOR FOUR: $10.92. That's for you big eaters who can polish this off between four of you. If we're talking six servings, we're looking at $1.82 per serving. The chicken should cost no more than $1.69 per pound. At 4 pounds, that's $6.76, though I am expecting you to be on the lookout for 99¢-per-pound chicken, okay? The olive oil is 48¢. The onion costs 33¢. The carrots cost 94¢ at $3.99 for 5 pounds of carrots, figuring that our soffritto carrot is at most ⅙ of a pound. The celery costs 20¢ at 10 stalks in a bunch costing $1.99. The cider was 56¢ using 1½ cups from 8 cups at $2.99. The broth was 2 cups of the 4-cup box that costs $2.19, so that's $1.10. The flour is 24¢ per cup, so that's 5¢. The mustard is 2 tablespoons from a bottle that costs $2.99 for 19 tablespoons, so that's 32¢. We'll throw in 18¢ for the thyme. If you serve this with the Buttery Mashed Potatoes (page 121) those will cost you around $2.50, keeping you well under the $15.00 dinner budget, and leaving a person or two in your family happy to have some Chicken in Cider Gravy leftovers.

PERFECT ROASTED CHICKEN WITH SPICY ORANGE SAUCE

{ Serves 4, $5.00 to $10.00 }

It is a bit audacious to call anything perfect, a fact of which I am well aware, but we have had such great success with this method of chicken roasting in our home that the name seems just to, well, fit. It also happens that a nicely roasted chicken makes for quite a delectable meal. So delectable, in fact, that the recipe that follows this one features another take on the Perfect Roasted Chicken. Enjoy—it's not often that one tastes perfection, after all, and yet, it is so simple to achieve here. For extra saucy goodness, this sauce is fantastic with ham and pork, and also can help you create a Chinese takeout-style meal at home for far less than that carryout would run you. Serve this chicken with steamed rice and broccoli, then top the whole lot with the spicy orange sauce, and none—save your bank account—will be the wiser.

Roasted Chicken

1 (3- to 4-pound) whole roasting chicken
Kosher salt
Freshly ground black pepper

Spicy Orange Sauce

2 cups orange juice
⅛ teaspoon crushed red pepper flakes
1 tablespoon honey
¼ teaspoon kosher salt
¼ teaspoon freshly ground black pepper

1 Preheat the oven to 400°F. We like the high heat for sealing in the tenderness while gifting us a crispy skin. This, my friend, is the key to perfection.

2 Rinse the chicken and pat it completely dry. We want a dry heat in the oven to avoid steaming the bird, which would then deny us our crispy skin. Place in a roasting pan or lasagne pan and season generously with salt and pepper. You may place the chicken on a small roasting rack if you like, though we roast the chicken sitting in the pan at our house. Place the chicken in the oven with the breast side facing out, the legs toward the back of the oven, and roast until

the skin is crispy and lightly browned, and when the chicken is pierced, clear juices run from it, 55 minutes to 1 hour. Remove the chicken from the oven and allow it to rest for at least 5 minutes before carving away.

3 While the chicken roasts, prepare the sauce. Combine the orange juice, crushed red pepper flakes, honey, salt, and pepper in a medium saucepan and bring to a gentle simmer over medium heat. Simmer—gently now, okay?—until the sauce is reduced by two-thirds and has darkened to a deep, rich rust-like orange, 35 to 40 minutes. When the time has come to serve the perfection on a plate, drizzle just a touch of this sauce over each of your friends' or family members' share, and bask in the warm glow of having done something perfectly. And know that you can do it again. Anytime you please, in fact.

POOR GIRL GOURMET TIP: If you find yourself intrigued at the prospect of Vegetable Scrap Stock (page 1), you may also become entranced at the idea of making homemade chicken stock with what would otherwise land in your trash bin. This saving of scraps applies not only to vegetable peelings, but also to chicken carcasses and other meat bones. Roasted bones lend additional flavor to meat stock, so to make chicken stock, you can salvage this chicken carcass and freeze it its own food storage bag or container—not together with the vegetable scraps—until you're ready to make your next batch of chicken stock. It certainly does make the best use of the whole bird, that is for certain.

ESTIMATED COST FOR FOUR: $7.91. The chicken should cost no more than $1.69 per pound. At that rate, 4 pounds costs $6.76. The orange juice costs $3.49 for 8 cups, we are using 2 of those cups, which costs us 87¢. The crushed red pepper flakes cost us 3¢. The honey is 25¢.

CINNAMON ROASTED CHICKEN WITH ORANGE-CINNAMON SAUCE

{ **Serves 4 to 6, $5.00 to $10.00** }

While I do love cinnamon in nearly any combination with fruit—really, just take a glance at the Bakery and Desserts chapter—many cultures use cinnamon in their savory dishes, so it occurred to me that cinnamon would pair nicely with chicken. Hence, I present you with this variation on Perfect Roasted Chicken. Serve the chicken forth with a spoonful or two of the Orange-Cinnamon Sauce, ideally with the Israeli Couscous with Chickpeas and Almonds (page 112) and Roasted Carrots with Thyme (page 92); or with Basic Polenta (page 118) and Roasted Carrots with Thyme, and sit back as the cinnamon bird transports your family's dinner routine to new heights.

Cinnamon Roasted Chicken

1 (3- to 4-pound) whole roasting chicken

Kosher salt

Freshly ground black pepper

1 teaspoon ground cinnamon

Orange-Cinnamon Sauce

2 tablespoons extra virgin olive oil

½ medium yellow onion, coarsely chopped

1 cup orange juice

1 teaspoon ground cinnamon

¼ cup raisins

1 Preheat the oven to 400°F.

2 Rinse the chicken and pat it dry. Place the chicken breast side up in a roasting pan or lasagne pan. Season the bird with salt and pepper, and then rub the cinnamon all over the skin. If you are looking at your teaspoon full of precious, powdery cinnamon and considering how ever will you rub it on the chicken skin, I can assure you it will be easier if you place it in a bowl first and pinch out what you need as you go.

3 Once the oven is up to temperature, slide the chicken in its pan into the oven with the legs toward the back wall and the breast facing the oven door. Roast until the skin is crispy and when the bird is pierced, clear liquid runs from it, 55 minutes to 1 hour. Remove your cinnamon bird from the oven and allow it to stand for at least 5 minutes prior to carving.

4 Approximately 20 minutes before the bird is scheduled to come out of the oven, heat the olive oil in a large sauté or fry pan over medium heat. Add the onion and sauté until it is translucent, 3 to 5 minutes. Add the orange juice, cinnamon, and raisins, stir to combine, and simmer gently until the liquid is reduced by half, 8 to 10 minutes.

ESTIMATED COST FOR FOUR: $8.31. One whole chicken should cost no more than $1.69 per pound, if we're being fancy about it. For a 4-pound bird, then, we're talking $6.76. The cinnamon for this dish will set us back approximately 37¢. The olive oil is 24¢, the orange juice is 44¢. The onion is half of an onion that will weigh around ½ pound, so at 65¢ per pound, we're talking just over 16¢, which we'll round up and call 17¢. The raisins cost $1.99 for 24 tablespoons; 4 tablespoons costs us 33¢. So for $8.31, you and your family are enjoying an exotic, Spice Road–style dinner. Not bad for the price of admission.

The Cinnamon Bird

Cinnamon has been an important spice since antiquity. It was thought to have curative powers, was commonly given as gifts to royalty, and was burned in Roman funeral pyres. In the early years of trading along the Spice Road, the traders apparently concocted elaborate stories of how spices were collected, helping to justify the high prices. One such tale surrounding cinnamon was that cinnamon birds harvested the spice in order to construct their nests, and then particularly daring humans had to fake out the birds in order to collect the cinnamon from those nests before it could even begin its journey along the Spice Road.

Eventually, word spread that cinnamon is actually the bark of a small evergreen tree that is indigenous to Sri Lanka, which, during colonial times, was known as Ceylon. Both the Portuguese and Dutch colonized Sri Lanka early on—separately, of course—and the Dutch created a monopoly on the export of Ceylon cinnamon. By the time the British took control of Ceylon from the Dutch in 1796, Ceylon cinnamon had competition from its relative, Cassia, which is what we most often find in our grocery stores. No cinnamon birds or daring bird tricksters required.

ROASTED CHICKEN LEGS WITH OLIVES

{ **Serves 4, $5.00 to $10.00** }

Continuing in my usual inspired-by-Italy theme, this recipe arose from my desire to recreate—in a budget-conscious fashion—the flavors of a meal of roasted duck with olives that I had on vacation in, yep, Italy. The olives alone were an epiphany—I had never before had roasted olives and was swooning over the dance of mellowed salty and buttery flavors that the roasting had imparted. Though you are welcome to try this with duck legs, I have substituted the more readily available—and don't you just know it—inexpensive, chicken legs. We enjoy this dish at our house with either Basic Polenta (page 118) and Roasted Garlic Collard Greens (page 94) or Buttery Mashed Potatoes (page 121) and Roasted Cauliflower (page 108). Uncork yourself a Sangiovese wine, and imagine you and your beloved sitting in a Tuscan piazza, warm breezes and the smell of roasting meats wafting through the air.

4 chicken legs, approximately ¾ pound each

2 tablespoons extra virgin olive oil

1 teaspoon dried thyme, or 1 tablespoon fresh

Kosher salt

Freshly ground black pepper

¼ pound good-quality olives, such as Kalamata or Castelvetrano, unpitted

1 Preheat the oven to 400°F.

2 In a large baking dish or lasagne pan, arrange the chicken legs in a single layer, skin side up. Using a basting brush or your hands—your hands are the best tools you have, remember—lightly coat the skin with the olive oil. Sprinkle the legs with thyme, and season them with salt and pepper.

3 Scatter the olives around the chicken such that they have their own space in which to live. It is okay if a few olives reside in the fold of a leg, but you do want to try to get the majority of them onto their own space in the baking dish so that they are marinated with the chicken fat as they cook.

4 Roast the chicken until the skin is crispy and juices run clear when the legs are pierced, 55 minutes to 1 hour. Serve each leg forth with one-quarter of the olives per person, even to the olive haters, for they need to taste and then find themselves transformed to olive lovers, or at least roasted olive lovers. Be certain to remind your dinner companions that the olives are not pitted so that no one loses a tooth. That's no way to start a meal, or inspire a love of roasted olives.

ESTIMATED COST FOR FOUR: $6.67. The chicken legs should cost no more than $1.49 per pound. Rounding up, we'll call it $4.50 for the 4 legs. At $6.99 per pound, ¼ pound of olives will cost roughly $1.75. The olive oil will cost us 24¢, and the thyme approximately 18¢. If you do not have a good Italian or specialty deli in your area, jarred olives (with pits) are fine to use. In that case, you will use approximately half of the jar, and at $3.59 per jar, that's an increase in price of approximately 30¢.

SPICY PANCETTA AND PEAS

{ **Serves 4, $5.00 to $10.00** }

Quick Meal

This dish is quick to prepare, which is a nice feature, as though being inexpensive and delicious weren't enough. Including the time it takes for the water to come to a boil, the first bite of pasta, pancetta, peas, and runny egg yolk is on your fork in about 35 minutes. If you aren't a big fan of spicy heat, scale the crushed red pepper flakes back to 1/4 teaspoon—and if you find that the spice is still not to your liking, which I think is nearly impossible, omit the pepper flakes the next time you make it. Because believe you me, there will be a next time.

1 pound spaghetti or orecchiette

5 tablespoons extra virgin olive oil

½ pound thinly sliced pancetta (specify this when you purchase it), cut into roughly 1-inch squares

1 medium shallot, coarsely chopped

½ teaspoon crushed red pepper flakes

2 cups peas

Kosher salt

Freshly ground black pepper

4 large eggs

1 Fill a large pot with salted water and set it on the stove over medium-high heat. Just before the water comes to the boil, heat 3 tablespoons of the olive oil over medium heat in a large sauté or frying pan. Add the pancetta, and stir to spread it evenly throughout the pan. Start cooking the pasta once the water comes to a boil, and continue to cook the pancetta until the fat begins to melt, 5 to 6 minutes. Add the shallot and crushed red pepper flakes, stirring to combine with the pancetta. Cook the pancetta, shallot, and crushed red pepper flakes until the shallot is softened and becoming translucent, 2 to 3 minutes, then add the peas, stirring to combine them with the pancetta mixture.

2 When the pasta is al dente, drain it, reserving 1½ cups of the pasta cooking water (for the best way to do this, see page xv), and then add the pasta to the pan with the pancetta mixture. Add 1 cup of the pasta cooking water into the sauté pan, then stir to combine the pasta and pasta cooking water with the pancetta mixture. Reduce the heat to medium-low. If it looks like the pan is drying out at any time while you're working on the next step, go ahead and add the remaining ½ cup of pasta cooking water to the pan. Add salt and pepper to taste.

3 In another frying pan, heat the remaining 2 tablespoons of olive oil over medium heat and add the eggs, being careful not to crack the yolks. If you do happen to crack a yolk, it's not the end of the world. I'm sure either someone in your family thinks runny yolks are icky (this person is likely under ten years old) or some other person will take one for the team and volunteer to eat the broken-yolk egg. And that person is probably you, who are cooking this, for it would be me at my house. The cook goes down with the broken-yolk ship, as it were. Cook the eggs until they are set but the yolk is not cooked through, also known as sunny-side up.

4 Transfer one-fourth of the pasta with pancetta and peas to each of four plates, top each mound of pasta with an egg, and serve them forth.

Pancetta

Pancetta is an Italian cured pork product. It is also produced in Spain, and in both cases, it comes from the same cut of the pig—the belly—that is used to produce bacon. Unlike bacon, pancetta is not smoked, so it doesn't present itself in as pronounced a manner as bacon, though it does add a nice saltiness to a dish without overwhelming it.

Pancetta is a natural companion for peas as its saltiness pairs beautifully with the sweetness of the peas. It is slightly more expensive than bacon, but it is worth it for the nuance of flavor it provides, and you don't need more than two ounces per person to produce an incredibly satisfying dish of Spicy Pancetta and Peas. In fact, you could probably get away with closer to an ounce each, but just in case you have a large appetite, we'll go with two ounces per *mangiatore* (eater, in Italian).

ESTIMATED COST FOR FOUR: $9.15. The pasta shouldn't be any more than $1.99, and if you choose to use orecchiette, that should be no more than $1.79. The olive oil is around 60¢ for both the pancetta and the egg portion of the meal. The pancetta is $8.29 per pound, so ½ pound is $4.15. The shallot costs roughly 25¢, the crushed red pepper flakes put us out 12¢, and the peas are just about two-thirds of a bag that costs $1.49, which costs us $1.00. The eggs are no more than 26¢ each, so that's $1.04, and the richness of the yolks replaces the need for any Parmigiano-Reggiano shaving, or even grated Pecorino Romano sprinkling, which is why it is employed here. To save a buck or two.

BRAISED PORK SHOULDER

{ **Serves 4, $5.00 to $10.00, and then you get to have pulled pork sandwiches with a scrumptious barbecue sauce for $5.00 to $10.00, y'all** }

I think I'm channeling my inner Paula Deen. *Y'all* just isn't in my normal vocabulary, but for this recipe, it just seems a natural fit. In any case, pork shoulder is an absolutely delicious cut of the pig, the secret being to slow cook it at a nice, gentle simmer so that the meat does, very literally, fall off the bone. For the first feeding session—ahem, meal—from this shoulder, serve it up with Basic Polenta (page 118) and Roasted Garlic Collard Greens (page 94) or Roasted Carrots with Thyme (page 92). Then enjoy the leftovers on your favorite sandwich roll with the tangy barbecue sauce that follows, and try—just try—not to use *y'all* in your next sentence.

¼ cup extra virgin olive oil

Kosher salt

Freshly ground black pepper

1 (4- to 5-pound) pork shoulder (see Note)

2 medium yellow onions, cut crosswise into ¼-inch rounds

1 tablespoon Dijon mustard

1 teaspoon dried thyme, or 1 tablespoon fresh

4 cups apple cider

1 Warm the olive oil over medium-high heat in a large Dutch oven or other large, heavy pot with a tight-fitting lid. Season the pork shoulder on all sides with salt and pepper. Brown the pork shoulder on all long sides (don't worry about the short ends, you'll be wrestling pork shoulder and oil, and it's not necessary), 3 to 5 minutes per side. Remove the pork shoulder from the pot—with a friend's help if necessary—and transfer it to a plate. Reduce the heat to medium. Place the onions in the pot and cook until they are softened and translucent, 5 to 7 minutes. Add the mustard and thyme, stirring to combine. Return the pork shoulder and any accumulated juices to the pan, and add the apple cider. Bring to a gentle simmer over

medium heat, cover, and cook at a gentle simmer until the meat does what? Falls off the bone. That's right, people. At that point, the meat is also fork-tender, meaning it does not require a knife to be cut. To achieve this will take 3 to 3½ hours. Pull yourself some pork from the pot, put it on a plate, top with a bit of the cooking liquid, and start thinking about pulled pork sandwiches, even as you enjoy the braised pork.

NOTE: I prefer a shoulder that is cut flat, rather than with a protruding leg bone. You want as small a bone as you can get your butcher to rustle up. Pork butt, also called Boston butt, would also work here.

ESTIMATED COST FOR THE BRAISED PORK SHOULDER FOR FOUR: $7.97. The pork shoulder should cost you no more than $1.99 per pound. And you know you won't get exactly 5 pounds even if you tried, so we'll call it $10.00. Even if you are four very hungry people, you will only eat around half of that, so that's $5.00. The braising ingredients only have the one time to shine, so we'll factor those in addition to the cost of meat for the Braised Pork Shoulder, but they don't come into play for the leftovers, which are quite good as pulled pork sandwiches. The onions weigh approximately 1 pound, and so they cost 65¢. The olive oil is 48¢, the apple cider is $1.50 at 8 cups for $2.99, the mustard is 16¢, and the thyme is 18¢.

TANGY BARBECUE SAUCE

{ **Serves 6 to 8 from a yield of 1½ cups, $5.00 or less** }

So here you are, a pile of pork left over (page 77), and you need a casual dinner, or, heck, perhaps even lunch. I'll tell you what to do: Mix up a batch of this sauce, get yourself some sandwich rolls, and serve up some pulled pork sandwiches.

I'm sure you already have a good idea of other uses for the barbecue sauce, but lest you be at a loss, I am here to help: Slather on grilled chicken, any other cut of grilled pork, grilled beef, dip some French fries in it, or get right back to the market and get ye another pork shoulder and do it all again. Remember as you use the sauce for those grilled items, you want to wait until *after* the meat has been grilled to load it on. The sugar in the sauce will cause the meat to char if you grill with it already on your selected cut, which is fine if you prefer the taste of char over the taste of chicken, pork, beef, and the barbecue sauce, but I don't imagine you do.

2 tablespoons extra virgin olive oil

1 medium shallot, finely chopped

2 cloves garlic, peeled, very finely chopped

½ cup distilled white vinegar

3 tablespoons packed brown sugar

2 tablespoons honey

1 (6-ounce) can tomato paste

2 tablespoons Dijon mustard

2 tablespoons Worcestershire sauce

¼ teaspoon chili powder

¼ teaspoon kosher salt

Freshly ground black pepper

1 In a large saucepan over medium heat, heat the olive oil. Sauté the shallot and garlic until softened and the shallot is translucent, 2 to 3 minutes. Add the vinegar, sugar, and honey, and stir until the sugar and honey are dissolved. Add the tomato paste, mustard, and Worcestershire sauce, stirring to combine. Add the chili powder, salt, and pepper, give it a good stir, and then simmer on medium-low heat, stirring occasionally, until the sauce has thickened, 18 to 20 minutes. Okay, now, dole it out—first onto reheated pork shoulder leftovers, and then, later this week, onto any other protein that you want to jazz up with delicious barbecue taste. I'm no barbecue expert, but I'm pretty certain that when your family and friends groan in a happy way with each bite of their sticky, tangy barbecue scrumptiousness, you'll know you done good.

ESTIMATED COST FOR THE WHOLE DARNED BATCH OF BARBECUE SAUCE: $3.05. The olive oil cost 24¢, the shallot 25¢, and the garlic cloves, we like to estimate two at 10¢ from a 50¢ head of garlic, but you know that's rounding up, don't you? The vinegar was $1.99 for 4 cups, so that's 25¢. Three tablespoons of brown sugar is 12¢, two tablespoons of honey is 50¢. The tomato paste should cost you no more than 80¢, two tablespoons of Dijon mustard is 32¢, the Worcestershire is 37¢. Add in that chili powder for 10¢, and there we are. You'll get enough for two meals, so the cost of the barbecue sauce for this meal is $1.53. Now we add the leftover pork shoulder cost to this, and that is $6.53. Then you all will need a roll each, y'all, which we'll figure is 50¢ per roll, so that's $2.00. The sandwiches then total $8.53 for four, and they are so, so worth it.

HONEY MUSTARD AND CIDER—MARINATED PORK SPARERIBS

{ **Serves 4, $5.00 to $10.00** }

Country-style pork spareribs are one of those so-called lesser cuts of meat that benefit greatly from a little extra attention. They add all that tasty pork flavor to your dinner without the tenderloin price. This recipe is ideal for a weeknight because it's simple and uses only a few ingredients. You come home from work, whip up the marinade, relax—or not—for an hour, and then you're off to the pork sparerib races. Oh, and it's also easily modified—you could always substitute apple juice, orange juice, or pineapple juice for the cider if you don't have any on hand. These ribs would work well with Roasted Carrots with Thyme (page 92) and Buttery Mashed Potatoes (page 121), or Smashed Sugar-Roasted Sweet Potatoes (page 116) and Caramelized Onions (page 110).

2 tablespoons honey

2 tablespoons Dijon mustard

¼ cup extra virgin olive oil

¼ cup apple cider

Kosher salt

Freshly ground black pepper

4 boneless country style pork spareribs, ¾-inch to 1 inch thick, approximately 1½ pounds

¼ cup packed brown sugar

1 In a medium mixing bowl, whisk the honey, mustard, oil, and cider together. Add salt and pepper to taste. Place the spareribs in a large food storage bag or large shallow dish, such as a pie dish, cover with the marinade, and refrigerate for 1 hour and up to 24 hours. You could get this going a night earlier and even speedier goes the meal.

2 Preheat the oven to 375°F. Line a 9 by 13-inch rimmed baking sheet with aluminum foil.

3 Space the ribs evenly across the baking sheet. Sprinkle enough brown sugar to lightly cover the top of each rib. Bake until the ribs reach an internal temperature of 140°F, 40 to 45 minutes, flipping the ribs over midway through the cooking time and sprinkling brown sugar over the top of that side as well. Once the ribs are done, do not be afraid to give each rib a swirl through the caramelized brown sugar that is sitting on the foil, and then serve them forth.

NOTE: I'm sure I don't need to tell you—though I am about to do so just the same—that this marinade and sugar dusting would work just as well with chicken or other cuts of pork. For we like treatments that multitask, do we not?

ESTIMATED COST FOR FOUR: $7.56. The honey is 50¢ for 2 tablespoons. The Dijon mustard is $2.99 for 19 tablespoons, so that's 32¢. The olive oil is 48¢ at $7.99 for 67 tablespoons. The apple cider is $2.99 for 8 cups, so ¼ cup is approximately 10¢. The spare ribs are $3.99 per pound, and 1 ½ pounds, that will run us $6.00 or so. The brown sugar is 4¢ per tablespoon, so 16¢ for our dusting here.

RIGATONI WITH ROASTED BUTTERNUT SQUASH, SWEET ITALIAN SAUSAGE, AND FRIED SAGE

{ Serves 4, $10.00 to $15.00 }

Because my farming neighbors grow butternut squash, I tend to have a healthy stock of it stowed away for autumn and winter use, and so I am always working on new ways to incorporate this stalwart winter squash into my dinner plans. As it happens, I also love sweet Italian sausage and the combination of sweet and savory, so this dish works on all levels for me.

Many times, I prepare this dish with leftover roasted butternut squash, which makes for a quick preparation on a weeknight. If you aren't feeling inspired to fry the sage leaves, you may omit them. Their addition is well worth the effort, however.

Butternut Squash

1 pound butternut squash, peeled, seeded, cut into 1-inch cubes (approximately 3½ cups)

2 tablespoons extra virgin olive oil

Fried Sage

2 tablespoons extra virgin olive oil

12 fresh sage leaves

Rigatoni and Sausage

1 pound sweet Italian sausage or hot Italian sausage

1 pound rigatoni

3 tablespoons extra virgin olive oil, plus more for drizzling

1 medium leek, white and light green parts only, cleaned (see page xiv), finely chopped

Kosher salt

Freshly ground black pepper

¼ cup grated Pecorino Romano cheese

1 Preheat the oven to 375°F.

2 To roast the squash, toss it with the olive oil and spread in a single layer on a 9 by 13-inch rimmed baking sheet. Roast until it is soft and some browning has occurred, approximately 30 minutes. You can do this a day in advance to speed up weeknight preparations if you so desire; transfer the squash to an airtight container and refrigerate until you're ready to use it.

3 While the butternut roasts, make the fried sage. Heat the olive oil in a medium frying pan over medium-high heat until the oil shimmers. Working in small batches, 2 to 3 leaves at a time, add the sage leaves to the pan and fry until they're crisp, 1 to 2 minutes. Transfer the sage leaves to a plate lined with a paper towel to allow any excess oil to drain. Likewise, the fried sage may be stored in an airtight container until you're ready to use it up.

4 Preheat the broiler or light the grill, and set a large pot of salted water on high heat to bring to a boil.

5 Broil or grill the sausage until it is browned. Alternatively, you could cook the sausage in the sauté pan until it is cooked through, though I like the additional flavor

that broiling (or grilling) imparts to this dish, as it contrasts nicely with the sweetness of the squash. Transfer the sausage to a cutting board and slice it crosswise into ½-inch rounds.

6 Cook the rigatoni in that large pot of boiling, salted water according to the manufacturer's directions until al dente. Drain the pasta, reserving 1½ cups of the cooking water (for the best way to do this, see page xv).

7 Heat the olive oil in a large sauté pan over medium heat. Add the leek and sauté until it's translucent, 3 to 5 minutes. Add the squash, the rigatoni, 1 cup of the reserved pasta cooking water, and the sausage. Stir to combine and cook for 2 minutes more. If the sausage mixture is drying out at all, pour in the remaining ½ cup of cooking water. Add salt and pepper to taste, then crumble the fried sage leaves over the top. Serve immediately with a sprinkle of grated Pecorino Romano cheese and a drizzle of olive oil if you so desire.

ESTIMATED COST FOR FOUR: $10.86. The butternut squash costs 79¢ per pound during its season, which is autumn. Reserve any remaining butternut squash for another use—perhaps this same dish a few days from now? The sage will be less than half of the leaves on a bunch available from the supermarket costing $1.99, but we'll call it $1.00 just the same. The total amount of oil costs 84¢. The leek should cost no more than $1.00, the sausage is available in prices ranging from $2.99 per pound to $4.99 per pound, and, as you probably know all too well by now, I always buy mine on sale for $2.99 per pound. However, we'll use the higher figure, and call it $4.99. The rigatoni should cost no more than $1.99, and the grated Pecorino Romano, a tablespoon per person will do, so that's ½ ounce at $7.99 per pound, and that adds 25¢ to our bill.

SWEET ITALIAN SAUSAGE WITH APPLE AND FENNEL SEED

{ **Serves 4, $5.00 to $10.00** }

I love the classic combination of sausage and white beans, and this dish dresses it up just a bit. Fennel seeds are a traditional seasoning for Italian sausages, and here, they've toasted for a little extra boost in flavor. At my house, we serve this alongside the Pan-Sautéed Cabbage with Roasted Garlic (page 106), and it is delicious, filling, and comforting all at once.

1 teaspoon fennel seeds

4 (6-inch) links sweet Italian sausage (approximately 1 pound)

¼ cup extra virgin olive oil

1 medium yellow onion, quartered lengthwise, layers separated

¼ cup dry white wine (not dessert wine)

1 Macintosh apple, peeled, cut into ½-inch cubes

1 (15-ounce) can cannellini beans, drained and rinsed

Kosher salt

Freshly ground black pepper

1 Alrighty now, at the start of this recipe, you must focus solely on the stovetop for the first 2 minutes, lest you burn your fennel seeds and deny yourself the sweet, toasty, mild anisette flavor they bestow upon this dish. In a medium sauté pan over medium heat, toast the fennel seeds, stirring constantly, until the majority are lightly browned and you are enjoying the aroma of toasty fennel in the air, 1 to 2 minutes. Remove the pan from the heat, transfer the seeds to a bowl, and set aside.

2 Next, prepare the sausage. Remove the meat from the casings by using a sharp knife or kitchen shears to cut the casings away, then discard them. Break the meat up into 1-inch pieces such that the pieces resemble small meatballs.

3 Heat the oil in a large sauté pan over medium heat. Add the onion, and cook for 2 minutes before adding the sausage. Add the sausage and cook until the sausage is browned, 6 to 8 minutes. Add the wine, apple, and beans, and give them all a good stir. Simmer until the sauce thickens, 2 to 3 minutes, then add salt and pepper to taste.

Serve four equal portions out and top with a sprinkle each of the toasted fennel seeds. I'll advise you to bring the remaining toasted fennel seeds to the table because it is highly unlikely that your family or friends will not want to scatter a few more over their plates once they get underway with the eating.

ESTIMATED COST FOR FOUR: $8.00. The fennel seeds are 1 teaspoon of a container that costs $4.29 for 5.12 tablespoons, and that means the teaspoon costs us 29¢. The olive oil costs 48¢. The onion was around ½ pound, and a pound costs 65¢, so rounding up, that's 33¢. The sausage would be $4.99 if we did not buy it on sale, but we surely do buy it on sale, which would save us a couple of dollars from the tally here. Of course, I'm still using the higher price for this accounting session. The apple was just about 50¢, and the beans were 99¢. The wine is one-twelfth of a bottle containing 3 cups—which is the approximate cup measurement for 750ml, so, knowing that we would not spend more than $5.00 per bottle on wine we are cooking with, that would be 42¢, or it's leftover wine that you either stashed in the refrigerator for a week, or it is leftover wine that you froze in an ice-cube tray for a use such as this.

GINGER SOY SIRLOIN TIP STIR-FRY WITH MUSHROOMS

{ Serves 4, $10.00 to $15.00 }

Quick Meal

Truly, there are times when carnivorous folks crave beef, even if on a restricted budget. And these very same carnivores quite likely also crave takeout, but know that $35 in random Chinese food isn't the best use of, well, $35. Enter this dish. It's simple to make, coming together a mere 10 or 12 minutes from the moment the water comes to a boil, and it is just as good the next day—even as a cold dish—unlike some of that pricey takeout you get.

Marinated Sirloin

1 pound sirloin tips, sliced crosswise into ¼-inch-thick strips

¼ cup low-sodium or reduced-sodium soy sauce

1 ½ teaspoons freshly grated ginger

⅛ teaspoon crushed red pepper flakes

1 clove garlic, crushed

Noodles and Stir Fry

1 tablespoon sesame seeds

1 pound linguine

3 tablespoons extra virgin olive oil

1 ½ teaspoons freshly grated ginger

⅛ teaspoon crushed red pepper flakes

1 clove garlic, finely chopped

1 medium leek, white and light green parts only, cleaned (see page xiv), coarsely chopped

1 (10-ounce) package white mushrooms, rinsed, trimmed, sliced ¼ inch thick

¼ cup low-sodium or reduced-sodium soy sauce, divided

1 tablespoon toasted sesame oil

Kosher salt

Freshly ground black pepper

1 Combine the sirloin tips, soy sauce, ginger, crushed red pepper flakes, and garlic in an airtight container or 1-gallon-capacity plastic food storage bag. Marinate in the refrigerator for 1 hour and up to 24 hours.

2 Toast the sesame seeds in a small saucepan or sauté pan over medium heat until they are lightly browned, 1 to 2 minutes. Remove the pan from the heat, transfer the sesame seeds to a bowl, and set them aside.

3 Cook the linguine in a large pot of boiling, salted water according to the manufacturer's directions, overcooking it by 1 to 2 minutes. Whereas I love the texture of cooked yet slightly firm—the famous al dente—pasta in Italian dishes, it turns out that slightly overcooking regular old 99¢ pasta replicates the texture of noodles used in Chinese takeout. Now you know.

4 While the pasta cooks, heat the olive oil in a large sauté pan over medium heat. Add the ginger, crushed red pepper flakes, and garlic, and cook for 1 minute. Remove the sirloin from the marinade, discard the remaining marinade, then add the sirloin, leek, mushrooms, and 2 tablespoons of the soy sauce to the pan, and sauté until the mushrooms are softened and the meat is cooked through, 10 to 12 minutes.

5 Drain the pasta and toss it with the remaining 2 tablespoons of soy sauce and the toasted sesame oil. Place one-quarter of the noodles on each of four plates. Top with one-quarter of the sirloin-mushroom mixture, drizzling the pan sauce onto each plate. Sprinkle one-quarter of the toasted sesame seeds over the whole lot, and serve it forth, asking your family to guess where you ordered from—unless, of course, they saw you in the kitchen. In that case, the guessing game will be a tremendous failure.

VARIATION: This treatment would also work well with chicken, substituting teriyaki sauce for the soy and 1 pound of broccoli for the mushrooms. Likewise, mixed vegetables and tofu would also be a satisfying variation on this dish. Just like that—three make-at-home takeout options, there you have 'em.

ESTIMATED COST FOR FOUR: $14.58. The sirloin tips cost $7.99 per pound. The total ginger used in this dish will cost you around 12¢. You're looking for a piece of ginger that is about a 1-inch cube, knowing, of course, that ginger makes for a very misshapen cube, being a root and all. The garlic for the entire dish is 10¢, and the crushed red pepper total is 6¢. The soy sauce total for the dish is ½ cup at just about 11¢ per tablespoon; the 8 tablespoons that make up ½ cup cost us 88¢. The olive oil is 36¢, the sesame oil costs $4.19 for 10 tablespoons, we're using one, so that's 42¢. The leek should cost no more than $1.00, and the mushrooms cost $1.99 for 10 ounces. The pasta really is 99¢ pasta, as I use the regular old Whole Foods 365 Everyday Value linguine rather than the fancier Whole Pantry linguine that costs $1.99 per pound. Sesame seeds cost $5.49 for a container holding 8 tablespoons, so that adds 67¢ to the tally.

vegetables and sides

MUSHROOMS IN CREAM SAUCE

{ **Serves 4, $5.00 to $10.00** }

This is one of the first dressed-up vegetable side dishes I made once I moved out on my own as a mid-twenty-something. A bit of a late starter am I, apparently. However, JR was rather impressed by this dish, and for weeks after I served it to him, he would tell any and all friends and acquaintances that I made cream of mushroom soup from scratch. Granted, he thought that mushrooms in cream sauce were about the same as, though slightly fancier than, canned condensed cream of mushroom soup, but brag he did. I still remember some looks of disbelief, but then, those friends and acquaintances probably didn't realize just how easy it is.

These mushrooms work particularly well to gussy up roasted chicken or pork, so you could use it as JR once enjoyed, ahem, *condensed* cream of mushroom soup, on a piece of roasted chicken, such as Perfect Roasted Chicken (page 69) sans the Spicy Orange Sauce, or perhaps with some oven-baked pork chops.

2 tablespoons extra virgin olive oil

2 tablespoons unsalted butter

1 medium shallot, finely chopped

1 (10-ounce) container white mushrooms, rinsed, trimmed, sliced ¼ inch thick

½ teaspoon dried thyme, or 1 ½ teaspoons fresh

2 cups light cream

Kosher salt

Freshly ground black pepper

1 Heat the olive oil and butter in a large sauté pan over medium heat. Once the butter has melted, add the shallot and cook until it is translucent and softened, 2 to 3 minutes. Add the mushrooms and thyme and cook, stirring occasionally, until they are just softened and browned, 5 to 7 minutes. There may be a point at the start of the mushroom cooking that you think, "Hey, this could use more oil—or butter—or something." No need to fret, the mushrooms will start releasing their juices soon, and all will be good, and nothing will be dried out.

2 Add the cream, stir to combine with the mushrooms, and bring to a gentle simmer. Simmer until the liquid is reduced by half, 25 to 30 minutes, stirring occasionally. Add salt and pepper to taste, and serve your homemade cream of mushroom "soup" side dish forth.

ESTIMATED COST FOR FOUR: $5.44. The olive oil is 24¢, the butter is 18¢, and the shallot is 25¢. The mushrooms cost $1.99. The thyme runs us 9¢ and the light cream costs $2.69.

ROASTED CARROTS WITH THYME

{ **Serves 4, $5.00 or less** }

While I do love fresh-from-the-garden carrots straight out of the soil—well, okay, with a good rinsing first—even in the off-season, I always have a bag of carrots at the ready. They are a good, low-cost vegetable side dish—and roasted as they are here, their sweetness is accentuated. As one of the three primary ingredients of soffritto, they are the base of many a soup, stew, or sauce, hence it is good to have them on hand throughout the chilly months.

These carrots pair nicely with a slew of dishes, but in particular with Perfect Roasted Chicken (page 69), and the occasional thaw-in-the-winter-freeze grilled Sunday steak. I mean, we are watching our spending here, but every so often, a carnivore might like a steak. Am I wrong?

2 pounds carrots (approximately 12 medium), peeled and trimmed

3 tablespoons extra virgin olive oil

½ teaspoon dried thyme

¼ teaspoon kosher salt

¼ teaspoon freshly ground black pepper

1 tablespoon salted sweet cream butter, quartered

1 Preheat the oven to 400°F.

2 Cut the carrots in half and then halve them lengthwise. In a large mixing bowl, toss the carrots with the olive oil, thyme, salt, and pepper. Transfer to a 9 by 13-inch rimmed baking sheet and roast until the carrots begin to brown, 45 to 50 minutes, flipping the carrots midway through the cooking time.

3 Remove the carrots from the oven, transfer them to a serving dish, and top with the tablespoon of butter.

POOR GIRL GOURMET TIP: Let's not forget when peeling the carrots for this dish—as well as when you peel them for soffritto or even when snacking from the garden—to save the peels and trimmings for Vegetable Scrap Stock (page 1). After all, you and I are parsimonious, and we've already paid for the carrots, so why waste when you can get the stock for free?

ESTIMATED COST FOR FOUR: $2.14. The 2 pounds of carrots cost $1.60, as they come from a 5 pound bag costing $3.99. The olive oil is 36¢, the thyme is in the neighborhood of 9¢, and the sweet cream butter is 9¢.

ROASTED GARLIC COLLARD GREENS

{ Serves 4, $5.00 or less }

Collard greens and kale are in the same family as cabbage, but are likely the older cousins as they were grown by ancient Greeks and Romans. They are incredibly easy to cook, are ready in just about fifteen minutes, and have a pleasant bitter flavor. You might be surprised to know that I—gasp—leaned toward Italian preparation for this dish, and, as luck may have it, this same preparation would work well with kale as well. Or turnip greens. Or, heck, even spinach. And I love these collard greens with Honey Mustard-Marinated Pork Chops with Peach Salsa (page 176) or Roasted Chicken Legs with Olives (73).

1 bunch collard greens (approximately 1¼ pounds)

3 tablespoons extra virgin olive oil

5 cloves roasted garlic (page xvii)

⅛ teaspoon crushed red pepper flakes

Kosher salt

Freshly ground black pepper

1 Collard greens and their kale brethren require that their woody stems be removed prior to cooking. First, be certain to wash the leaves well, as they grow close to the ground and soil can be attached to them. Then cut the stems from the center of each leaf. Once the leaves are trimmed, cut them crosswise into ½-inch strips.

2 Heat the olive oil in a large sauté pan over medium heat, then add the roasted garlic and cook for 1 minute. Add the collard greens and the crushed red pepper flakes and cook until all of the leaves are wilted, stirring frequently, 13 to 15 minutes. Add salt and pepper to taste, and serve forth this stalwart of Southern cuisine that also just happened to be a favorite of southern European antiquity. So I hear, anyway.

Seasonal Tip: Both collards and kale are crops that fare well in the autumn, and their flavor benefits, even, from a bit of crisp air and frost. Therefore, you will find them plentiful late in the harvest season, though both are available year-round.

ESTIMATED COST FOR FOUR: $3.15. The olive oil costs 36¢. The roasted garlic costs approximately 27¢. One bunch of collard greens costs $2.49 just about anywhere you go—grocery store, farm stand, or farmers market, so be sure to spread some love around to your local growers if you have the chance—and the crushed red pepper flakes will be added in at 3¢.

HONEY-MUSTARD COLESLAW

{ Serves 4, $5.00 or less }

The moment JR and I bit into pulled pork sandwiches with Tangy Barbecue Sauce (page 79), we knew there absolutely had to be a coleslaw recipe in this book to accompany them. Cabbage has a habit of shrinking once you douse it in dressing, so don't be alarmed by the quantity of chopped cabbage when you start this recipe. If you don't have a bowl quite large enough to handle all of the prior-to-having-shrunk cabbage, you can work in stages, or use a large stockpot instead. If you're working in stages, add half of the cabbage to your largest bowl, add the dressing, and then work in the remaining cabbage. In fact, if you find that you must use this method, *that* is the most complicated moment of executing this recipe. Quickly, quickly, it comes together, and oh, it goes so darned well with those pork sandwiches. And any other summer party or barbecue food, for that matter.

2 to 2½ **pounds green cabbage**
   (from one small head)
⅓ **cup extra virgin olive oil**
⅓ **cup Dijon mustard**
⅓ **cup honey**
Kosher salt
Freshly ground black pepper

1 Ah, cabbage. So simple, and yet it has such mass, it requires a bit of explaining. In order to achieve that familiar shredded cabbage look that you recall from experience of coleslaws past, you will first need to remove the external leaves from each head until you get to the clean interior. Don't get too crazy about this—if you see some bruised or not-so-appetizing-looking bits once you're in the interior, you can cut around them—you don't want to decimate the entire head in search of a perfectly clean leaf, after all. Cut the stem from the bottom of the cabbage, and then cut the cabbage in half lengthwise, from the top

to the base where the stem once was. Now place the cut side down on your cutting surface, and cut ¼-inch slices crosswise. I find that a serrated knife works well for this. When cutting near the base, simply remove the bits of the solid part, which is the core, and add them to your compost heap if you have one. Place the cut cabbage ribbons into a large serving bowl and move on to the making of the dressing.

2 Whisk the olive oil, mustard, and honey together in a medium mixing bowl until the honey has dissolved and the dressing is

smooth. Pour the dressing over the cabbage, turning the cabbage over itself to be sure the dressing is coating every cabbagey bit. Heed my advice at the top of the recipe if, like me, your largest bowl is not large enough. Once the coleslaw is dressed, add salt and pepper to taste. Serve it forth—perhaps even on a pulled pork sandwich—and enjoy the summer day. Or night.

ESTIMATED COST FOR FOUR: $4.30. Green cabbage is apparently not quite as fancy as its red counterpart and retails for 59¢ per pound, rather than the 69¢ per pound that red commands, so 2½ pounds costs us $1.48. The olive oil is 64¢. The mustard is $2.99 for 19 tablespoons, and we used 5⅓ tablespoons, so that's 85¢. The honey is $3.99 for 16 tablespoons, and so that costs us $1.33.

PAN-SAUTÉED CORN AND TOMATOES

{ **Serves 4, $5.00 to $10.00** }

Corn is a late-summer favorite that usually conjures up images of warm days with friends and family at a barbecue or clambake. But it doesn't have to be relegated solely to steamed or grilled on-the-cob servings; it is sublime sautéed, accompanied by the complementary and delicious flavors of tomatoes and basil. Funny how they all ripen around the same time, isn't it? It's Nature's way of telling us to serve them together. And so we oblige, and in this case, transform three tastes of summer into one scrumptious dish.

3 tablespoons extra virgin olive oil

1 medium shallot, finely chopped

2 cups corn kernels, shaved from 4 ears of corn (see Note)

1 pint grape or cherry tomatoes

Kosher salt

Freshly ground black pepper

¼ cup basil leaves, stemmed, coarsely chopped

1 Heat the olive oil in a large sauté pan over medium heat, then add the shallot and sauté until it's translucent, 3 to 5 minutes. Add the corn kernels you have so diligently shaved and cook for 2 minutes. Add the tomatoes, and cook until they are heated through, 3 to 5 minutes. Remove the pan from the heat, and add salt and pepper to taste. Once this summery combo hits the plate, sprinkle the basil over the whole bright mound, and serve it forth.

NOTE: Don't be put off by the idea of shaving kernels from their cobs. It's quite easy. Shuck the ears of their husks and silks, leaving the stem intact, as it becomes your handle. Place the ear of corn tip-downward in a large bowl, using the stem to hold it steady. Using a serrated knife, start at the top and cut downward, keeping the knife as close as possible to the cob. You may have some random bits of silk in the mix; pick them out if they bother you, but otherwise, not to worry.

Work around the ear until all of the kernels have been shaved off, and away we go. Because corn starches quickly transform into sugars, giving older corn that less-than-desirable mealy texture, it's best to use fresh corn and to cut the corn just prior to starting the sauté. I promise it doesn't take that long. And if you have other things to do, perhaps you can persuade another member of your household to shave kernels for you.

ESTIMATED COST FOR FOUR: $5.80. The olive oil costs 36¢, and the shallot 25¢. The corn should be no more than 55¢ per ear, so that's $2.20. The tomatoes are $1.99, and the basil is half of a bunch that costs $1.99, so that adds $1.00. Though, of course, I highly recommend you have a potted basil plant of your very own awaiting this and many other summery dishes' preparation.

ZUCCHINI WITH PECORINO ROMANO

{ Serves 4, $5.00 or less }

During the short New England growing season, I become what some might consider a squash beetle vigilante, quickly smooshing each yellow and black winged offender that dares land on my zucchini and summer squash plants. My bordering-on-the-obsessive pest management rewards us with a bounty of squash. Fortunate are we that we never tire of this recipe, first introduced to us by JR's niece, and now a staple at our house. Serve alongside Perfect Roasted Chicken (page 69) sans orange sauce or an "I-got-a-good-deal-on-this-for-I-shop-sales" grilled steak, and start picturing yourself obsessively tending to zucchini plants. It's well worth the effort.

2 pounds zucchini (approximately 2 large or 4 medium), sliced into ¼-inch rounds

2 tablespoons extra virgin olive oil

Kosher salt

Freshly ground black pepper

¼ cup grated Pecorino Romano cheese

> Psssst . . . "in season" for zucchini is summer. In fact, if you aren't growing them yourself, you may find a neighbor or eight who are *giving* them away.

1 Preheat the oven to 400°F.

2 In a large bowl, toss the zucchini rounds with the olive oil to coat them. Season with salt and pepper and arrange the zucchini in a single layer on a 10 by 15-inch rimmed baking sheet.

3 Sprinkle the grated Pecorino Romano over the top of the rounds and bake until the zucchini is soft and the cheese is golden brown, 30 to 35 minutes.

ESTIMATED COST FOR FOUR: $2.99. In season, zucchini costs $1.25 per pound. We're using 2 pounds here, so that's $2.50. The olive oil costs 24¢, and the grated Pecorino Romano costs 25¢.

ROASTED BEETS WITH CARAMELIZED BEET GREENS AND ORANGE-WALNUT PESTO

{ Serves 4, $5.00 to $10.00 }

In my youth, the only time I ate beets was when I decided I needed to lose weight by eating solely beets, hot dogs, and vanilla ice cream. That was an actual diet. I believe it also involved grapes. But those diet beets always came out of a can. I imagine my mother didn't want to bother with roasting up actual, fresh beets if I was going to subscribe to such a gimmicky weight loss tactic. Served me right. Luckily, now that I'm older and oh-so-much wiser, I know that gimmick diets don't work and I also know that beets are delicious roasted, with orange and walnuts, in salads and with chicken. And this dish has all but the chicken—and okay, I *am* taking liberties by calling parsley "salad." Parsley is not salad, but it is green, and it adds an herbal flavor to this dish that I love. And while we're speaking of greens, beet greens are a lovely addition to salad, and a wonderful addition to this dish.

Roasted Beets

1 bunch beets of approximately 4 (2-inch-diameter) beet roots, peeled, trimmed, cut into ¼-inch slices

Juice of 1 Valencia or navel orange (approximately ¼ cup), zest reserved for making the pesto

Kosher salt

Freshly ground black pepper

Orange-Walnut Pesto

The zest of 1 orange (reserved from the beet preparation)

½ cup toasted walnuts (page xvi), coarsely chopped

¼ cup coarsely chopped parsley

1 tablespoon extra virgin olive oil

Caramelized Beet Greens

3 tablespoons extra virgin olive oil

Beet greens (from the beets in this dish), washed and stemmed

2 tablespoons honey

Kosher salt

Freshly ground black pepper

1 Preheat the oven to 375°F.

2 Now that I am so much wiser than I was in my fad-diet days, I'd like to share a helpful hint with you. It is easiest to cut the beets by putting the now-trimmed top end facedown on the cutting board so that you are working off of a flat—and therefore balanced—surface. Then cut the beet in half, place the new, larger flat side down, and proceed with your quarter-inch slices. As you are cutting, you may find that the beet's round edges may not comply 100 percent with the ¼-inch measurement, and that's okay. If some pieces are a bit larger than you'd like, simply cut them so that they are approximately ¼-inch pieces. See, I told you I was wise. Ish.

3 In a large bowl, toss those sliced beets with the orange juice. Add salt and pepper to taste. Transfer the whole lot to a

baking dish and cover with aluminum foil. Roast, covered, for 30 minutes, until the beets are softened. Remove the foil and roast for an additional 5 to 10 minutes, until the beets begin to brown slightly. Stir the beets midway through this last cooking stage to keep them dressed in orange juice.

4 While the beets roast, mix the zest, walnuts, parsley, and olive oil together in a small bowl.

5 Now, prepare the beet greens. They come together quickly, and by using them rather than tossing them out or adding them to compost, it's as though you get two vegetables for the price of one. Heat the olive oil in a large sauté pan over medium heat. Add the beet greens and sauté them until they have wilted, 2 to 3 minutes. Add the honey, stir to distribute among the greens, and sauté for an additional 2 minutes. Remove the pan from the heat, and add salt and pepper to taste.

6 When it is time to serve—ideally on a plate containing Honey-Balsamic Chicken Thighs (page 65) or Perfect Roasted Chicken with Spicy Orange Sauce (page 69), place one-quarter of the greens on each plate. Then place one-quarter of the beets over the greens, and, finally, top each pile of beets and greens with a tablespoon or two of the walnut-orange mixture. Then start thinking how all of these items would work really well in a salad for lunch tomorrow. Yes, yes, they would.

ESTIMATED COST FOR FOUR: $6.05. A bunch of beets can be yours for $2.49. Beets have two seasons, the early summer and the fall, as they enjoy cooler temperatures for growing. The orange should cost you around 50¢, and, yes, that includes both the juice and the zest. It's another two-for-one bonus produce item, that citrus is. The walnuts were ½ cup from a bag containing 4 cups and that cost $8.69, so $1.08. The parsley is half of a store-bought bunch of fresh parsley, and that will cost us $1.00 for the half-bunch. The olive oil was 48¢, and the honey was 50¢. If you'd like to splurge, you could toss 2 tablespoons of crumbled blue cheese into the mix for an added cost of 38¢, at $4.49 for 6 ounces, and approximately ½ ounce contained in 2 tablespoons.

CIDER-BRAISED FENNEL

{ Serves 4, $5.00 or less }

As mentioned elsewhere in this very book, fennel does not receive the recognition or the accolades it deserves. As far as I'm concerned, anyway. This treatment is the perfect accompaniment to pork or roasted chicken, or even roasted turkey—can you say, "I am a holiday side-dish innovator!"? Yes. Yes, you are. So go on, test-drive this dish once the air gets crisp and your thoughts turn to roasting, and then see if you aren't compelled to bring it to your aunt's, sister's, brother's, parents', or in-laws' during the holiday season.

2 medium fennel bulbs (approximately 2 pounds)

3 tablespoons extra virgin olive oil

1 cup apple cider

2 tablespoons raisins

1 tablespoon salted sweet cream butter at room temperature

Kosher salt

Freshly ground black pepper

1 Here is a fennel-cutting lesson: Take a good gander at the fennel, particularly if you aren't terribly familiar with our vegetable du jour. It has stalks sticking up from the rounded base, but we don't want to cook the stalks. Notice how the stalks grow such that they are a bit angled off of the bulb. Well, we're going to lie the bulb down on its side and cut the stalks at an angle so as to preserve as much of the bulb as possible. There's no need to cut squarely across and waste precious bulb. I like to use the stalks in my Vegetable Scrap Stock (page 1) as they add a pleasant yet subtle anise (licorice) flavor to the broth. Try it once and see if you like it. Now, thinly slice off the base of the bulb to remove any dark-colored fennel flesh. Next, stand your de-stalked and de-based bulb back up and cut 1-inch slices lengthwise from the previous home of the

fronts to the former home of the base. It's just that simple. If you see baby fronds (the fern-like leaves) within the bulb, feel free to cut those out before cooking, but they won't hurt you if you don't.

2 Heat the olive oil over medium heat in a large sauté pan. Add the fennel, arranging it in one layer, and brown it on both sides, 8 to 10 minutes per side. Add the cider and raisins, being certain to push the raisins into the liquid so that they soften up as they cook. Continue cooking until the cider is reduced by half, 18 to 20 minutes. Remember, cooking is not a race. You do not win for finishing more quickly, and besides, you are roasting something in the oven to accompany this dish, which means you should settle in and enjoy the experience, not to mention the aroma of fennel and cider mingling about in the kitchen air. Once the cider is reduced by half, transfer the fennel to a serving platter, or even your dinner plates. Remove the sauté pan from the heat and swirl in the butter until it is completely melted. Add salt and pepper to taste, spoon the sauce over the lovely braised fennel, and serve it forth.

ESTIMATED COST FOR FOUR: $3.98. The olive oil is 36¢. The fennel should be around 2 pounds at $1.49 per pound, and that is $2.98. The apple cider costs $2.99 for 8 cups. We are using 1 cup, and that adds 38¢ to the total. The raisins are $1.99 for 24 tablespoons, we are using 17¢ worth. The butter costs $2.79 for 32 tablespoons, we are using one lone tablespoon, and that costs 9¢. Not bad for a dish worthy of a holiday celebration, now, is it?

PAN-SAUTÉED CABBAGE WITH ROASTED GARLIC

{ Serves 4, $5.00 or under }

In M.F.K. Fisher's essay "The Social Status of a Vegetable" (a germane topic as we undertake our eating-well-for-less strategies, and I, for one, feel that no vegetable is of a lower status than another—however, back to Fisher), she writes that her dining companion is horrified by the presence of cabbage on Fisher's plate. Her reason for such vehement dislike of our hero cabbage? The scarring experience of a rainy night's walk through what she terms "the slums," which also happened to smell of cooking cabbage; she queries Fisher as to whether she *really* likes cabbage. Fisher, no vegetable status snob herself, responds, "But we *do* like it, really."

I often think of Fisher's cabbage-disdaining friend when I prepare this dish—oh, what she was missing out on with her fancy-pants pretension! Sautéed cabbage is so very satisfying and goes well with meat dishes of every type, though I think it is particularly well suited to grace a plate that also includes sausage—grilled or broiled—such as Sweet Italian Sausage with Apples and Fennel Seed (page 85) and Quick White Beans with Bacon (page 120). It is the royalty of low-cost comfort food, in my opinion. And I can't be alone. If you would like more detail on the cabbage slicing, please have a look at the Honey-Mustard Coleslaw recipe (page 96).

½ cup extra virgin olive oil

The cloves from 1 head roasted garlic (page xvii), coarsely chopped

1 small head cabbage (approximately 2 pounds), outer leaves removed, cored, cut into ½-inch pieces

Kosher salt

Freshly ground black pepper

1 Heat the olive oil in a large sauté pan over medium heat. Add the flavor-boosting roasted garlic, and immediately add the cabbage. Cook over medium heat, frequently turning the cabbage on the bottom of the pan over to the top of the cabbage pile—and, oh, it *will* be a pile. Resist the urge to increase the heat, as cooking, my friend, is not a race—have you heard this somewhere before?—and you must be patient so that the cabbage browns slightly but does not burn whatsoever. Cook until the cabbage is softened and has the occasional lightly browned piece, 55 minutes to 1 hour. It's a fantastic cold-weather event, this cabbage sautéing is. Add salt and pepper to taste, and serve it forth.

ESTIMATED COST FOR FOUR: $2.68. And a hearty side dish this is—you may even find yourself with leftovers if you aren't diligent in your eating. The olive oil will run us 96¢, the roasted garlic is 54¢, for that is what it costs to prepare it. The cabbage costs 59¢ per pound, and we are using around 2 pounds, so that's $1.18 or so.

ROASTED CAULIFLOWER

{ Serves 4, $5.00 or less }

I am confused by people who profess their undying hatred of cauliflower. "Are we talking about the same cauliflower?" I wonder, sometimes using my external incredulous voice—it's beyond my control, so shocked am I by statements of cauliflower contempt. Especially given that I think roasted cauliflower may, in fact, deserve its very own cookbook. Roasted Cauliflower pie, anyone? My next words after the thinking-out-loud blunder are usually, "Have you not tasted the nutty perfection that is roasted cauliflower?" Ahhh, but you must, and then let me know how you feel.

1 head cauliflower, stemmed, green leaves removed

¼ cup extra virgin olive oil

Kosher salt

Freshly ground black pepper

½ cup grated Pecorino Romano cheese

1 Preheat the oven to 400°F.

2 Cut the cauliflower head lengthwise into 4 approximately equal parts—we're making 4 handy individual serving-sized pieces of cauliflower here.

3 In a large mixing bowl, toss each quarter individually with the olive oil. Do not fret if you don't completely cover the quarter in oil, everything will still turn out just fine. Transfer that first quarter to a 9 by 13-inch rimmed baking sheet, and repeat with the remaining cauliflower-head quarters. Season generously with salt and pepper, and place each quarter cut side down.

4 Start roasting. About 20 minutes into the cooking process, flip the cauliflower-head quarters so that the other cut side rests on the baking sheet. Roast another 15 to 20 minutes, until all cut sides are browned at the edges and the florets have begun to brown.

5 Remove the cauliflower from the oven, place a floret quarter on each individual's plate, ideally next to a Roasted Chicken Leg with Olives (page 73) or steak of some sort, and then sprinkle each serving with 1 tablespoon of the grated Pecorino Romano cheese. Be prepared for the nearly unbearable nutty-tasting scrumptiousness that roasted cauliflower gives as its gift to you. You have been warned. And I dare say transformed, should you have been one of those cauliflower haters to start.

VARIATION: For a very, very satisfying meal, chop the roasted cauliflower after you roast it. Then toss the pieces with about 14 ounces of whole-wheat spaghetti and 8 tablespoons of melted, unsalted butter, and top with the cheese. The wheat pasta and cauliflower combine for a very satisfying concert of toasted, nutty flavors, and the dish comes together quickly and easily. Add to that, it's meat free, and you won't but barely notice, so satisfying is the nuttiness of this combination.

ESTIMATED COST FOR FOUR: $3.97. The cauliflower head cost $2.99. Four tablespoons of olive oil are 48¢ at 67 tablespoons from a 33.8-ounce bottle that costs $7.99 using Whole Foods store brand olive oil. Grated Pecorino Romano from my favorite Italian market is $7.99 per pound, we are using approximately 50¢ worth of cheese here.

If you're feeling a bit fancy, substitute grated Parmigiano-Reggiano cheese, which costs $18.99 per pound. One ounce therefore costs $1.19, adding 69¢ to the tally.

CARAMELIZED ONIONS

{ **Serves 4, less than $5.00** }

In the neighborhood where JR lived as a child, there was a family that he insists ate caramelized onions at dinner every night. This makes me believe that they must have also eaten either beef or pork every night as well, as caramelized onions best complement meaty dishes—you wouldn't normally think of having caramelized onions with catfish, after all—so perhaps caramelized onions were their budget concession so they could afford meat with such regularity. Or perhaps JR only imagined that they enjoyed caramelized onions each and every day. And I can see why he might dream that dream, for in addition to going well with meat, caramelizing elevates the humble onion to a sublime comestible, one that happens to top off mashed potatoes rather nicely, to boot, which is of infinite value if you are a meat-and-potatoes lover.

8 tablespoons unsalted butter

4 medium yellow onions (approximately 2 pounds), peeled, sliced into ¼-inch rings

¼ cup sugar

3 tablespoons balsamic vinegar

Kosher salt

Freshly ground black pepper

1 In a large sauté pan or skillet, melt the butter over medium heat. Add the pile of onions and cook until they are softened and translucent, stirring constantly. This could take up to 20 minutes, as you have quite a few onion rings here. Not to worry, they will shrink considerably as they cook.

2 Once the onions are soft and translucent, sprinkle them with sugar, and stir to combine. Cook until the sugar begins to caramelize. If you haven't previously caramelized sugar, this is a fun process to watch unfold. The first time I did it, I belted out, "Hey, wow, it's making caramel!" Yeah. Apparently the "caramelized" in the

description didn't clarify it nearly enough for me. In any case, the mixture will bubble and turn a golden brown. Once it is golden brown, stir in the vinegar. Cook for 2 to 3 minutes more to meld the flavors. Add salt and pepper to taste, and serve them up alongside something meaty. But be sure to alternate with other vegetables from night to night. Even though these are addictive, you need some variety in your diet as well.

NOTE: Caramelized onions also happen to be quite versatile—think toppings for pizza, salad, focaccia bread, an addition to a frittata— and, as mentioned once or twice above, as a side dish for meats. Have I mentioned their affinity for mashed potatoes?

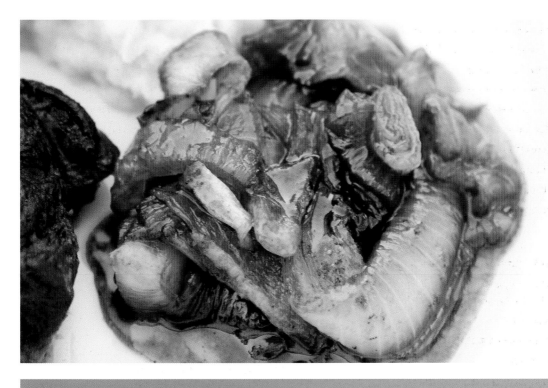

ESTIMATED COST FOR FOUR: $2.76. The onions should be the least expensive you can find—there's no need to spend your money on sweet onions for this, as the onions will be made sweet by caramelizing. A 2-pound bag of yellow onions at Whole Foods costs $1.29. The butter is a quarter of a package that costs $2.79, so that's 70¢. The balsamic is not the fancy-schmancy aged balsamic, it is the more common type found in every grocery store and was $7.99 for a 16.9-ounce bottle containing 33 tablespoons. Break that down, and for 3 tablespoons, it costs 73¢. And the magical sugar that creates the caramel was 4¢.

If you'd like to get the price down to $2.03 or so, eliminate the balsamic vinegar. The onions will be just as good, and you'll be able to brag about a gourmet side dish for less than 50¢ per person. Not that you're the bragging type, of course. But if you were, you might feel compelled.

ISRAELI COUSCOUS WITH CHICKPEAS AND ALMONDS

{ Serves 4, $5.00 to $10.00 }

This dish is fabulous warm or cold, so it's a great make-ahead dish. It is also super fantastically easy to make, so much so that by the time the couscous cooks, all of the other ingredients will be awaiting its arrival in the toss-it-around bowl. You know that party you have this weekend? The one you have no idea what to bring along, only you know it has to be quick, delicious, and inexpensive? Yeah, this is the dish you've been looking for. Yes, it is. You could also serve it up at home with Cinnamon Roasted Chicken with Orange-Cinnamon Sauce (page 71) or on the side of lamb kebabs. Delicious in either case.

1 ⅓ cups Israeli couscous, sometimes called giant pearl barley or Middle Eastern couscous

½ cup toasted whole almonds (page xvi)

½ cup raisins

1 (15-ounce) can garbanzo beans, drained and rinsed

The zest and juice of 1 Valencia or navel orange (approximately ¼ cup juice)

1 tablespoon extra virgin olive oil

Kosher salt

Freshly ground black pepper

1 Cook the couscous according to the manufacturer's directions.

2 So here it goes: While the couscous is cooking, combine the almonds, raisins, and garbanzo beans in a large bowl. Once the couscous is thoroughly cooked, drain it and add it to the bowl. Stir in the orange juice and zest, then pour in the olive oil and stir it about to coat the whole mixture. Add salt and pepper to taste. And just like that, you're done. Put some type of seal over the bowl, and walk into the party a proud, proud side dish and/or salad maker.

ESTIMATED COST FOR FOUR: $6.24. The Israeli couscous costs $3.19. The almonds are $6.99 for a bag containing 4 cups, so ½ cup costs us 87¢. The raisins cost $1.99 for 24 tablespoons, we are using 8, so that runs us 67¢, and the garbanzo beans cost 89¢. The orange should cost you no more than 50¢, and the olive oil is a mere 12¢.

RED POTATO AND GREEN BEAN SALAD THREE WAYS

{ Serves 4, $5.00 to $10.00 }

In the Liguria region of Italy, the Italian Riviera, where pesto was invented, green beans and potatoes are often combined with pasta and pesto sauce for a summery, meat-free meal. Now that you've got that idea in your head, I'd like to share a recipe—actually three recipes—for those same potatoes and beans, sans pasta. In the first variation, we'll stick with the traditional basil pesto. This treatment works well with chicken—I'm thinking grilled chicken legs would complement the potato salad nicely, a bit of smoky grill flavor to complement the fresh flavor of the pesto. Yes. Sounds good. The second variation, parsley-walnut pesto, goes well with grilled meats like lamb and beef. And the third, with mustard-dill sauce, is quite complementary to the Olive Caper Fish Cakes with Lemon-Dill Sauce (page 183). As an added bonus—and I like me an added bonus—you can serve any of these variations hot, at room temperature, or cold, so you can make any one of them ahead of time while it's still cool in the kitchen and bust out with a substantial starch-and-veggie side dish come dinnertime.

Potatoes and Green Beans

8 medium red potatoes (approximately 2 pounds), quartered

½ pound green beans, trimmed, cut into 1-inch pieces

Basil Pesto

½ cup packed basil leaves

¼ cup pine nuts

¼ cup grated Pecorino Romano cheese

¾ cup extra virgin olive oil

Kosher salt

Freshly ground black pepper

Parsley-Walnut Pesto

½ cup finely chopped packed parsley leaves

½ cup finely chopped walnuts

¼ cup grated Pecorino Romano cheese

¾ cup extra virgin olive oil

Kosher salt

Freshly ground black pepper

Mustard-Dill Sauce

½ cup Dijon mustard

½ cup extra virgin olive oil

The zest and juice of 1 lemon

¼ cup chopped fresh dill

Kosher salt

Freshly ground black pepper

1 As you might have surmised, the technique for the potatoes and beans remains the same regardless of the variation. Place the quartered potatoes in a large pot with enough water to cover them by 1 inch. Bring to a boil over medium-high heat—it will take 18 to 20 minutes to reach the boil—and cook until the potatoes are easily pierced with a fork, 4 to 5 minutes. Add the beans to the pot and cook until they are bright green, 1 to 2 minutes. Drain the potatoes and beans in a large colander and place in a serving bowl.

2 While the potatoes boil, make the dressing of your choosing.

3 For the Basil Pesto, you first must finely chop the basil and pine nuts. This may be done in any of three ways. There is, of course, the *a mano* method—using a knife and your own energy. You could also use a small food processor to chop them, working in separate batches to avoid creating a liquid basil pesto—you still want some heft to those leaves, not a puree. Or you may also go all old school—like, pre-Renaissance old—and use a mortar and pestle to grind the basil and pine nuts.

4 Whichever method you choose, combine the chopped basil, pine nuts, cheese, and olive oil in a small bowl, and then add it to the potato-bean bowl, stirring to dress the potatoes and beans evenly in basil pesto goodness. Add salt and pepper to taste, and serve it alongside that chicken we discussed.

5 As the Parsley-Walnut Pesto is also a pesto-style sauce—you might have suspected so given its name—you may use

any of the three methods listed for the basil pesto to achieve a finely chopped pile of parsley and walnuts. Combine the parsley, walnuts, Pecorino Romano, and olive oil in a small bowl, sneak a bite—a small one, you don't want to take too much away from your dinner mates after all—and then add the pesto to the potato-bean mixture, giving it a good, hearty stir to be sure it is evenly distributed throughout. Add salt and pepper to taste, and serve it next to your summer Sunday steak. This is what we do in my house. Even a family on a budget should have a grilled steak splurge a few times a summer.

6 Perhaps after reading the instructions for the two dressings above, you have already reached for your small bowl. That's very good. You'll be needing it for the Mustard-Dill Sauce. Place the mustard, olive oil, lemon zest and juice, and chopped dill into that small bowl. Whisk it until the mustard and olive oil become a cohesive dressing. Now pour that dressing over the potatoes and beans, stir well, for we like dressing on all bits of the spuds and legumes, add salt and pepper to taste, and finish frying those Olive Caper Fish Cakes with Lemon-Dill Sauce (page 183).

ESTIMATED COST FOR FOUR: The potatoes cost 99¢ per pound, so we will use no more than $2.00 worth. The beans are $1.75 per pound, and we used ½ pound, so that's 88¢. The base of our salad, therefore, costs $2.88.

WITH BASIL PESTO: $7.56. To the $2.88 we'll add $1.99 for a bunch of basil purchased at the supermarket, though I don't need to remind you that basil grows quite voraciously in a pot or in your garden, where it will cost you much less. The pine nuts cost $7.99 for 8 ounces with ¼ cup weighing approximately 1 ounce, so that's $1.00. The cheese costs 25¢. The olive oil costs us $1.44, as we are using 12 tablespoons from a 33.8-ounce bottle that costs $7.99 and contains 67 tablespoons.

WITH PARSLEY-WALNUT PESTO: $7.64. The parsley, should you not be growing it yourself, will cost $1.99. The walnuts are ½ cup of a bag costing $8.69 that contains 4 cups. Therefore, they cost us $1.08. The olive oil and cheese are the same deal as discussed above in our conversation about Basil Pesto, and so they add $1.69 to the tally.

WITH MUSTARD-DILL SAUCE: $6.54. The mustard costs $2.99 for 19 tablespoons. We are using 8 tablespoons, so that's $1.26. The olive oil is 90¢, as we are using just 8 tablespoons for this sauce. The lemon costs 50¢, and the dill would be about half of a store-bought bunch costing $1.99, so $1.00 to the bill for the dill.

SMASHED SUGAR-ROASTED SWEET POTATOES

{ **Serves 4, $5.00 or less** }

Even a fan of sweet and savory like me has to appreciate a little sweet, spicy, and starchy every now and again. These potatoes nail it. They are easy as sweet potato pie to make, and go along for the ride just beautifully with the Braised Pork Shoulder (page 77) or Honey Mustard-Marinated Pork Chops with Peach Salsa (page 176) and Roasted Garlic Collard Greens (page 94).

¼ **cup extra virgin olive oil**

3 **tablespoons packed brown sugar**

¼ **teaspoon cayenne pepper (ground red pepper, not red pepper flakes)**

3 **medium sweet potatoes (approximately 2½ pounds), peeled, cut into ½-inch cubes**

2 **tablespoons salted sweet cream butter, softened**

Kosher salt

Freshly ground black pepper

1 Okay, now, just as I said, easy, easy, easy. Preheat the oven to 375°F.

2 While the oven revs up, whisk together the olive oil, brown sugar, and cayenne pepper in a small bowl, and mix them up well now, please. Place the sweet potato cubes in a large mixing bowl, pour the brown sugar mixture over the whole lot of them, and stir well to coat. Spread the potatoes on a 9 by 13-inch rimmed baking sheet, and roast until they are softened and beginning to brown, 40 to 45 minutes.

3 Let the sweet potatoes sit for just one minute while you gather your smashing wits about you. I suppose I could have called these potatoes mashed, but doesn't "smashed" just sound so much more, well, fun? And I'm sure you've already noticed

that it helps the title alliteration along as well. Yes. I knew you had. So now we'll transfer the potatoes back to the bowl from whence they came prior to roasting. We'll add the butter—I find sweet potatoes don't require a whole lot of butter to render them creamy—and we will smash them to our desired consistency. I like to leave a few hefty bits in the mix, but you do as you see fit. Once they are smashed to your liking—by which time you have hopefully worked out some of the day's stress—add salt and pepper to taste, and serve them forth.

NOTE: If you so desire, you may also make the sweet potatoes the day before, omitting the butter. When the time comes for you to partake of them, simply reheat them for 15 to 20 minutes in the oven—preheated to 350°F—with the butter cut into bits and laid atop the orange, spicy, sweet potato mound.

ESTIMATED COST FOR FOUR: $3.33. Two and a half pounds of sweet potatoes at 99¢ per pound will run us around $2.50. The olive oil costs us 48¢, the brown sugar is 4¢ per tablespoon, so that's 12¢, and the cayenne was but a pinch, though we'll call it 5¢. The butter costs an additional 18¢. Sweet, indeed.

BASIC POLENTA

{ **Serves 4, less than $5.00** }

On a trip to Columbia, South Carolina, I had my "ah-ha" moment for polenta, which is also known as corn grits throughout the southern United States. Before this moment, I had not truly loved polenta, despite my best attempts. I had always found it too bland to consider a go-to dish. On the fateful love-inducing night, JR and I had dinner at a Columbia restaurant serving what they promised was the best of the area's bounty, and it did not disappoint. I ordered cornmeal-crusted oysters with creamy grits, and much to my surprise, the grits (ahem, polenta) were the best I had ever had—not bland as all grits prior had been—in fact, they actually tasted of toasty corn—and deserving of my amour. The waitress agreed with me, adding, "They cook them in chicken broth." Ahhhhh ... haaaaaaaa. If you are unable to find stone-ground polenta, finely ground will do.

4 cups chicken broth

1 cup stone-ground polenta (corn grits), such as Bob's Red Mill

½ cup grated Pecorino Romano cheese

1 tablespoon salted sweet cream butter

Kosher salt

Freshly ground black pepper

1 Bring the chicken broth to a simmer in a large saucepan over medium heat. Add the polenta (*ahem*, corn grits, for my Southern friends) in a slow, steady stream, stirring continuously to prevent the polenta from clumping. Clumping is less likely with stone-ground polenta, and I prefer the overall texture of stone-ground to finely ground polenta, so I do recommend seeking it out for this dish. If you are only able to find finely ground polenta, pay particular attention to this initial pour to avoid the aforementioned clumps.

2 Although polenta is not risotto, it does require continuous stirring while it cooks, lest it start to spit out angry polenta pellets at you. Maintain medium heat, and stir

continuously for 10 to 12 minutes, until the liquid has been absorbed, and a path cut by your stirring spoon through the center shows the bottom of the pan. Remove the pan from the heat, and stir in the grated cheese and the butter. Add salt and pepper to taste, then allow the polenta to sit for 5 minutes prior to serving it out.

VARIATION: Another delicious option for this recipe is to substitute 2 tablespoons crumbled Gorgonzola cheese for the Pecorino Romano. It pairs particularly nicely with the Roasted Beets with Caramelized Beet Greens and Orange-Walnut Pesto (page 101), and doing so adds a mere 38¢ to the total.

ESTIMATED COST FOR FOUR: $3.35. The chicken broth costs $2.19. The stone-ground polenta is 57¢ per cup at $2.69 for 4 ¾ cups. The Pecorino-Romano costs $7.99 per pound, and approximately 1 ounce is contained in ½ cup of grated cheese, which adds 50¢ to the tally. The butter is 9¢ at $2.79 for 32 tablespoons.

If you feel you'd like to splurge and spend more on your creamy polenta/grits, substitute freshly grated Parmigiano-Reggiano at $18.99 per pound in place of the Pecorino Romano, which will add $1.37 to the total.

QUICK WHITE BEANS WITH BACON

{ Serves 4 to 6, $5.00 or less }

"Quickness" is relative. Dried beans require soaking overnight, and therefore are decidedly not quick. Sure, they're less expensive to make than are canned beans, there is no disputing this. But sometimes, one craves the creamy heartiness of beans when nary a soaking bean may be found in one's home. It is those times when one should turn to this recipe. Try it with grilled sausage and Roasted Garlic Collard Greens (page 94).

4 slices bacon, cut into ½-inch pieces

2 cloves roasted garlic (page xvii), coarsely chopped

2 (15-ounce) cans cannellini beans, including liquid

1 teaspoon crushed dried sage, or 1 tablespoon finely chopped fresh sage

⅛ teaspoon crushed red pepper flakes

Kosher salt

Freshly ground black pepper

1 Cook the bacon to your desired crispness in a medium saucepan over medium-high heat, turning frequently to ensure even cooking. Using tongs or a slotted spoon, transfer the bacon to a paper towel-lined plate, leaving the cooked fat in the pan.

2 Add the garlic, the beans including their juices, sage, and crushed red pepper flakes, stirring well to combine. Cook at a very gentle simmer over medium heat, stirring frequently, until the liquid has thickened, 18 to 20 minutes. Remove from the heat, add salt and pepper to taste, and serve them forth—sprinkling one-quarter of the bacon over each serving.

ESTIMATED COST FOR FOUR: $4.05. Four slices of fancy bacon will be approximately 4 ounces. At $6.99 per pound, that costs $1.75. The roasted garlic costs 11¢. The beans cost 99¢ per can, so that's $1.98. The sage is 18¢ if using dried, the crushed red pepper flakes cost 3¢. And you should have leftovers, so someone can make a snack for him or herself tomorrow while no one else is looking.

BUTTERY MASHED POTATOES

{ Serves 4, $5.00 or less }

It's hard not to love a classic comfort food like mashed potatoes, and it turns out, they are a fantastically economical side dish as well as a soothing, soul-warming taste of home. I've found that if you use a good, buttery-flavored potato like a Yukon Gold—and it's worth asking at your local farm stand if they grow a similar type near you, as you could be in for additional locally grown flavor—you can cut back on the milk. Just as pasta cooking water helps thicken sauces, potato cooking water can help give these mashed bad boys some moisture. In fact, in the event that you find you have no milk in the house, you can use the potato cooking water for the entire moistening process, and all will be good. It's all about finding options to help you get past those annoying little setbacks. Though I do not skimp on butter. Oh, no—not the butter.

2 pounds Yukon Gold or similar potatoes (approximately 4 large), peeled, cut into 1-inch cubes

2 teaspoons kosher salt, plus more for seasoning

4 tablespoons salted sweet cream butter, softened, cut into ¼-inch pats

¼ cup milk

Freshly ground black pepper

1 Place the cubed potatoes into a large saucepan. Add enough water to cover the potatoes by 1 inch. Bring the water to a boil over medium-high heat, add the salt, and boil until the potatoes are softened. The whole process from turning the burner on to mashable potatoes should take 20 to 25 minutes.

2 Reserve ¼ cup of the cooking water so you can moisten the potatoes. Use the same method for this task as you did for reserving pasta water (page xv).

3 Return the potatoes to the saucepan, and mash well. Add the butter, then pour the milk and cooking water over the potatoes, mash a bit more, then add salt and pepper to taste, and *voilà*—you have a buttery, comforting starch at the ready.

VARIATION: For an easy variation on this theme, just before you add salt and pepper to your heart's delight, throw in the cloves from an entire head of roasted garlic (page xvii), mashing them well in a small bowl before adding them to the potatoes. It adds a mere 54¢ to the bill. This variation goes quite well with a number of items, some of which I will leave to your imagination, but, in particular, it pairs nicely with the Beef Short Ribs in Mushroom Gravy (page 188).

ESTIMATED COST FOR FOUR: $2.49. The potatoes should cost no more than 99¢ per pound on the high end, though you have and I have seen foolishly inexpensive potatoes on sale. I have also had great potato success with locally grown potatoes that cost 58¢ per pound—the more pounds one purchased, the more one saved, so a 10-pound bag was $5.75, but we do like to be on the high end to avoid scorn and disappointment, so we will call the 2 pounds of potatoes $2.00. The milk cost 12½¢ at $1.99 for 8 cups, so we'll just round that up and call it 13¢. The butter costs 36¢. There. That's it. Now, if you add the roasted garlic, it's another 54¢. So for $3.03, you're eating a steak house–style side. All four of you are, in fact.

RISOTTO FORMAGGIO DI CAPRA (GOAT CHEESE RISOTTO)

{ Serves 4, $5.00 to $10.00 }

Risotto may be prepared in a huge variety of ways—with seafood, with saffron (alla Milanese), with peas, with artichoke hearts, with asparagus, with mushrooms, and with Parmigiano-Reggiano and butter (risotto Bianco), just to name a few. Or, you can improvise and make it whatever way you like once you've got the basic steps down. Risotto can be used for almost any occasion, and dressed up with whatever ingredients are around. This risotto is designed to complement Lamb Shanks in an Orangey Fig Sauce (page 186), but any cut of lamb would be welcome with it, as would roasted vegetables in place of meat. JR and I enjoy leek risotto when leeks are in season, and Butternut Squash Risotto (page 126) is a great holiday side dish. If you don't like goat cheese, feel free to make the risotto with Parmigiano-Reggiano instead—though it is worth trying this with locally made goat cheese, which is a change from the type you'll usually find in the market and an opportunity to learn about cheese that's available in your area. No matter if you go the Formaggio di Capra or the Bianco route, it's easy to master this staple of northern Italian cuisine.

5 cups low-sodium chicken stock (see Note)

7 tablespoons unsalted butter

1 medium shallot, finely chopped

1 cup Arborio or Carnaroli rice

½ cup dry white wine, plus 1 glass for sipping (optional)

2 ounces fresh goat cheese, crumbled to the best of your ability, or ¼ cup grated Parmigiano-Reggiano cheese

Kosher salt

Freshly ground black pepper

1 In a medium saucepan, heat the stock over medium heat until warmed through. Keep a ladle at the ready for transferring the stock to the risotto pot.

2 In a large saucepan over medium heat, melt 6 tablespoons of the butter. Once the butter is completely melted but before it starts to brown, add the shallot. Cook the shallot until it is translucent, 2 to 3 minutes. Maintain the medium heat—you don't want to use too hot a flame (or coil, as the case may be) because overheating the rice will cause it to harden. Don't be nervous, it's really quite easy, but you should know that you must be patient. Now, pick up that glass of wine (or water), have a sip, put it back down, take a deep breath, and add the rice to the pan. Stir the rice to coat it in butter, and cook for 1 to 2 minutes at medium heat to warm the rice through before adding liquid.

3 Add the ½ cup of wine, stirring constantly until it has been completely absorbed into the rice. Once the wine has been absorbed, add the first ladle of stock and stir, yes, constantly, until it has been completely absorbed into the rice. By completely absorbed, I do not mean that the rice is dried out and sticking to the bottom of the pot—you should still see a little bit of moisture surrounding your rice—but you do need to let the liquid be absorbed before adding the next ladleful. It's a balancing act, but one that you are perfectly able to handle.

4 Your first 3 or 4 additions of stock will be about a cup each. After that, you may want to add a little less liquid—say, a little over ½ cup. So here you are, stirring and admiring the rice as it plumps up. You will stir and admire for 20 to 25 minutes or so, but the true test is in the tasting.

5 As you get toward the bottom of your stock supply, which is very likely around 20 minutes into the cooking process, take a little bit of the rice out and cool it so you can test it without burning your mouth. The rice should be firm but not chewy. Once I get to that 20-minute mark, I test before each new addition of stock to see how it's going. If this is your first time preparing risotto at home, not to worry. If you've had it in a restaurant, you have a pretty good idea of what the texture should be; and if you've never had it anywhere before because you live in a secluded mountainous and wooded area with not one road out of the wilderness, yet somehow you've managed to get yourself some superfino rice, just use your best judgment. Is it pleasantly firm to the bite or does it stick to the inside of your molars when you test it? If it sticks to your teeth, you probably want to add more stock. But, hey, if you like rice stuck in your teeth, just move on to the next step at that point.

6 The next step is to remove the pot from the heat and stir in the cheese. Now, add the remaining tablespoon of butter. Stir it into the rice until it has melted. Let the rice sit for a few minutes, then stir, add salt and pepper to taste, and serve it out.

NOTE: If you're using store-bought chicken stock, make sure it's low-sodium; otherwise, the salt flavor may be overpowering. Both of the rices are superfino. Fino rice is also acceptable, but do not use regular rice for this dish. It will be a mushy disaster and you'll be left wondering what all the fuss is about with this risotto junk.

ESTIMATED COST FOR FOUR: $7.76. Six tablespoons of butter at $2.79 for 32 tablespoons is 54¢, plus the additional 9¢ for the last bit of butter added at the end. One medium shallot should run you around 25¢. One 4-cup box of Whole Foods store brand broth is $2.19 plus another cup from a second box is 55¢, so $2.74. If you aren't going to use the remaining 3 cups of broth anytime soon, go ahead and put the box up in the freezer, or you can parcel it out into an ice cube tray and freeze it for smaller serving sizes. One cup of risotto out of a 2-pound bag that sells for $5.19 is $1.30. One-half cup of white wine—which I recommend you purchase for no more than $5.00 for a 750ml bottle—but do be sure that it is meant to be drunk—costs 84¢. The two ounces of goat cheese, at $3.99 for 4 ounces, is $2.00.

If you were to go the Risotto Bianco route using Parmigiano-Reggiano, the cost would come down to $7.16 as ¼ cup of grated Parmigiano-Reggiano is about ½ ounce of cheese and costs $18.99 per pound. Double bonus jackpot recipe, indeed.

BUTTERNUT SQUASH RISOTTO

{ Serves 4, $5.00 to $10.00 }

As you learned when you read the notes on our *Goat Cheese Risotto* (page 123), there are nearly infinite variations on risotto, and this is one that consistently receives *ooohs* and *ahhhhs* whenever it is served at my house. It pairs as beautifully with a holiday turkey or roast as it does with chicken or pork, and is a lovely dish for cold weather, or even simply crisp weather. It has the additional benefit of including a vegetable within, and so a side vegetable is not required when you serve this forth. Unless you feel strongly about eating many vegetables at each sitting. That's up to you.

2 pounds butternut squash, peeled, seeded, cut into ½-inch cubes

2 tablespoons extra virgin olive oil

5 cups low-sodium vegetable stock (see Note)

6 tablespoons plus 1 tablespoon unsalted butter

1 medium shallot, finely chopped

1 cup Arborio or Carnaroli rice (see Note)

¼ cup grated Pecorino Romano cheese

Kosher salt

Freshly ground pepper

1 Preheat the oven to 350°F.

2 Toss the butternut squash with the olive oil. Spread it out on a 9 by 13-inch rimmed baking sheet and bake for 25 to 30 minutes, until the squash is softened and is beginning to brown. Remove from the oven and set aside.

3 In a medium saucepan, heat the stock over medium heat until warmed through. Keep a ladle at the ready for transferring the stock to the risotto pot.

4 In a large saucepan over medium heat, melt 6 tablespoons of the butter. Once the butter is completely melted but before it starts to brown, add the shallot. Cook the shallot until it is translucent, 2 to 3 minutes.

ladleful and continue stirring and adding and stirring some more. When the rice is getting close to done—our goal is al dente—add the roasted squash with the next addition of stock. And stir, stir away while the rice is transformed to a lovely orangey color that promises sweet autumn flavors.

6 As you approach the end of the stirring, the rice has less absorption capability, so you do not need to add quite as much stock as you did in those early stages.

7 Take this glorious pot of rice from the heat and add the Pecorino Romano cheese. Work the cheese in completely, and then stir in the remaining tablespoon of butter. Allow the rice to sit for 2 to 3 minutes, add salt and pepper to taste, give it another swirl, and serve it forth.

Add the rice to the pan, stir to coat it in butter, and cook for a couple of minutes at medium heat to warm the rice through before adding the vegetable stock.

5 Add a ladleful of the stock and stir constantly until it is completely absorbed. And I do mean completely, but I do not mean so much so that your rice begins to stick to the bottom of the pan and burn, which it should not even be at risk of, for you, my friend, are stirring constantly and therefore paying attention. Add the next

NOTE: If you're using store-bought vegetable stock, make sure it's low-sodium; otherwise, the salt flavor may be overpowering. Both of the rices are superfino. Fino rice is also acceptable, but do not use regular rice for this dish lest you end with an unappetizing bowl of rice mush.

ESTIMATED COST FOR FOUR: $7.26. A pound and a half of butternut squash, peeled and seeded, should come from a 2-pound butternut squash. At 79¢ per pound, we'll round up and call it $1.60. Two tablespoons of olive oil are 24¢. Six tablespoons of butter at $2.79 for 32 tablespoons is 54¢, plus an additional 9¢ for the tablespoon with which we finish the butternutty goodness. One medium shallot should cost around 25¢. One and a half 4-cup boxes of Whole Foods store brand vegetable broth costs $2.39 plus 60¢, so $2.99. One cup of risotto out of a 2-pound bag that sells for $5.19 is $1.30. A quarter cup of Pecorino Romano cheese is approximately ½ ounce, and at $7.99 per pound, that adds 25¢ to the tally.

The Smell of Warm Sugar

During the summers when I was six and seven years old—back in the freewheeling 1970s—my parents sent me off to stay with a family who, by comparison, lived in the country. How they came to know this family makes these trips slightly dubious, as they met while my father sought to purchase an antique car from them. From that lone meeting over a 1948 Ford sedan—or some similarly old vehicle—my parents decided that a week in their country home each summer would serve me well.

That their decision was likely influenced by the fact that the husband was the retired Chief of Police in that country town provides me some solace, and, again, it was the freewheeling 1970s. Children played in the street until dark; parents only knew that they were outside with other children. Those other children's backgrounds weren't checked as though they were about to join the Secret Service. I'm fortunate that it was so, for my time at their horse farm remains among my favorite childhood memories.

The Chief's house—his name was Mr. Werme—was a circa 1600s cape with wide wood floors, exposed beams, and a red brick hearth framing the fireplace in the dining room, the dining room and kitchen one and the same. The house sat close to the road, but their horses roamed hilly, stonewall-enclosed fields. At the perimeter of these fields grew boysenberries—a cross between a raspberry and the Pacific blackberry—cascading from their brambles to the ground, resting from time to time on the stone walls, a perfect height for a seven-year-old to pick.

I would gather as many ripe berries as I could find, careful of the thorns, as I had been warned, and avoiding any gnarly-looking or unripe fruit. Fingers sticky and tinged purple, Mrs. Werme and I would return to the house, spreading our loot out over the broad honey-colored wooden kitchen table that served as counter, too. While I picked through the berries once more—popping a few into my mouth in the name of quality control—Mrs. Werme prepared the preserving accoutrement: glass jars in the hot water bath, linen kitchen towels illustrated with calendars from 1951, 1963, and 1970 dampened and warmed, jar grabbers to protect us from burns, all at the ready.

The kitchen window fogged as the berries cooked down, the scent of warm sugar filling the room. I would help stir, and when I grew tired of the task, would sit on the brick hearth and listen to Mrs. Werme's tales of raising four children—always sliding in life lessons about responsibility and respecting others—subtly, though, so as to keep me from knowing it was so.

When I said good-bye to the rolling hills, the horses, my four-poster feather bed complete with stepstool, and Mr. and Mrs. Werme, a jar of boysenberry preserves was always tucked into the back seat of my parents' wood-paneled station wagon with me, a taste of summer, country life, and the wisdom of a sixty-year-old woman all held in the quilted crystal glass.

The garden at our house is surrounded by bramble—the remains of the ill-conceived plan of an owner back in those freewheeling 1970s—bramble from which JR and I are convinced we will never be free. It rises up between the lettuce and squash, the raised beds no protection from the sprawling root systems these marauding stalks cast out. Of the hundreds of brambles that make up the thicket next to our garden, only three are raspberries, a small prize for such a menacing area.

While sitting in our usual spot in the garden, making note of said dearth of raspberries, JR informed me that he had noticed a stand of blackberries in a neglected area of the corral attached to our barn—a small corral at that, only a quarter acre or so in size. In years prior, he had always been sure to cut these "weeds" back, and before that, when there were cows in the corral, cutting back was unnecessary. Yet here is the success of those 1970s homeowners who lived here before us—edible berries, and slews of them at that.

The morning after the discovery, I donned one of JR's long-sleeved work shirts, durable enough to protect my arms from thorny scrapes during the harvest, though he

thought it might be advisable for me to wear his beekeeping suit, and began the process. Slowly at first—I had been picking for what seemed like a long time, only to find that the bottom of the basket, though small, wasn't yet covered. Then the berries began to make themselves more obvious—or perhaps I slowed down enough to see them more readily—and eventually, I chanced upon a thicket rich with ripe berries; placing my basket under them, they would all but fall off of the vine. Suddenly, I had enough berries for preserves, as well as one spider trapped under the weight of the berries and one slug that was dispatched to the field on sight. Fingers purple and slightly sticky, I repeated the process learned so many years ago— pick through the berries—in this case, free the spider—gobble up a few for purposes of quality control, and prepare the quilted jelly jars for canning.

BLACKBERRY (BOYSENBERRY, RASPBERRY, BERRY-BERRY) PRESERVES

{ Makes 2 cups }

2 cups sweet, ripe berries, picked over
1 ½ cups sugar
The juice of 1 lemon

1 Prepare your canning goods for the canning process. Be sure to first wash the jars and lids in hot, soapy water, then sterilize the jars in a hot water bath that covers all parts of the jars. Start with the jars in the water, then bring the water to a boil, and boil them for 10 minutes.

2 Remove the jars only when you're ready to use them, and cover them with a clean kitchen towel, preferably linen with some long-ago calendar printed upon it.

3 I also use a funnel, which must be cleaned prior to canning, a magnetic lid fetcher (that's the name I made up for it—it grabs the lids from the hot water bath that I use to prepare those—they're smaller than canning jars, and therefore fit into a smaller pot), and a jar grabber. I line my countertop with kitchen towels as well, so as to easily clean up sticky preserves that miss

their mark—this missing is inevitable, as far as I can tell.

4 In a large saucepan or stockpot—for the hot sugar and berries will bubble and you want some distance between the two of you, as hot sugar burns are not desirable— combine the berries, sugar, and lemon juice. Allow the mixture to sit for a half hour to draw out some of the blackberries' juice, a process known more formally as macerating. During this maceration phase, resist the temptation to eat up half of the berries and jar the other half; beautiful though they may be, it is worth the effort of cooking them. Bring them to a boil over medium-high heat and cook, stirring frequently to help avoid the hot sugar spray of unattended preserves in progress, until a candy or oil thermometer registers 220°F, 12 to 15 minutes.

5 See, it's not time consuming at all. Just like that, you have the preserves ready to be canned. So can we must. Transfer the preserves to the sterilized jelly jars and place the lids on. If you plan to use the preserves *tout de suite*, you can just put them into the refrigerator now. If you're not using them within a month, process the jars in a hot water bath for 10 minutes to seal the lids.

6 The hot water bath sealing process is also quite simple. Before you begin cooking the preserves, get out your boiling water canner. Remove the rack upon which the jars will sit—you'll be lowering it back into the water once the jars are filled—and pour water into the canner until it is about halfway full, then bring it to a boil. Take the filled jars, with lids securely on, place them on the rack, and lower the rack into the water, adding additional water if necessary to cover the jars by at least 2 inches. Cover and process for 10 minutes, being certain that the water is always at a boil. If at any point it stops boiling, bring the water back up to a boil and begin timing the 10 minutes over again. Remove the lid using oven mitts, being careful to release the steam away from your face. Let the jars cool for at least 5 minutes before removing them, pressing down on the lids once cooled to be sure they have sealed properly. If they have not sealed properly, the middle of the lid will yield to the pressure of your finger. Allow the jars to cool completely on a rack for 12 to 24 hours, then store them in a cool, dark spot until you're ready to spoon some preserves out, but be sure to use them within a year. Once they've been opened, store them in the refrigerator and use them up within a month.

NOTE: Should you lack an oil or candy thermometer, all is not lost. Simply place a small ceramic or porcelain plate into the freezer for 20 minutes. When you're ready to test the preserves to see if they'll firm up, place a small amount of the hot liquid onto the cold plate. If the liquid doesn't run all over the plate—and behaves like you expect preserves to behave—they're ready for canning.

RHUBARB-GINGER CHUTNEY

{ **Makes approximately 3 cups** }

Another way to gussy up simple grilled or roasted meats—for those days when you don't have the inclination to get too involved in the kitchen—is to use chutney as an accompaniment. This rhubarb chutney is extremely easy to make—there isn't even a test to see if it's jelled, it is simply cooked until the rhubarb falls apart, which takes somewhere in the 12- to 15-minute range. Likewise, this may be jarred up and the lids sealed for longer-term storage, for those winter evening meals that would benefit from instant fanciness. You will be grateful that you have it when you make the Perfect Roasted Chicken (page 69) and find you haven't a bit of orange juice on hand for the sauce. It would also be wonderful with nearly any cut of pork, and grilled chicken of any type would also benefit from its inclusion at your dinner table.

3 cups chopped rhubarb (4 to 5 stalks, cut into ¼-inch slices)

1 medium Vidalia or other sweet onion, coarsely chopped

½ cup raisins

2 tablespoons freshly grated ginger, from approximately 1 ounce of ginger root

½ cup sugar

1 Combine the rhubarb, onion, raisins, ginger, and sugar in a large saucepan or stockpot. Let sit for 15 minutes until the rhubarb releases its liquid. Cook over medium heat until the rhubarb becomes mush (desirable in this case) and the onions are softened, 12 to 15 minutes.

2 Transfer to sterilized jars, cover with sterilized lids, and process in a hot water bath for 10 minutes. Allow the jars to cool, and store them in a cool, dark spot for future use, but no more than a year into the future, and then, to be a bit redundant, refrigerate it after opening and use it within a month. The chutney will thicken as it cools.

bakery and desserts

SAVORY PIE CRUST

{ **Makes 1 thick or 2 thin (12-inch) crusts, $5.00 or less** }

We start this chapter with a recipe that will change your life—or, at the very least, will help you stretch your food budget all while appearing quite fancy, thank you very much. It is imperative that you know about savory pie crust.

Let's just say you have some leftovers—perhaps a beef stew, perhaps some chicken in, oh, I don't know, cider gravy—and you're thinking, "Boring! I can't possibly eat that again." Well, my friend, should this happen to you, simply whip up a savory pie crust. In about a half an hour, you will be placing into your oven a dish worthy of company. If you happen to be a guest at my house during the winter months, you need not worry about being gauche by asking if the meat and gravy part of the pie are leftovers. They most assuredly are. And yet, you will be overwhelmed with the transcendent buttery flakiness of the crust, and will not care that I am serving you leftovers, my dear guest.

The number of dishes that can be fancied up with this dough is practically limitless. Ok, so you're a vegetarian. How about a vegetable stew, or a lentil and carrot stew? You there, Ms. Carnivore, let's make a chili con carne and top it off with a layer of shredded pepper Jack cheese and then the crust. Or maybe a lamb and carrot stew would be more to your liking. Why not add a bit of goat cheese under the crust for that dish? You see what I mean? Practically limitless.

So, now, just forget that you've ever read anything that implies pie dough is challenging to craft. Get thee to thy pantry and gather up the flour and butter and vegetable shortening. We're going to make a meal-saving, savory pie crust.

3 cups unbleached all-purpose flour

1 ½ teaspoons kosher salt

1 teaspoon baking powder

8 tablespoons (½ cup) very cold vegetable shortening

8 tablespoons (1 stick) very cold unsalted butter

½ to ¾ cup ice water

1 large egg yolk

1 tablespoon milk (any kind)

1 Now, you do not need a food processor for this, but I will provide instruction for both the by-hand method and the food processor method. It must be due to the fact that I have to hand-wash my dishes (that's right, I have no newfangled dishwashing machine) that I'm not fully embracing the food processor method, but in the interest of full disclosure, I thoroughly enjoy working with dough by hand, or *a mano*. It's soothing and also gratifying to know your two warm palms and ten cold fingers put it all together.

2 To make the dough by hand, mix together the flour, salt, and baking powder in a large mixing bowl. Now, not to scare you about the dough, because we all know now that the dough is your friend and is infinitely useful, but the reason why the very cold items must be very cold is because you want a flaky crust, and that can't happen if the fats blend into the dough completely. It is the little bits of fat that create flakiness and give you that buttery crust we all hold so dear. This is also why you should use your fingers, the cold part of your hands, and not your palms, which are the warm part of your

hands, to work the dough. If it makes your life easier, you can put the butter and shortening into the freezer for 5 or 10 minutes to ensure that they are both very cold for the next step.

3 Cut the very cold vegetable shortening and the very cold butter into approximately ½-inch cubes and add them to the flour mixture. Using the tips of your fingers, blend the butter and shortening into the flour. What this means is, you plunge your fingers into the flour, coating the fats with flour, while breaking up the fats until they are roughly pea-sized. It is perfectly okay for some of them to be larger than pea-sized, you just don't want them to be close to the same size as the cubes you initially placed into the flour. Remove your fingers from the flour and fats mixture. Get yourself a fork. Pour ½ cup very cold ice water (yes, I know I've mentioned "very cold" before—I am trying to make a point) into the flour and fats mixture and blend the water into the dough with the fork. You are trying to moisten the dough just enough that it holds together, so if there are still dry spots in your bowl, and I'm pretty certain there will be, add very cold, oh, absolutely frigid, ice water to the dough, 1 tablespoon at a time, blending in gently, until the dough is just holding together. On a lightly floured surface, form the dough into a ball, wrap it in plastic wrap, and refrigerate it for 30 minutes.

4 And now, the food processor version: In a food processor fitted with the metal blade, add the flour, salt, and baking powder. Then add the very cold butter and the very cold shortening, and pulse for about 10 seconds until the fats are pea-sized. Pulsing the motor, add ½ cup of the ice water

to the flour mixture until it begins to form small balls. If there is still a fair amount of flour laying about in the processor, add ice water, 1 tablespoon at a time, until dry has become moist. Turn the small balls of dough out onto a lightly floured surface, being very careful of the metal blade—that thing is sharp—and form them quickly and gently into a ball. Cover the dough completely in plastic wrap, and place it in the refrigerator for 30 minutes.

5 Now, let's just say that you're transforming Chicken in Cider Gravy (page 67) into pot pie, but let's also say that you decided to use a rotisserie chicken that you picked up from the grocery store on your way home, and you're going to make a cider gravy on the stovetop. You could pick the chicken clean and make the gravy in about the amount of time it takes for the savory pie dough to firm up in the refrigerator. Now, let's pretend that your grocery store sells rotisserie chicken for $7.99 each. And that your cider gravy costs $4.16 as described in the Chicken in Cider Gravy recipe (page 67). And that the pie crust costs $2.60 to make. And that the pie serves at least six. Now, how much does that cost us? That's right, people. It costs us $14.75 for the whole thing, or $2.46 per serving. With purchased rotisserie chicken.

6 Preheat the oven to 375°F.

7 So now your gravy is done; it and the chicken are in the pie pan, and you need only to get the savory pie dough out of the refrigerator and, on a lightly floured surface, roll it out to approximately ¼-inch thickness in some approximation of a circle (or a rectangle, or a square; whatever shape baking dish you're using). As soon as the dough is rolled out, gently lift it and place it atop your baking dish. Push the dough down the sides of the dish to firmly cover the filling as though you're tucking someone you love into a toasty bed, allowing for an inch or so of dough overhanging the edges of the baking dish. Crimp the overhanging dough over itself to create a thicker crust edge. Beat the egg yolk and milk together and brush it over the top of the crust. Cut five 1-inch slits in the dough over the filling—be decorative with it if you like—and place your masterpiece into the oven. I advise you to put the baking dish on a foil-lined baking sheet in order to prevent spillage on the bottom of the oven, which might result in copious amounts of smoke in your kitchen, and might require you to set the oven to clean the next day. Ahem. Not that this is has ever happened at my house or anything. Bake until the crust is golden brown, approximately 40 minutes.

What About Sweet Crust, You Ask?

It is simple enough to modify this recipe to craft a lovely dough for sweet dishes. Simply reduce the salt to 1 teaspoon and add 2 tablespoons of sugar to the mix, follow the very same process, and impress friends and relations all year-round with your clearly superior bakery skills. The recipe yields enough for a top and bottom for a sweet pie, unless you fancy a thick crust, in which case you'll probably want to make a double batch. P.S. Adding sugar increases the tally by a whopping 4¢. Rounded up, of course.

NOTE: When making pot pies, be certain that there is some liquid in those leftovers you're transforming. Don't go putting meatloaf slices sans gravy in a pie dish and topping it with pie crust. No. In fact, you should wrap the meatloaf slices in this pie crust as though you're mailing them off in savory little envelopes and call it *pain de viande en croute*. Now, that's fancy.

ESTIMATED COST FOR ONE PIE CRUST: $2.60. The flour is 71¢ for 3 cups from a bag that costs $4.49 for 19 cups. The baking powder costs 1¢. The vegetable shortening is 90¢ for our 8 tablespoons at $5.49 for 49 tablespoons. The butter used is 8 of 32 tablespoons at $2.79, so that's 70¢. The egg yolk is from 1 egg, which is 26¢, and the milk for the wash is 3¢, ¹⁄₆₄ of $1.99.

CALZONE DOUGH

{ **Makes 1 (12-inch) calzone crust, $5.00 or less** }

One good way to stretch leftovers is to fashion them into another satisfying and delicious meal. Calzone fits that bill exactly; it's a hit at my house with a couple of Mom's Meatballs and Not My Nana's Red Sauce (page 61) leftovers, but do feel free to use any other protein or vegetable that might tickle your fancy. If you have a whole slew of leftovers requiring transformation into calzones, or if you want to stretch some deli meats to get through the week, this recipe is easily doubled. My mother was the queen of dual-calzone baking, always a meatball side by side with a ham and cheese calzone—just be sure to coat the interior of the ham and cheese with some spicy mustard before rolling it up—that's the secret ingredient that made hers so addictive.

Though there were indications of it in my youth—the clandestine eating of bread and cookie dough while my mother's rear-view eyes weren't looking—in adulthood, all has been revealed, and I am, in fact, an admitted dough freak. I love everything about dough—the smell of the yeast, the magical alchemy of flour and liquids transforming into dough before my eyes, the upper-body workout that kneading provides, and, of course, the blissful eating of that which my hands have wrought—sometimes, still prior to the actual baking. That said, this dough, which I adapted from a recipe on the King Arthur Flour Web site, is gorgeous. Silky and smooth from the get-go, and light and fluffy once cooked. Can you stand it any longer? Let's get started, shall we?

1 ½ teaspoons turbinado sugar (sold as Sugar in the Raw)

1 cup warm water, between 105° and 115°F (see Note)

1 ½ teaspoons active dry yeast

1 tablespoon extra virgin olive oil

1 ½ teaspoons kosher salt

2 ¼ cups unbleached all-purpose flour, plus ¼ cup or more for kneading

¼ cup whole-wheat or unbleached all-purpose flour

1 large egg yolk

1 tablespoon milk (any kind)

Sesame seeds or poppy seeds, for dusting

1 In a large mixing bowl, dissolve the sugar in the water. Sprinkle the yeast over the water and allow it to sit for 5 minutes. It will begin to ferment, bubbling to indicate that it is so. Perhaps the scent will remind you of Sunday morning outside your favorite college bar. Perhaps not. But it does have a distinct smell that is worth sticking your nose into the bowl—not into the water mixture, the bowl—to savor. This is the smell of the yeast getting ready to give that flour a lift.

2 While the sugar, water, and yeast are doing their thing, measure out the oil, salt, and flours. This way, you are at the ready the moment the yeasty mixture is.

3 After the 5 minutes have passed, add the olive oil and salt and give the mixture a stir. Add the flours gradually, a cup or so at a time, stirring well with each addition.

4 Grease a large bowl—one large enough to hold double the dough's bulk—with olive oil, and set aside.

5 Dust the countertop with the flour for kneading. This dough is sticky, so you will also need to flour your hands in order to move it to the counter. Knead the dough for 5 to 6 minutes, until the flour used for dusting has been incorporated into the dough and the dough isn't fully adhering to your hands with each touch. Allow the dough to rest for 1 to 2 minutes, dust your work surface with additional flour, then knead once more for 1 to 2 minutes.

6 Place the dough into the large bowl, turning to coat with the olive oil. We do this to prevent the formation of a crust on the dough. Cover the top of the bowl with

a clean kitchen towel or plastic wrap that has been lightly greased on the side facing the dough so that when the dough rises up to the bowl edge and touches the plastic wrap, it does not adhere to it, and place it in a warm, draft-free area to rise. Rising times are contingent upon the temperature of your home, but in a room with a temperature of 70°F, the dough should have risen to twice its original size in 1 to 1½ hours.

7 Line a 9 by 13-inch rimmed baking sheet with parchment paper.

8 Punch down the dough and turn it out onto your lightly floured counter. Gently stretch the dough out to 12 inches by 15 inches or so. I do not expect you to use a ruler for this exercise unless you feel strongly about achieving exact measurements. That's your business. However, when I tell you to leave an inch border around the edge of the dough on all sides as you fill it, I really do mean that. Otherwise, you will find yourself with a disaster of oozing fillings that no one wants to contend with. It just takes the fun out of calzone construction to have them explode on you. Fill the calzone with whatever fillings you desire, but make sure that they aren't too runny—there is such a thing as too much sauce, for instance (see previous comment on oozing fillings not being fun, please). Arrange your chosen fillings in a single layer—you want to keep them right around ¼ inch thick at the most—and leaving that at-least-1-inch-topping-free zone we discussed around the perimeter. Once your fillings are in place, treat the calzone as though it were a business letter; you are going to fold it over itself in thirds from the long side. In some areas, this is

known as a stromboli, but where I grew up, both the business-letter fold and the half-moon types are referred to as calzone. So, now, fold down the topmost side so that only one-third of the filling is exposed, then take that exposed side and fold it over again, crimping the dough to seal it. Be sure to tuck the dough edges on the short sides under the mass of calzone and crimp them to prevent, yes, oozing filling.

9 Carefully put your calzone on its baking sheet, and cover your creation with your clean kitchen towel or a lightly greased piece of plastic wrap. Set it aside to rise once more, this time for 1 hour.

10 Thirty minutes before you are going to bake the calzone, preheat the oven to 450°F. At the moment you preheat the oven, place a metal—metal, metal, metal, not glass, *metal*—roasting pan on an oven rack set to the lowest position. Why metal? You will be pouring water into this pan. And glass will shatter if one measly drop of cool water touches its 450°F surface, leaving you and your significant other to first scream in shock at the sound and sight of glass shattering in your oven, and then forcing you both to clean shards of shattered glass from your oven. And not just in order to get this calzone in the oven. Oh, no. This will go on for months, this discovery of glass shards will.

11 While waiting to place the calzone into the hot, hot oven, make 5 slits in the top of the calzone using a sharp knife. Mix together the egg yolk and milk to form a wash. This will help adhere your topping of choice—sesame seeds or poppy seeds—to the top of your calzone. If you choose not

to top with seeds, the egg wash also helps create a nice, brown crust. As does the following trick.

12 Just as you are about to add the calzone to the oven, pour 4 cups of water into the metal roasting pan. Quickly place the calzone in the oven, and shut the door, quick-quick. If this step seems curious, you may want to read What's With the Water? while you bake the calzone until that crust is nicely golden and crisp, which will take 25 to 30 minutes.

13 Remove the calzone from the oven and allow it to rest for 10 to 15 minutes to set the filling—see, we continue in our avoidance of runny filling—and then dig in. Perfect for lunches, for a picnic, for the beach, for anytime you need a portable treat. *Perfetto!*

NOTE: The water temperature is very important, as too high a heat will kill the yeast and prevent you from enjoying that glorious yeasty-fermenting smell at the start. Oh, and your bread will be flat as a cracker as well.

What's With the Water?

Adding water at the beginning of the cooking helps us home cooks to simulate steam-injection ovens that professional bakeries use to get that crisp crust we all love. Now, while this may seem counterintuitive, here, my friend, is why it happens. Think of it as though you are wearing black on a hot, summer day. The darkness of your clothing absorbs the heat and warms you. Too much. Which is why everyone around you is wearing white, and linen, at that. Well, when calzone—or any bread using this trick, in fact—enters the oven, the water steams and creates condensation on the bread surface. This steam also helps the bread to expand, so the loaf is lighter in the end. The condensation on the bread surface cools the bread slightly, allowing the yeast enzymes to continue working a bit longer to convert carbohydrates into simple sugars, which then caramelize. Boy, do I love caramelization. It's like magic. And here is where the black outfit on a hot day comes in: The caramelization darkens the crust, and so the heat from the oven is better absorbed by the crust, thereby causing it to become crispy. See, science made simple. By the time you are done reading this explanation of the process, your calzone will probably be nearly done baking.

ESTIMATED COST FOR THE DOUGH PLUS EGG WASH AND DECORATIVE SEED TOPPING: $2.43. Water is free from the tap, of course, so we start off on a positive note with this recipe. The turbinado sugar costs around 2¢ per teaspoon, so we're using 3¢ worth here. Yeast costs 67¢ per 2½-teaspoon package, and to be fair, considering you are likely not saving the remainder of the package—though you should—we'll just leave it at 67¢. The olive oil costs 12¢. The all-purpose flour and whole-wheat flour both cost the same per 5-pound bag, so for 2¾ cups, we're looking at 65¢. The egg wash runs us 28¢, and sesame seeds cost $2.69 for just over 4 tablespoons. We'll use 1 tablespoon of sesame seeds for topping, and that adds 68¢ to the total.

OATMEAL-WHEAT BEER BREAD

{ 1 loaf, 10 to 12 slices, $5.00 or less }

I love making yeast breads—I am particularly fond of kneading dough, which perhaps says something about my need to work out frustration through pushing dough around. That notwithstanding, even I, a lover of dough and dough kneading, sometimes prefer a speedy bread—a quick bread, as they are commonly known—but not always banana or pumpkin or zucchini. For while I love any of those types of produce-based breads, they do not necessarily speak to me about tomorrow's sandwich for lunch. So when I need a quick sandwich loaf, I turn to this beer bread, which happens to include a little fiber in the form of rolled oats and wheat flour. In my house, the most time-consuming part of making this bread is letting the beer unchill, as we want to use room-temperature beer here, and we keep our cans of beer in the refrigerator. You may use any type of beer that suits your fancy. Lighter-style beers will result in a lighter flavor, while ales and stouts will result in a more robust flavor.

2 cups unbleached all-purpose flour

¾ cup whole-wheat flour

½ cup old-fashioned rolled oats (not quick-cooking oats)

3 tablespoons packed brown sugar

1 tablespoon baking soda

1 teaspoon kosher salt

12 ounces beer, at room temperature

1 Preheat the oven to 375°F. Grease a 9 by 5 by 3-inch loaf pan and set it aside.

2 In a large mixing bowl, mix the all-purpose flour, wheat flour, oats, sugar, baking soda, and salt, stirring well to combine. Add the warm beer in one quick pour, which, you may remember from some previous experience with warm carbonated beverages, will be quite foamy. Quickly stir to combine the beer with the flour mixture, paying no mind to lumps—they're perfectly acceptable in this bread. Scrape the whole beery mixture into the loaf pan—this entire process is so speedy, you may find yourself waiting for the oven to preheat with a loaf pan full of batter in hand— and bake until golden brown and a toothpick inserted into the middle of the loaf emerges clean, 40 to 45 minutes. Cool the bread in its pan on a cooling rack, 10 to 15 minutes, then turn the bread out of the pan onto the cooling rack until ready to serve.

Waste Not the Wrapper

I save wrappers from sticks of unsalted butter in the refrigerator for greasing pans. No need to chop into those handy, premeasured sticks when you can use residual butter from their spent packaging, after all.

ESTIMATED COST FOR 1 LOAF, 10 TO 12 SLICES: $2.26. The unbleached all-purpose flour and whole-wheat flour both cost $4.49 for 19 cups. We used 2 cups, or 47¢ worth of all-purpose flour, and ¾ cup, or 18¢ worth of the whole-wheat flour. The oats cost 21¢ per ½ cup at $2.69 for 13½-cup servings. The brown sugar costs 4¢ per tablespoon, and so that adds 12¢ to our tally. The baking soda costs just less than 1¢ per teaspoon, and 3 teaspoons is equivalent to 1 tablespoon, so we'll add 3¢ to the bill. We don't count salt in our mathematics, though we do count the beer, which, if purchased as a lone beer, would run around $1.25.

BUTTERHORNS

{ **Makes 24, $5.00 or less, approximately 13¢ per butterhorn** }

This recipe has been a favorite in my friend Amy's family, the Marrs family of Harveyville, Kansas, since at least the late 1920s. Amy's grandfather, Harvey Marrs, enjoyed these butterhorns on his family farm during the Great Depression; when the family had a little extra money, they'd make cinnamon rolls from the same recipe. In fact, these rolls are so versatile, you could add herbs, roasted garlic, cinnamon sugar, or jam before rolling them up, and satisfy all manner of fresh-baked-good cravings. Fancy enough for company, but easy enough for every day, and as always, inexpensive to craft. Perfection in butterhorn form.

¾ cup milk (not skim)

¼ cup sugar

¼ cup (4 tablespoons) vegetable shortening

1 teaspoon kosher salt

¼ cup warm water (105° to 115°F)

2¼ teaspoons (1 envelope) active dry yeast

3¾ cups unbleached all-purpose flour, sifted

1 large egg, at room temperature

6 tablespoons unsalted butter

1 Grease a large mixing bowl with butter or olive oil. Set aside.

2 Warm the milk in a small saucepan over medium heat until steam just begins to rise from it and the milk at the edge of the pan is just starting to bubble. This is called scalding, which traditionally was done in order to prevent the milk from souring, and in the case of this recipe, the heating helps to dissolve the sugar and shortening before incorporating the rest of the ingredients.

3 In another large mixing bowl, combine the milk, sugar, shortening, and salt, and stir well. You'll now want the milk mixture to cool slightly so the heat doesn't kill the yeast when it is added.

4 Meanwhile, mix together the warm water—which can be obtained by running hot tap water for a minute or so, or

by heating the water in a small saucepan over medium heat for 2 to 3 minutes—with the yeast in a small bowl. Allow the yeast to dissolve for 5 minutes. At first, this mixture will resemble khaki-colored paint and then will bubble as the yeast dissolves. If it doesn't bubble, the water is either too hot and has killed the yeast, or the yeast is past its prime. If either of those are the case, toss the yeast and water mixture out and make another batch.

5 While the milk mixture is cooling and the yeast is dissolving in the water, sift the flour. Add 1½ cups of the sifted flour to the milk mixture, and mix until it is well blended. Add the egg and then the yeast mixture, and mix until you no longer see the yellow of the egg. Add the remaining flour gradually, until it is fully incorporated with the wet ingredients and your dough has formed, meaning that no flour is hanging out at the bottom of your bowl and the dough is adhering to itself. Transfer the sticky, yet beautiful dough to a lightly floured surface, dust your hands well with flour, and knead gently until the dough comes together and is silken, 1 to 2 minutes. Form the dough into a ball, place that ball in the greased bowl, and roll it around to coat the surface of the dough lightly with the oil or butter used for greasing. You are doing this to prevent forming a crust on the dough, as that would detract from the buttery deliciousness of the butterhorns down the line.

6 Cover the top of the bowl with a clean dishtowel or plastic wrap that has been lightly greased on the side facing the dough. Set the bowl in a warm, draft-free area and allow it to rise until the dough is doubled in bulk, 1½ to 2 hours, depending upon how warm your household is kept. This estimate is for a room temperature of 70°F in your house, so be sure to take a look at the dough to determine whether it has risen to twice its mass.

7 Line two 9 by 13-inch rimmed baking sheets with parchment paper or grease them lightly. Set them aside.

8 Once the dough has risen to double its original bulk, transfer it to a lightly floured surface and divide it in half. Form each half into a ball, and then roll each ball out into a 12-inch round. Cut each round in half with a large, sharp knife or a pastry scraper, and cut each half-circle into 6 equal wedges. Melt the butter and brush about half of it onto the wedges, reserving the remaining butter for a second butter application once the butterhorns are rolled up and have had their second rise.

9 Now, let's form up some horns, shall we? Beginning at the wide end of each wedge, roll the dough toward the pointed edge. Place your rolled horn point down on the baking sheet to keep it from unraveling. Cover once more with your clean kitchen towel or lightly greased plastic wrap, and let the butterhorns rise again until double in size, 30 to 45 minutes.

10 When the rising time is nearly over, preheat the oven to 400°F. Brush the tops of the butterhorns with the remaining melted butter and bake until they are golden brown, 12 to 15 minutes. Allow the butterhorns to cool slightly before transferring them to a breadbasket. And be sure to clock how quickly they all disappear. These things are Good with a capital G.

NOTE: In the Marrs family, the butterhorns are prepared two ways in every batch: Twelve remain buttery butterhorns and twelve are made into cinnamon rolls. You can do this by sprinkling cinnamon sugar over the rolls after you've brushed them with butter but before you've rolled them up. However, don't stop at cinnamon rolls. In addition to jam rolls, herb rolls, and roasted garlic rolls, these could also be fashioned into Pecorino Romano rolls or finely chopped onion rolls. Or olive tapenade rolls. Or pesto rolls. Or toasted sesame seed rolls. Or pretty much any-other-type-of-flavoring-you-can-dream-up rolls.

ESTIMATED COST FOR 24 BUTTERHORNS: $3.04. The milk costs $1.99 for 8 cups, so ¾ cup costs 19¢. The sugar is nearly given away, at just over 4¢ per ¼ cup, so we'll call it 5¢. The shortening is organic Whole Foods store brand, which costs $5.49 for a 24-ounce container that yields 49 tablespoons, so we add 44¢ to our total to account for the 4 tablespoons we're using. One package of yeast is 67¢, though I advise you, if you expect to be doing a lot of yeast bread baking, to purchase yeast in bulk as it reduces the cost from 67¢ per 2¼ teaspoons to less than 10¢. The flour costs $4.49 for 19 cups, therefore, 3¾ cups costs 89¢. The egg should cost no more than 26¢, and the butter is 6 tablespoons from a package containing 32 tablespoons for $2.79, so that adds 54¢ to the tally.

HARVEY MARRS'S HOMEMADE BUTTER

{ **Makes just less than 2 cups of butter and just less than 2 cups of buttermilk, $5.00 to $10.00** }

This is the butter recipe that the Marrs family used on their Kansas farm during the Great Depression. I'm not implying that you need to make butter from scratch, but you have to admit, butter from scratch is pretty cool. Especially now that it's optional. I've adapted Harvey's recipe so that you can make it with a hand mixer or stand mixer, but we'll start with the recipe as it was executed on the Marrs family farm in the late 1920s and early 1930s, using a butter churn and butter paddles:

"In a large bowl, let whole milk sit long enough that the cream rises to the top. The cream should be cooled to approximately 55 degrees Fahrenheit and then poured into a wooden cask or butter churn. Agitate the cream until little particles of fat—which are butter—form together and float to the surface. The solid chunks of butter should then be removed from the churn with a strainer, rinsed with cold water and placed in a large wooden bowl for paddling. The remaining liquid can be stored for use as buttermilk. The wooden butter paddles are then used to squeeze out and separate any excess buttermilk still inside of the butter. You do not want any pockets of liquid or air left in the butter as these can cause rot. Butter paddles can be used to firm the butter, allowing it to be easily packed into butter molds. Once the excess buttermilk is separated from the butter, add salt to the mixture for flavor and to help preserve the butter."

Now, because you and I are not likely to have access to whole, unfiltered milk from our own herd of dairy cows, or a wooden butter churn, for that matter, we'll start this process with cream and our handy stand mixer or hand mixer. And so here we go:

32 ounces heavy cream

1 teaspoon kosher salt

1 Allow the cream to come to 55°F—it will be around 40°F when it is removed from the refrigerator.

2 Pour the cream into the bowl of your stand mixer or into a large mixing bowl, if you're using a hand mixer. Using the wire whip attachment and starting off at low speed, increase the speed to medium-high (setting 6), and beat the cream until the fats congeal and become butter, 10 to 15 minutes. This is a truly remarkable process. Before your very eyes, you will watch the cream go from liquid to soft peak whipped cream, to firm peak whipped cream, to pale yellow chunks, to butter yellow, um, butter. It is highly advisable to drape a kitchen towel over the mixing bowl, or, as I did with my stand mixer, create a shield of plastic wrap, to stave off the splatter of cream that will later be followed by the splatter of buttermilk, the buttermilk splatter indicating clearly that what once was cream now is butter.

3 Once the butter has formed, strain off the buttermilk to another container for future use—as in the next 5 to 7 days. I did this by transferring the butter and buttermilk to a fine-mesh strainer placed over a large bowl and then pressing on the butter with a wooden spoon to compress it, though a colander lined with 100 percent cotton cheesecloth would also do the trick.

4 Now that you have strained most of the buttermilk from the butter, rinse the butter with cold water from the tap to remove any residual buttermilk—for keeping the buttermilk in contact with the butter could cause spoilage later. Consider this step the hand-moisturizing portion of the process.

5 After rinsing the butter the first time, return it to the bowl and mix on medium-low speed to remove any additional liquid contained within the butter. Repeat the rinsing and mixing process 3 to 4 times, until no more buttermilk can be extracted from the butter.

6 Add the teaspoon of salt, mix it into the butter, and, if you so desire, add herbs, garlic, onion, or any other seasoning that suits your fancy. Place in an airtight container, and use at will within the next 2 weeks, though it will likely be devoured in far less time. Don't forget to tell everyone that you made the butter yourself. This used to be a fact of life, and now it's a great dinner party conversation piece. Imagine?

ESTIMATED COST FOR NEARLY 2 CUPS OF BUTTER AND NEARLY 2 CUPS OF BUTTERMILK: $5.98. Two pints of heavy cream cost $2.99 each. It's a little more costly than purchasing buttermilk and a pound of butter separately, but, then, you wouldn't have this fascinating experience to discuss, would you?

BANANA-WHEAT MUFFINS

{ **Makes 12 muffins, $5.00 to $10.00, 45¢ per muffin** }

If you're like me, you probably routinely end up with at least one banana that has seen less ripe days, but a collection of three gives us a reason to make these delectable, and extremely moist, morsels. Though I was raised on banana bread—my mother also abhors food waste—and there is a bit of an obsession with it for some members of my family, I make muffins in an effort to keep portions in mind. I'm not saying that I'm one of the family members with a banana bread problem, but any time I bake banana bread, half of it mysteriously disappears, and when I awake from my trance, there I am, serrated knife in hand, half a loaf remaining and virtually no recollection of the deed. These muffins are just as addictive, only you'll be very well aware when you've eaten more than the recommended serving size, which, incidentally, is one muffin baked in a standard 12-muffin (2½-inch diameter per each muffin) tin.

8 tablespoons (1 stick) unsalted butter, softened

1 ¼ cups granulated sugar

¼ cup packed brown sugar

3 overripe medium bananas

2 large eggs

½ teaspoon vanilla extract

1 cup unbleached all-purpose flour

½ cup whole-wheat flour

1 ½ teaspoons baking powder

¼ teaspoon kosher salt

¼ teaspoon ground cinnamon

1 cup chopped walnuts (optional)

1 Preheat the oven to 350°F. Grease the muffin tins or line them with baking paper, preferably in fun patterns if you have them. Breakfast should be fun, after all, otherwise, we might dread mornings more than we do.

2 In a large mixing bowl, beat the butter and sugars together until they are light, fluffy, and no longer look like two separate ingredients. Add the bananas, blending until well combined. It's okay if there are random chunks of banana, though you want to blend most of the banana into the sugar mixture. Add the eggs, one at a time, beating until each is fully incorporated into the batter. Add the vanilla and mix well.

3 Combine the flours, baking powder, salt, and cinnamon in a large bowl, then add those dry ingredients to the banana mixture, stirring well to combine. Gently mix the walnuts into the batter.

4 Spoon the batter into the prepared muffin tins until each is filled nearly to the top. Bake for 25 to 30 minutes, until the muffins are golden brown and a toothpick inserted into the middle comes out clean. Allow them to cool in the pan for 5 minutes, then transfer them to a cooling rack, but not before you snag one for yourself (no one is looking, and besides, *you* baked them—you deserve it. Oh, and they *are* portion controlled.) and slather some sweet cream butter over it. Yum.

ESTIMATED COST FOR 12: $5.37. The butter is 70¢ for 1 stick out of a package of 4 that costs $2.79. The granulated sugar costs 23¢, the brown sugar costs 16¢. I buy Fair Trade bananas, which are only slightly more expensive than those not certified Fair Trade. The cost of 3 bananas averages around 98¢, so we'll just call that a dollar. However, in the scheme of things, you might have otherwise thrown these overripe bananas out, so don't be afraid to consider this a net gain as you are actually avoiding food waste by baking them into muffin form. The eggs are no more than 26¢ each, so 52¢. The vanilla extract costs 11¢ for ½ teaspoon. The all-purpose flour is 24¢ per cup, the whole-wheat flour is 12¢ for the ½ cup. The baking soda costs 1½ cents, but we round up, so that's 2¢. The cinnamon is 10¢. The walnuts are $8.69 for a bag containing 4 cups, so that adds $2.17 to the total. If you'd like to avoid that extra expense in nuts, go right ahead and omit them, and tuck that $2.17 back into your pocket. With walnuts, you're looking at 45¢ per muffin, and without, a mere 27¢.

BROWN SUGAR CHOCOLATE CHIP COOKIES

{ **Makes 24 cookies, $5.00 or under, 13¢ per cookie** }

I'm fairly certain it was chocolate chip cookies that started me on a lifetime of dough love. My mother made chocolate chip cookies she called "elephant ears," and I know that in each batch she got a few less of those elephant ears than was intended as a result of me slinking across the kitchen to the dough she had hidden in the corner, tucked away from the counter's edge—as though that would be enough to save it.

In my first apartment, one of my greatest pleasures was making chocolate chip cookies and eating however much dough I wanted to—oooph, not always the best idea. I used my favorite chocolate chip cookie recipe for at least ten years, until one day I considered how it might benefit from a little molasses-y flavor. And how turbinado sugar (sold as Sugar in the Raw, among other brands) might also jazz them up a bit. And you know what? The two of them did.

This is my new perfect chocolate chip cookie recipe—for eating both raw and baked (though there is that whole risk of salmonella thing, so I advise you strongly against it, okay?). Now, I hope you realize that this must be a pretty special cookie to replace a decade-old, tried-and-true recipe. Oh, and it is. Yes. It is.

1 cup plus 2 tablespoons unbleached all-purpose flour

½ teaspoon baking soda

½ teaspoon kosher salt

8 tablespoons (1 stick) unsalted butter, softened

½ cup turbinado sugar

½ cup packed brown sugar

1 large egg

1 ½ teaspoons vanilla extract

¾ cup semisweet chocolate chips (such as Whole Foods 365 brand)

1 Preheat the oven to 350°F (for crispy cookies, preheat to 375°F). While you're there, check to see if you can fit two 9 by 13-inch cookie sheets on the middle rack of your oven. If you can't, set the racks to the positions just above and just below the middle. Grease those two 9 by 13-inch cookie sheets with butter.

2 In a medium mixing bowl, mix the flour, baking soda, and salt together to be sure that the baking soda and salt are evenly distributed. Set the dry ingredients aside.

3 In a large mixing bowl, mix the butter and sugars together until they are light, fluffy, and well combined—also known as creaming the butter and sugar. Add the egg and vanilla, and mix well to combine.

4 Mix the flour mixture into the creamed butter-sugar mixture. Stir until combined, then add the chocolate chips and mix those bad boys in.

5 Using two spoons or a small ice-cream scoop, scoop out the dough and place it on the cookie sheet so that each ball of dough is approximately 2 inches from any neighboring balls of dough. Bake for 10 to 12 minutes, or until the cookies are golden brown, turning the cookie sheets midway through the baking time. If you were unable to fit both cookie sheets on the middle rack, then in addition to turning the sheets midway through baking, you should also switch the top sheet to the bottom rack and vice versa.

6 Allow the cookies to cool on the pan for a few minutes before transferring to a cooling rack, and enjoy, perhaps with a big glass of cold milk, or maybe a coffee or hot chocolate.

ESTIMATED COST FOR 24 COOKIES: $4.20. The flour costs 24¢ per cup, so with the additional 2 tablespoons, that's 27¢. The baking soda is less than a penny—a ha'penny, in fact—but we'll round up and call it 1¢ just the same. The butter costs $2.79 for a package containing 32 tablespoons, and 8 tablespoons is 1 stick, so that's 70¢. The turbinado sugar costs $3.99 for just over 75 tablespoons, so it costs us 32¢ for our 8 tablespoons here. The dark brown sugar costs 4¢ per tablespoon, so that's also 32¢. The egg runs us 26¢. The vanilla extract is 11¢ per ½ teaspoon, so it adds 33¢ to our tally here. The chocolate chips are approximately half of a bag that costs $1.99, so that's one lone dollar added to the tally.

However, if you are a dough eater such as myself, this recipe may yield closer to 22 than 24 cookies. You know, sometimes that wee bit of dough just doesn't seem like enough for a whole other cookie. But this is one of the joys of adulthood. You can eat the dough if you want and no one can reprimand you for it. Except for the USDA, of course.

OATMEAL COOKIES WITH DRIED CRANBERRIES AND CRYSTALLIZED GINGER

{ **Makes approximately 40 cookies, $5.00 to $10.00, 20¢ per cookie** }

As it is well established that I suffer from a raw dough obsession, it also turns out that I have what some may term an obsessive sweet tooth that carries over into dough that has been baked as well. When I make these cookies, it is highly likely that I will eat nothing but these cookies for breakfast and lunch. I blame it on the cookie. They're just so darned tempting. And, in my land of make-believe, the oats and cranberries almost convince me that eating these is kind of like eating granola bars. Almost. Try for yourself and tell me I'm wrong. Though I expect that you might have a slightly less compulsive obsession than I, and probably do not reside in a fantasyland of sweets-eating justification.

1 ¾ cups unbleached all-purpose flour

¾ teaspoon baking powder

¾ teaspoon baking soda

½ teaspoon kosher salt

½ teaspoon ground cinnamon

½ teaspoon ground nutmeg

16 tablespoons (2 sticks) unsalted butter, softened

1 ½ cups packed brown sugar

¼ cup granulated sugar

2 large eggs

2 ½ teaspoons vanilla extract

3 cups old-fashioned rolled oats (not quick-cooking oats)

1 cup dried cranberries

⅓ cup finely chopped crystallized ginger

1 Preheat the oven to 350°F. Grease two 9 by 13-inch rimmed baking sheets using that yet-to-be-thrown-away butter wrapper we've discussed before.

2 Combine the flour, baking powder, baking soda, salt, cinnamon, and nutmeg in a bowl and stir to distribute the baking powder and seasonings evenly.

3 Mix the butter and the sugars until they are light, fluffy, and well combined. Add the eggs and vanilla, and mix until well blended.

4 Stir in the oats, dried cranberries, and crystallized ginger. Using a small ice-cream scoop or two spoons, scoop the dough into mounds and place it onto the baking sheets. Space the mounds of dough approximately 2 inches apart, and bake one baking sheet at a time until the cookies are lightly browned, 8 to 10 minutes, turning the sheet midway through cooking. Let the cookies cool on a rack, and then store them in an airtight container, where they will fare very well for 4 to 5 days.

NOTE: This recipe makes about 40 cookies, so I make 24 cookies (5 of which are promptly eaten out of the oven—egads) and wrap the remaining dough in waxed paper after rolling the dough into a log shape. The dough can then be frozen or refrigerated for future use—baking, eating out of hand (though not advised by me, as there is a health risk involved, people), you name it. The dough will keep for 2 to 3 days in the refrigerator and up to a month in the freezer. In either case, allow the dough to come to room temperature before baking.

ESTIMATED COST FOR 40 COOKIES: $8.11, OR 20¢ PER COOKIE. The flour is $4.49 for 19 cups, so 42¢ for 1¾ cups. The baking powder and baking soda each cost around 1¢, so that adds 2¢. The cinnamon and nutmeg we will add in at 30¢ total. The butter costs $1.40 being 16 tablespoons from 32 at $2.79. The brown sugar is 4¢ per tablespoon, so 24 tablespoons costs 96¢. The granulated sugar is 1¢ per tablespoon, so that's 4¢. The 2 eggs are 52¢. The vanilla extract costs 11¢ per ½ teaspoon, so that adds 55¢ to our tally. The oats cost 21¢ per ½ cup, so $1.26 for the 3 cups we're using. The cranberries are $1.89 per cup. The crystallized ginger is $4.99 for 10 ounces, ⅓ cup is just over 1 ounce, so we round up to 1½ ounces, and that costs 75¢.

VANILLA ICE CREAM

{ **Serves 6 to 8, $5.00 to $10.00** }

When I first got my ice cream maker, I attempted to make chocolate ice cream. When I got to the bit about "freeze the ice cream according to the manufacturer's instructions," things got a little rough. Seems I had misplaced—okay, lost forever—the manufacturer's instructions. So I put the custard, which is what is frozen to make the ice cream, into the ice cream maker freezer bowl, then placed bowl and liquid custard into the freezer, and wondered for years why my chocolate ice cream was so horrible and had to be chiseled out of the ice cream maker. I'm not even completely sure when I realized what I had done wrong, but I can assure you, it was years later. Years. Which would have been highly disappointing to my Nana McCoy, who was famous in her hometown as "The Ice Cream Lady" for the ice cream truck she owned and buzzed about town in, spreading joy with every creamy cupful.

As it turns out, making ice cream is incredibly simple. There are very basic steps that you'll follow each and every time, and rarely are there more than a handful of said steps per recipe, so once you've mastered the basics, you're pretty much set for life. Just be certain to actually follow those manufacturer's freezing instructions, okay? Just like making bread dough, after a few forays into ice cream making, you'll instinctively know when the mixture is ready. In the case of ice cream, this is the point at which it will freeze properly—when the milk proteins are going to work with you and coagulate. With this ice cream, it's the moment when the cream and egg combination no longer appears foamy, when it looks like a smooth pool of vanilla. There is a thickening that happens when the milk or cream is finally cooked to the point that it is ready, and the more you practice—oh, such a horror to have to make more ice cream from scratch in order to practice—the more easily you'll recognize that pancake-batter consistency. And you and yours will be greatly rewarded with tasty, wholesome dessert treats.

I've adapted this recipe from *Ice Creams & Sorbets* by Lou Seibert Pappas.

3 cups heavy cream

1 (4-inch) vanilla bean

4 large egg yolks

⅔ cup sugar

1 Pour the cream into a medium non-reactive (stainless steel) saucepan. Slice the vanilla bean lengthwise, scraping out the vanilla seeds from the pod and adding them to the cream. Once you have removed as many of the vanilla seeds as possible from the pod—don't make yourself crazy about this; remember, ice cream making is *easy*—add the pod to the cream.

2 In a separate heatproof bowl, beat the egg yolks well, then add the sugar and whisk together until the sugar is well blended with the yolks, at which point the mixture will be a light yellow color.

3 Over medium-low heat, stirring continuously, warm the cream, vanilla seeds, and vanilla seedpod until the cream just scalds, which is the point at which steam begins to rise from the cream and foamy bubbles surface around the edge of the pan. At my house, this takes 3 to 5 minutes. You don't want to hit a simmer or a boil, so please do pay attention the entire time you're heating the cream, as this 3- to 5-minute window may vary and it's a short step from scalded to boiling. Once the cream is scalded, remove the pan from the heat.

4 Using a spoon or ladle, slowly add 1 cup of the hot cream to the egg mixture, stirring continuously. The reason you are doing this is to prevent the eggs from cooking to a scramble as a result of heating them too quickly, for scrambled eggs will most definitely ruin the custard. And make for an oddly chewy ice cream.

5 Return the saucepan to medium heat, and now slowly pour the egg and cream mixture into the saucepan with the cream, stirring continuously as you pour. You're still on scrambled-egg-avoidance duty at this point.

6 Keep stirring continuously until the mixture thickens to the consistency of pancake batter and coats the back of a spoon, 15 to 20 minutes. Remove the pan from the heat, and pour the custard into a non-reactive bowl, covering it with plastic wrap so the plastic wrap is touching the top of the custard to keep it from forming an unappetizing crust. Refrigerate until chilled completely, at least 2 hours and up to 24 hours.

7 Once the cream mixture is completely chilled, remove the vanilla bean pod and churn the cream mixture in an ice cream maker according to the manufacturer's directions. The ice cream maker I use requires that I freeze the ice cream maker bowl for many hours before churning the ice cream itself. This would have been handy to know that first time I attempted to make ice cream. Be sure to check the directions on yours so that you don't find yourself with a warm freezer bowl and cold custard. Or a freezer bowl full of ice cream that never gets churned, and instead must be chiseled into bowls. That would be bad.

8 Once the ice cream is churned, move it to an airtight container and place in the freezer for an hour or two until it is fully set, though I am a fan of the soft-serve effect that one gets immediately after churning the ice cream. However, with nearly a quart of ice cream in the end, you'd best freeze some of it to share with others.

NOTE: If you're looking for a fun dessert idea, I highly recommend making ice cream cookie sandwiches with either the Brown Sugar Chocolate Chip Cookies (page 151) or the Oatmeal Cookies with Dried Cranberries and Crystallized Ginger (page 153). Even adults will swoon, so don't save this treatment for children's parties only. Place one cookie smooth side up and spread about ¼ cup of this vanilla ice cream on top of it. Take another cookie, place it smooth side down on top of the ice cream, promptly wrap the ice cream cookie sandwich in plastic wrap, and store it in the freezer until it's time to bring glee to the crowd. I'm telling you. These are always a hit at my house. Always.

ESTIMATED COST FOR ONE BATCH OF VANILLA ICE CREAM: $9.66. The vanilla bean can be yours, with a companion bean for the next batch, for $7.99, so that's $4.00. The cream is $4.50 at $2.99 for 2 cups of heavy cream. The egg yolks, we'll call 26¢ each, even though you should be saving those egg whites for a separate use; but, in the event that you are not, we'll add in the full cost of eggs, which is $1.04. The sugar costs 1¢ per tablespoon, so 10.66 tablespoons cost 12¢.

SWEET CORN AND BASIL ICE CREAM

{ **Serves 6 to 8, $5.00 to $10.00** }

Think back to grade school. Remember that sweet, puffed corn cereal you loved? Now, think back to whenever you last had fresh, local corn. Pretty sweet, right? Exactly. Sweet corn ice cream is actually a common flavor in Mexico, and I love basil with corn. When you're stirring the custard, which is what we call the cream and egg mixture prior to freezing, try not to fall in love with the smell, okay? So to get started enjoying the scent of sweet corn custard, you'll need to fetch yourself some 100 percent cotton cheesecloth and a bit of kitchen twine.

¼ cup packed basil leaves, from
    approximately 3 stems of basil (see Note)

1½ cups corn kernels,
    from approximately 3 medium ears

2¾ cups light cream

4 large egg yolks

⅔ cup sugar

Thinly sliced strawberries, for topping

Whipped cream, for topping

1 Place the basil leaves in the center of an 8-inch-square piece of cheesecloth. Bundle up the cheesecloth around the basil leaves and tie it off as though you are preparing to run away from home or become a hobo with only a bindle—the technically correct name for a hobo's satchel—of basil to sustain you. By this, I mean, bring all four corners of the cheesecloth to the center, and tie the cheesecloth into a bundle using kitchen twine so the basil cannot escape.

2 Working in two batches, puree the corn with the cream. First, place ¾ cup of the corn in your blender or food processor, then add half of the cream and blend until the mixture is smooth. Transfer the first batch of puree to a large saucepan. Repeat with the remaining corn and cream, and transfer

the second batch to the saucepan. Add the basil to the saucepan and stir so it is submerged.

3 In a large, heatproof mixing bowl, combine the egg yolks and sugar, and beat until combined to the point that they begin to turn the color of late-summer golden corn. Set aside.

4 Over medium heat, warm the corn-cream mixture until it just scalds, which is a fancy term for warming until you see steam rising from the surface of the cream and you see foamy bubbles around the edge of the pot, 3 to 5 minutes. However, do pay attention the entire time you're scalding the cream, lest your scald time differs from mine. Once the cream is scalded, remove the pan from the heat.

5 Spoon or ladle approximately 1 cup of the hot corn-cream mixture in a slow stream into the egg and sugar mixture, stirring continuously—you are doing this so that the eggs are gradually brought up to the same temperature as the cream and we can avoid the unpleasant business of scrambled eggs in our ice cream.

6 Once the cup of cream has been incorporated into the egg mixture, slowly pour the cream and egg mixture into the saucepan, stirring continuously. Cook the custard over medium heat, again stirring continuously, until the mixture is the consistency of pancake batter, 20 to 25 minutes.

7 Once the custard is the consistency of pancake batter, remove the pan from the heat. Transfer the custard to a non-reactive bowl, and cover it with plastic wrap so the plastic wrap is touching the top of the custard to keep it from developing a crust. Refrigerate until it is chilled completely, at least 2 hours and up to 24 hours. Remove and discard the bindle of basil leaves before moving on to the freezing process.

8 For a smooth ice cream, use either a fine mesh strainer, or a colander lined with 100 percent cotton cheesecloth and strain the custard into a bowl with a capacity of at least 4 cups. Discard the solids.

9 Churn the strained custard in your ice cream maker according to the manufacturer's instructions. Transfer to a freezer proof container, and freeze for an hour or two prior to serving if you can resist eating it straight from the ice cream maker.

10 Top with strawberries and whipped cream and serve it forth.

NOTE: "Packed" simply means that you're jamming the leaves into the measuring cup such that if you aren't applying some pressure, those leaves will pop back out.

ESTIMATED COST FOR THE BATCH OF ICE CREAM: $7.51. The ears of corn should cost no more than 55¢ each, so that's $1.65. The light cream costs $2.69 for a container holding 2 cups, so an additional ¾ cup adds $1.01, which gets us to $3.70. The basil—ahem—which you should have in a pot on your windowsill at the very least—is half of a supermarket bunch costing $1.99, so $1.00. The eggs—we'll consider the entire cost, though you could make lovely egg white omelets with what remains behind—are 26¢ each, so that's $1.04. The sugar is nearly 11 tablespoons' worth, so that adds 12¢, and there we have it.

WATERMELON-LIME GRANITA

{ **Serves 4, under $5.00** }

One of the quintessential tastes of the summers of my childhood was—no, not watermelon, I'm afraid—a certain tart hard candy that was sold by the shovelful at the snack bar of the pool my family frequented. While I won't bore you now with a rant about the nutritional value of said candy, I will say that this granita will bring you back to those sun-kissed, warm-breezed, poolside days of your youth. Try it and tell me I'm wrong.

4 cups cubed seedless watermelon, from 2¾ to 3 pounds of watermelon

½ cup sugar

The zest and juice of 1 lime

1 Before going a step further, pick through the cubed watermelon and remove any visible seeds. Yes, even seedless watermelon has seeds; it has to reproduce somehow. Now, place 2 cups of the watermelon and ¼ cup water into your blender and whir away. Pour the pureed watermelon into a large bowl (at least 4-cup capacity) and repeat with the remaining 2 cups of watermelon and another ¼ cup water.

2 Add the sugar, lime zest, and lime juice to the watermelon mixture. Stir to dissolve the sugar completely, then cover the bowl and refrigerate it until the watermelon mixture is chilled, at least 2 hours and up to 24 hours.

3 Once the mixture is good and chilly, process it in an ice cream maker according to the manufacturer's instructions. Transfer the now-frozen concoction that would make a rancher rather jolly to an airtight container, and freeze for an hour to allow the mixture to fully set. After eating picnic fare, or barbecue, or, heck, even after some penny candy, serve the granita forth.

ESTIMATED COST FOR FOUR: $2.84. The watermelon costs 75¢ per pound, therefore 3 pounds cost us $2.25. And I know and you know that during the dog days of summer, watermelon costs even less. We are not even talking about water costs here, because water flows from the tap and is free. The sugar costs 9¢ at 19 cups for $3.49. One lime runs us 50¢. Is it me, or does this almost cost less than the candies? Okay, perhaps not, but you see where I'm going with this. Easy, inexpensive—and made with love. Better than snack shack treats any day.

ESPRESSO GRANITA

{ **Serves 6 to 8, $5.00 or less** }

By now you know that I abhor food waste. And I feel strongly that this should also apply to beverage waste. You've probably already noticed a mention or ten of leftover wine being repurposed in many a dish upon these pages, but what about that coffee that gets left behind each morning? Why should we waste that as well? Well, heck, we don't have to— just store the leftovers in an airtight container and place them in the refrigerator for a day or two before you intend to make this, and then, on the appointed day, take the 5 or so minutes of actual active time it takes to fashion this refreshing dessert, which, with the addition of just a little milk in a glass, can also double as a fancy frozen coffee shop-style drink. So sit back and bask in your frugality. For you, my friend, you do not let a thing go to waste, no, you do not.

1 ½ **cups brewed espresso or coffee**

1 ½ **cups water**

¾ **cup granulated sugar**

1 **tablespoon Dutch process cocoa powder, plus additional for garnish (optional, but I do love a little chocolate flavor in my coffee)**

Whipped cream, for garnish

1 Combine the espresso, water, sugar, and cocoa powder in a large mixing bowl and get out your whisk. Whisk vigorously to ensure that all of the sugar dissolves and the cocoa is combined into the mix. If it isn't already cool, cool the espresso mixture completely in the refrigerator for at least 2 hours and up to 24 hours.

2 Now, here comes the personal choice part of the recipe. If you like a creamier texture, process the granita in an ice cream maker according to the manufacturer's instructions, then transfer it to an airtight container, and freeze for an hour before serving.

3 If you prefer a little more of the shaved ice-style texture, place the espresso mixture in a 9 by 13-inch freezer-safe roasting pan, such as Pyrex, and allow it to freeze for 2 hours. Scrape all of the contents of the pan up with a fork, and I do mean all of it. Do not leave any icy bit unscraped. Return it to the freezer for an hour, and then serve it forth with a dollop of whipped cream and a sprinkle of cocoa powder, in an espresso cup if you'd like to earn additional adorable points.

NOTE: I often have this as my morning coffee in the summer. Simply add enough milk to get it to your desired lightness, and there you have a super-inexpensive fancy coffee shop–style drink. Sweet.

ESTIMATED COST FOR FOUR: $1.57. Ding-ding-ding—this is the least expensive stand-alone recipe in the entire book (roasted garlic isn't exactly a snack—at least not for most people I know). And, the lowest cost way to make this is, of course, to use leftover coffee or espresso, but if you were to estimate the cost based on brewing four 6-ounce cups for this specific purpose, and using Fair Trade coffee that costs $12.99 for approximately forty 6-ounce servings, that would be $1.30. The water is free, my friend, for you have running water at your house, or at least I certainly hope you do. Three-quarters of a cup of sugar is 14¢, and 1 tablespoon of cocoa powder is 13¢ for the fancy, imported type.

HEIGHT OF SUMMER BLUEBERRY CRUMBLE

{ **Serves 6 to 8, $5.00 to $10.00** }

Each summer, it is with great excitement that I await blueberry season. My neighbors, a local farm family, grow the sweetest, plumpest blueberries in all the land—or at least in all the land that I frequent—and sell them from a patio table set up in their front yard. Blueberries are abundant and inexpensive at the height of their season, and I scarf up every single pint they place on their table; freezing some for future use, eating many—perhaps too many, if there can be such a thing—out of hand, and crafting this gooey, crumbly treat here. During blueberry season, this crumble travels with me to whatever home I am a guest in, and almost without fail, the hosts ask to keep the remainder when I leave. I am only too happy to oblige, for I have 8 more pints at home and know that 4 more will be on the patio table in the morning. But at least I seem generous.

And this dish seems rich. But it is, in fact, a great frugal treat, as our grandmothers knew all too well as they baked their fresh fruit pies. It doesn't matter the money put into it, so long as the fruit is fresh. And so do feel free to improvise with your favorite summer and fall fruits. Cherries? Peaches? Plums? The choice is yours. Just substitute the same amount of fruit for the blueberries and wow them at your next dinner party.

Filling

2 pints blueberries (approximately 4 cups), rinsed and picked over for under- and overripe berries

1 cup granulated sugar

¼ cup unbleached all-purpose flour

1 teaspoon ground cinnamon

The zest and juice of 1 lemon

Pinch of kosher salt

Crumb Topping

1¼ cups unbleached all-purpose flour

¼ cup granulated sugar

6 tablespoons packed brown sugar

¾ teaspoon ground cinnamon

¼ teaspoon kosher salt

1 stick plus 2 tablespoons unsalted butter, melted

¼ teaspoon vanilla extract

4 Line a 10 by 15-inch rimmed baking sheet with aluminum foil so as to avoid dripping gooey blueberry all over the bottom of your oven during the baking portion of this exercise. Place the crumble on the pan and bake until the topping is a golden brown and the blueberry mixture is bubbling, 55 minutes to 1 hour. If the top is browning too quickly and there is no bubbling to be seen, cover the crumble loosely with foil until it is done. Let the crumble cool for 15 minutes and then serve with Vanilla Ice Cream (page 155). Or with whipped cream. When you do serve it forth, be certain to—discreetly, now—bask in the glow of your dinner hosts' appreciation. Leave them the leftovers. But be sure you have another pie dish at home, for you'll be needing to make another crumble tomorrow.

1 Preheat the oven to 375°F. Grease a 9-inch pie pan with butter.

2 Combine the blueberries, sugar, flour, cinnamon, lemon zest, lemon juice, and salt in a large mixing bowl. Transfer the mixture to the prepared pie pan.

3 Mix together the flour, sugars, cinnamon, and salt in a medium mixing bowl. Add the melted butter and vanilla extract, mixing all until a moist crumb is formed. Cover the mass of berry goodness with the crumb mixture.

ESTIMATED COST FOR ONE CRUMBLE. $8.92. The blueberries are $2.99 per pint. We are using 2 pints, so that's $5.98. Remember we make this during blueberry season, which is early to midsummer. The sugar costs 18¢ per cup. The flour is barely a blip on our budgetary radar, but we shall call it 6¢ just the same. The cinnamon for the entire recipe is approximately 65¢. The lemon costs us 50¢. Moving on to the crumb topping, the flour costs 30¢; the sugar, around 5¢ as we round up here; the brown sugar, 24¢. The butter runs us around 90¢, and the vanilla costs 6¢ for ¼ teaspoon. We'll make like you eat enough per serving to call this a 6-serving crumble, and that renders each serving $1.49, but if you can show enough restraint to serve 8, the cost comes down to $1.12 per person. The addition of Vanilla Ice Cream (page 155) adds around $1.21 per person to the tab.

CORNMEAL CRUST PEACH CROSTATA

{ Serves 6 to 8, $5.00 to $10.00 }

There could be no easier pie in the world than the crostata—at least as far as I'm concerned. Years ago, I was quite intimidated by pie making. Hence, I strove for an early mastery of fruit crumbles, which is also a lovely skill to have. Crostata was the first pastry crust dessert I learned to make, and it is still a favorite. I love the flavor of peaches at their peak—at the end of summer here in New England—and tossed with just a bit of honey, there could not be a more carefree yet impressive summertime dessert. Don't let the simplicity fool you, this dessert here is a showstopper. And don't stop at peaches. This treatment is a friend to stone fruit, so test out plums, nectarines, or a combination of stone fruit and seasonal berries if you're looking to mix it up.

Cornmeal Crust

2¾ cups unbleached all-purpose flour

¼ cup finely ground cornmeal

2 tablespoons granulated sugar

1 teaspoon baking powder

1 teaspoon kosher salt

8 tablespoons (½ cup) very cold vegetable shortening, cut into ½-inch pieces

8 tablespoons (1 stick) very cold unsalted butter, cut into ½-inch pieces

½ to ¾ cup ice-cold water

Peach Filling

6 medium peaches (approximately 2 pounds), halved, pitted, cut lengthwise into ¼-inch slices

¼ cup honey

For Finishing

1 large egg yolk, lightly beaten

1 tablespoon milk (any kind)

1 tablespoon turbinado sugar (sold as Sugar in the Raw), for dusting the crust

1 If, after reading this, you are unsure at all as to how to combine the ingredients for the crust, a quick reading of the Savory Pie Crust recipe (page 134) will allay your fears. In the meantime, we will review the process here.

2 In a large bowl, combine the flour, cornmeal, sugar, baking powder, and salt, mixing well to distribute all of these dry ingredients. Add the shortening and butter to the flour mixture, and blend until the fats are incorporated into the flour yet remain the size of peas.

3 Using a fork or pastry blender if not using a food processor, add the ice-cold water a tablespoon at a time until the dough just comes together, meaning that no loose flour remains in your bowl. Form the dough into a ball. Place a piece of plastic wrap approximately 9 by 12 inches long on your work surface. Turn the dough out onto the plastic wrap, and flatten it into a thick round. Cover all parts of the dough round with the plastic wrap and place it in the refrigerator for 30 minutes and up to 24 hours.

4 In a large bowl, mix together the peaches and honey, allowing the peaches to release their juices, or macerate, for 30 minutes.

5 Preheat the oven to 400°F and get out your 10 by 15-inch rimmed baking sheet.

6 On a lightly floured surface, working from the center of the dough round, roll

out the dough to a misshapen rectangle approximately 10 by 15 inches. I like to do this on a piece of reusable silicone parchment, which makes the transfer of the dough to the baking sheet infinitely easier, as I also bake the crostata on this piece of parchment. You can do the same by rolling the dough out on regular parchment paper and then sliding the dough and parchment paper onto the baking sheet before filling it with the peaches.

7 Place the honeyed peaches and their accumulated juices in the middle of the misshapen dough rectangle, spreading the peaches around so that there is a 2-inch peach-free border of dough. Working from the long sides first, fold that 2-inch dough border back over the peaches, then fold the short sides' 2-inch dough border over the peaches, tucking the corners up and over the dough to be sure all peaches at the edges are sealed in and leaving a center of exposed peaches, like a window of golden summer fruit.

8 In a small bowl, combine the egg yolk and milk, and then brush the egg wash over the crust. Sprinkle the crust with the turbinado sugar, then bake until the crust is golden brown and the peaches are bubbling, 40 to 45 minutes. Remove from the oven and allow to cool for 15 minutes before serving it forth.

NOTE: At my house, we serve the crusty edges of the crostata as breakfast pastry—hey, we're all adults here, we can eat what we want for breakfast, right?—and the peach-laden centers with ice cream—sometimes vanilla (page 155), and sometimes some sale bin Ben & Jerry's Peach Cobbler—purchased with a coupon, of course. Or devoid of topping. It's wonderful any way you choose.

ESTIMATED COST FOR FOUR: $3.17. The crust is a variation on the Savory Pie Crust (page 134), though the addition of the sugar and cornmeal adds 31¢ for the cornmeal, costing $3.29 for 42 tablespoons as it does, and the sugar is an additional 2¢. However, we shave off 6¢ in flour expense as we are using ¼ cup less than in the Savory Pie Crust, so our tally ends up at $2.87 for the crust. Peaches cost $2.79 per pound, and we are using 2 pounds, so that's $5.58. The honey costs $1.00 for 4 tablespoons. The egg wash is factored into the overall modified Savory Pie Crust price, and the tablespoon of turbinado sugar costs 6¢, as it is one of 75 tablespoons in a package costing $3.99. This crostata contains 12 servings for the low, low price of $9.51, so we'll divide our total cost by 3, and that brings us to $3.17 for four.

APPLE CRUMBLE WITH DRIED CRANBERRIES

{ **Serves 6 to 8, $5.00 to $10.00** }

I couldn't resist. It's blueberry crumble during the summer, and apple crumble all fall and into the winter. Thank goodness for fruits that store well for the wintertime. And also for accoutrements such as crystallized ginger and dried cranberries that add variety to this difficult-to-improve favorite.

Apple Filling

3 pounds apples, peeled, cored, sliced into ¼-inch pieces

¾ cup dried cranberries

1 cup granulated sugar

3½ tablespoons unbleached all-purpose flour

1 teaspoon ground cinnamon

1 tablespoon lemon juice

Pinch of kosher salt

Crumb Topping

1¼ cups unbleached all-purpose flour

¼ cup granulated sugar or, for a very molasses-y effect, turbinado sugar

6 tablespoons packed brown sugar

¾ teaspoon ground cinnamon

⅓ cup finely chopped crystallized ginger

¼ teaspoon kosher salt

1 stick plus 2 tablespoons unsalted butter, melted

¼ teaspoon vanilla extract

1 Preheat the oven to 375°F. Grease a 9-inch pie pan employing your uber-resourceful method of using the wrapper from the butter you just melted to make the crumb topping.

2 Combine the apples, cranberries, sugar, flour, cinnamon, lemon juice, and salt in a large mixing bowl, allowing about 30 minutes for the apples to macerate while you make the topping.

3 Combine the flour, sugar, brown sugar, cinnamon, crystallized ginger, and salt in a medium mixing bowl and mix well. Pour in the melted butter and vanilla extract, mixing until a moist crumb is formed.

4 Transfer the apple-cranberry mixture to the pie pan, mounding the apples so that they are highest in the middle of the pan. Top with the crumb mixture, covering all of the apples. Some will try to find a way to make their presence known through their bubbling while baking, so best to tuck them in well now.

5 Bake for approximately 1 hour, or until the topping is a golden brown and the apple mixture is bubbling. Just as with the blueberry crumble (page 164), if the top is browning too quickly and there is no bubbling to be seen, cover the crumble loosely with foil until it is done. Let the crumble cool for 15 minutes and then serve with Vanilla Ice Cream (page 155).

ESTIMATED COST FOR ONE CRUMBLE: $8.11. The apples should be no more than 99¢ per pound, so that runs us $3.00. The dried cranberries cost $1.89 for 1 cup, so our ¾ cup adds $1.42. The sugar costs 18¢ per cup. The flour is 6¢. The cinnamon comes in at 65¢. The lemon costs us 50¢. The flour costs 30¢, the sugar 5¢, as we round up here, the brown sugar, 24¢. The butter costs 90¢, and the vanilla extract is 6¢ for ¼ teaspoon. The crystallized ginger costs $4.99 for 10 ounces. There is just over 1 ounce in ⅓ cup, so we'll call it 1½, and that adds 75¢ to the tally. With 6 servings, this costs $1.35 per person, and for 8 apple-crumble eaters, it's just over $1.01 per person; the addition of Vanilla Ice Cream (page 155) adds another $1.21 per serving.

CIDER-BAKED PEARS

{ **Serves 4, $5.00 to $10.00** }

Pears bruise so easily. They entice me into buying them with their pretty colors—jewel tone reds, soft new-grass greens, mottled sunset pink—and then, within a day of having them in my house, they look like they've been in a barroom brawl, all bruised skin and mushy flesh. But, as it turns out, this is exactly when to turn these formerly gorgeous little bruisers into baked pears.

This dessert, in addition to preventing the dreaded waste of food, is actually pretty healthful. You're upping your recommended daily count of fruits in a completely surreptitious fashion. And these bad boys are decadent enough that you might even forget you're eating within the USDA Food Pyramid for your after-dinner treat. Not to mention—oh, but whoops, I did; I seem to have that tendency—they are super easy to make, and utilize common pantry items you very likely already have on hand. A bite of these baked pears, and you will never resent a bruised pear—no, not ever—again.

1 ½ **cups apple cider**

⅓ **cup packed brown sugar**

⅓ **cup raisins**

⅓ **cup dried cranberries**

2 **tablespoons granulated sugar**

2 **teaspoons ground cinnamon**

4 **medium pears, approximately ½ pound each, unpeeled, halved, and cored (a spoon or a melon baller will do the trick)**

1 Preheat the oven to 350°F.

2 In a small saucepan, heat the cider and brown sugar until it is dissolved. Simmer over medium heat until the cider is reduced slightly, about 5 minutes. Add the raisins and dried cranberries. Simmer for about 2 minutes more, until the raisins and dried cranberries are softened, stirring occasionally. Remove the raisins and dried cranberries with a slotted spoon, and remove the cider-sugar mixture from the heat.

3 In a small bowl, combine the granulated sugar and cinnamon and stir well to combine.

4 In a shallow baking pan (a lasagne pan or similar), arrange the pears cut side up. Pour the cider-sugar mixture over the pears, and then fill the cavity of each pear with the raisins and dried cranberries. Sprinkle the cinnamon sugar over the tops of the pears.

Cover the dish tightly with aluminum foil and bake until the pears are soft and easily pierced with a fork, about 45 minutes. Check midway through the cooking time and add additional cider if necessary. You don't want the liquid to bake off completely.

5 Serve either warm or at room temperature, drizzling the cooking liquid over the top of the pears.

ESTIMATED COST FOR FOUR: $5.85. The apple cider is $2.99 for 8 cups, and we are using 56¢ worth with our cup and a half. The brown sugar is 4¢ per tablespoon. We are using 5.33 tablespoons, which costs us 21¢. The raisins are $1.99 for 24 tablespoons, so that cost is 44¢. The dried cranberries cost $1.89/cup at $4.99 for 12 ounces, so that adds $1.42 to our bill. The pears should be no more than $1.49 per pound, and therefore will come in around $3.00. The sugar and cinnamon mixture consists of 2 tablespoons sugar at 2¢, and the cinnamon is roughly 20¢ for two teaspoons.

   If you don't need a full serving of fruit added to your diet to attain the daily recommendation, and if you'd rather spend less on dessert, cut the serving size back to one pear half per person for an estimated savings of $1.50.

PRUNES IN RED WINE WITH CINNAMON MASCARPONE

{ **Serves 4 to 6, $5.00 to $10.00** }

Prunes are much maligned in certain circles—though not by you and me, for we are not produce snobs—and conjure up unpleasant talk at inappropriate times, do they not? The prune industry even insists that they be called "dried plums." I think it's time to shed this prejudicial thinking and embrace the prune. This dish was inspired by a dessert I had at Frankie's Spuntino in New York City, a tiny jewel box of a restaurant serving wonderful food that you partake of in quite close proximity to your dining neighbors. Their kitchen is even smaller than mine, and I have the cell phone pictures to prove it. Yet another opportunity to debunk the small-kitchen-equals-impossible-to-create-good-food myth—no excuses, people, just get in there and cook.

Oh, yes, so back to the prunes. They are surprisingly rich and filling, therefore the mascarpone is a light and refreshing counterpoint, though I have found that vanilla ice cream is an outstanding partner as well, and, should you find yourself with leftovers, these prunes pair nicely with fresh cheeses and crusty bread. Or, you could do as I do and have some with fresh ricotta and a drizzle of honey for breakfast. Ahhhh, red wine at breakfast? I'm going with the theory that the booze cooks off, okay?

11 to 12 ounces prunes (approximately 2 cups), each prune cut in half

⅓ cup packed dark brown sugar

1½ cups dry red wine

1 stick cinnamon

½ cup mascarpone (see Note)

1 tablespoon granulated sugar

¼ teaspoon ground cinnamon

1 Combine the prunes, brown sugar, red wine, and cinnamon stick in a medium saucepan and bring to a simmer over medium heat. Simmer gently, stirring occasionally, until the prunes are softened and two-thirds of the liquid has evaporated such that you see prunes sitting in liquid, not liquid completely covering prunes, 30 to 35 minutes. Let the prunes stand for 10 minutes prior to serving.

2 While the prunes cook, combine the mascarpone, sugar, and cinnamon in a bowl. Cover and refrigerate until the prunes are ready to serve.

3 Spoon ½ cup of the prunes into each serving bowl and top each serving with 2 tablespoons of the cinnamon mascarpone. Now ask around, does anyone still think poorly of prunes? I'm willing to wager they don't.

NOTE: Mascarpone is an Italian cream cheese. If you aren't able to find it, buy regular cream cheese, let it soften at room temperature, then whip it so that it's nice and fluffy.

ESTIMATED COST FOR FOUR: $7.28. The prunes cost $3.99 for 16 ounces, hence, it was $3.00 for the amount used here. The red wine should come from the least expensive bottle of wine intended to be drunk that you are able to find, and for our purposes here, we'll call that whole bottle $5.00. One and a half cups is just about half of a 750ml bottle, so that cost is $2.50. The brown sugar costs 21¢ at 4¢ per tablespoon for 5.33 tablespoons, and the stick of cinnamon was 1 out of 10 at $4.69, so we'll call that 47¢. The mascarpone was $3.99 for 8 ounces, and we are using 2 ounces at a cost of $1.00. The cinnamon we estimate at 9¢ and the sugar is 1¢ per tablespoon.

To spare waste and some cost, you may also use leftover red wine that you've stored in the refrigerator for a few days. This dish reheats well, and so it may be made a few days in advance to use up that leftover wine that would otherwise go down the kitchen drain. And if you don't waste it, let's just call it "free," shall we? If we agree, that saves $2.50, bringing the total to $5.79.

splurges

Entrées for Special Occasions and Otherwise, serving four for $15.00 to $30.00

HONEY MUSTARD— MARINATED PORK CHOPS WITH PEACH SALSA

{ **Serves 4, $15.00 to $20.00** }

This dish has found itself in the Splurges chapter because of the very official Poor Girl Gourmet policy of using the non-sale price for proteins. However, you can easily make this for less being certain—as you always should—that you purchase the chops on sale. You'll want to start them marinating a day ahead of when you're planning to cook this dish, for it really is worth having the honey mustard seep into the meat for a full day. JR and I enjoy these chops paired with the Smashed Sugar-Roasted Sweet Potatoes (page 116) and the Roasted Garlic Collard Greens (page 94). The contrast of sweet peach salsa, spicy sweet potatoes, and barely bitter collard greens—not to mention the beautiful colors—oh, but then I just did, didn't I?—makes for a happy groan-inducing summertime meal.

Pork Chops and Marinade

⅓ cup extra virgin olive oil

⅓ cup honey

⅓ cup Dijon mustard

4 (½-pound) bone-in pork chops, approximately 1 inch thick

Kosher salt

Freshly ground black pepper

Salsa

2 medium peaches (approximately 1 pound), pitted, chopped into ¼-inch pieces

1 medium shallot, finely chopped

2 tablespoons honey

1 teaspoon fresh thyme leaves, or ¼ teaspoon dried

1 In a small bowl, whisk together the olive oil, honey, and mustard. You're working to make a cohesive marinade here—which, by the way, also happens to be a honey mustard salad dressing—and you do not want pools of oil floating atop the mustard and honey.

2 Season the pork chops with salt and pepper. Place them in a large, airtight container or a 1-gallon-capacity plastic food storage bag. Pour the honey mustard marinade/dressing into the container, being sure to coat the chops completely. Seal your pork chop container of choice, and refrigerate for 3 hours or up to 24 hours.

3 In a small bowl, combine the peach pieces, shallot, honey, and thyme and stir well to evenly distribute the honey. If you'd like to get all of the prep work of marinating and salsa making out of the way at once, it is perfectly fine to refrigerate the salsa for a day prior to using it.

4 If you haven't already, clean your grill rack of debris—if it's like mine, it probably has some debris—and coat it lightly with oil. Now, preheat the grill—to medium if using a gas grill, or, if using charcoal, create an area for indirect grilling. At our house, we do this by cooking around the perimeter of our charcoal grill, the pile of high-heat embers in the center of the grill. Grill the pork chops until cooked through, 3 to 4 minutes per side. Discard the remaining marinade.

5 Serve forth to each of the eagerly-anticipating-pork-delights diners one chop per each. Top each with one-quarter of the salsa, brighten everyone's dish with those sweet potatoes and collard greens as we've already discussed, and now bask in the praise of your dining companions.

ESTIMATED COST FOR FOUR: $19.35. For the purposes of our math here, the chops cost $5.99 per pound. Therefore, you will spend just over $12.00 for 4 chops not on sale. The olive oil costs us 64¢, as it is 5.33 tablespoons from a 33.8-ounce bottle containing 67 tablespoons for $7.99. The mustard costs 84¢, and the honey for the marinade $1.33, coming as it does from a 16-ounce bottle for $3.99. The fresh thyme would be no more than $1.00 as it should be less than half of a supermarket package that costs $1.99. Oh, but why don't you grow some? The peaches cost $2.79 per pound, the shallot costs approximately 25¢, and the 2 tablespoons of honey for the salsa, 50¢.

ALMOND-CRUSTED CHICKEN BREASTS WITH CHERRY—RED WINE REDUCTION SAUCE

{ Serves 4, $20.00 to $25.00 }

JR and I were lying on the beach when I first came up with this recipe. Actually, we were sitting up, eating cherries out of hand as though we might never see cherries again. We've been making breaded, stuffed chicken breasts for years—all different variations on the theme—and we call them "JR's Famous (insert stuffed chicken breast variation name here)"—but these ones, these are our very favorite. The pairing of almonds and cherries in a savory dish is slightly unexpected, and oh so good. It also pairs well with the Risotto Bianco variation (page 123).

Almond-Crusted Chicken

¾ cup panko breadcrumbs

¾ cup whole almonds, ground or very finely chopped

Kosher salt

Freshly ground black pepper

½ cup unbleached all-purpose flour

2 large eggs, lightly beaten

4 (½-pound) boneless, skinless chicken breasts

1 (4-ounce) log goat cheese

½ cup extra virgin olive oil, for frying

Sauce

3 tablespoons extra virgin olive oil

1 medium shallot, finely chopped

1 cup red wine

1 tablespoon honey

8 ounces cherries (approximately 20 whole cherries, or 2 cups), pitted and quartered

1 tablespoon unsalted butter

Kosher salt

Freshly ground black pepper

1 First things first. We need to get our breading and dredging ingredients all arranged. So set up two large dinner plates, one for your breadcrumb-almond mixture, one for the flour, and then a bowl for the eggs.

2 Now, mix the breadcrumbs and ground almonds together on their plate and season them with salt and pepper, then place the flour on its plate, and finally, the eggs in their bowl.

3 Seemingly counter to what you would think, stuffing the meat is actually easier when you make the stuffing incision into the thin side of the breast, where the 2 breasts were once connected. You'll want to slice lengthwise into the middle of the breast, cutting only about halfway into the breast, and leaving the top ½ inch and the bottom ½ inch of the breast uncut so as to not have it fall apart on you.

4 Into the incision, spread 1 ounce of goat cheese, and then close it up as though you never made a cut. Cover the chicken breast with flour, then dip it into the egg in order to cover it completely. Allow any excess egg to drip off, and then coat the breast completely with the breadcrumb-almond mixture. Set the stuffed, breaded chicken breast into a baking dish and repeat the process with the remaining 3 chicken breasts.

5 Once the breasts are all stuffed and breaded, place them into the refrigerator for 30 minutes.

6 Ten to fifteen minutes before the chicken has chilled for the half-hour, prepare the sauce. Heat the 3 tablespoons of olive oil in a large sauté pan over medium heat. Add the shallot and cook until translucent, 2 to 3 minutes. Add the wine, honey, and cherries, and cook until the mixture is thick and syrupy

with about an equal ratio of cherries to liquid, 22 to 25 minutes. Remove from the heat, add the butter, swirling it throughout the sauce, and add salt and pepper to taste. Set aside until it's time to serve.

7 After the chicken has chilled for 30 minutes, preheat the oven to 375°F. Then heat the olive oil in a large, nonstick sauté pan or well-seasoned cast-iron skillet, and, working in small batches so that the breasts fit easily in one layer in the pan, fry them until they are golden brown on each side, 2 to 3 minutes. Place the breasts back in the baking dish, place them into the oven, and bake until they're cooked through, 13 to 15 minutes.

8 Serve each breast forth with the cherry sauce and perhaps start concocting your own "famous" stuffed chicken breast variations.

ESTIMATED COST FOR FOUR: $21.90. The chicken breasts cost $4.99 per pound in the prepackaged case at Whole Foods, so that's going to be approximately $10.00 for the 4 halves. The goat cheese costs $3.99 for a 4-ounce log o' cheese. The flour costs 12¢ for ½ cup. The eggs should cost no more than 26¢ each. The almonds are from a bag of Whole Foods 365 Everyday Value brand that costs $6.99 for 4 cups, so our ¾-cup amount costs us $1.31. The panko breadcrumbs are also Whole Foods 365 Everyday Value brand, and they cost $1.99 for 4 cups, so that's 38¢. The total olive oil used costs $1.32. The shallot costs 25¢, the red wine should be no more than $1.67 as you know to buy bottles costing no more than $5.00—for the purpose of cooking—but still a bottle you would drink, not one labeled "cooking wine." The honey costs 25¢, and the cherries cost $2.00, being that they are ½ pound of a fruit that costs $3.99 per pound. The butter costs a mere 9¢.

Now, you and I have both seen boneless, skinless chicken breasts on sale for less than $4.99 per pound, and I have also seen cherries on sale for half price, so be on the lookout for either, or even both, and save a little more on this summertime splurge.

SOUTHWESTERN-STYLE COBB SALAD

{ Serves 4, $15.00 to $20.00 }

And here is another use for the delicious Lime Corn Cream Dressing (page 25) that also happens to satisfy our avocado cravings, in a riff on Cobb salad. Not only do we have the avocado and black beans for a little Southwestern flair, but we also enjoy the classic combination of hard-boiled eggs and bacon, and together, it's a brightly flavored combination that just about screams "summer"!

2 heads Boston or Bibb lettuce, cored, washed, leaves torn

1 (15-ounce) can black beans or kidney beans, drained and rinsed

2 cups corn kernels (see Note)

1 medium tomato (approximately ½ pound), cored, seeded, finely chopped

4 large eggs, hard-boiled, peeled, halved lengthwise

2 avocados, peeled, pitted, and quartered

4 slices bacon, cooked to desired doneness

Kosher salt

Freshly ground black pepper

½ cup Lime Corn Cream Dressing (page 25)

1 On each of four plates, create a lovely, fluffy base of torn lettuce. Top each with one-quarter of the beans, ½ cup of the corn kernels, one-quarter of the finely chopped tomato, 1 egg each—I like to place them at, say, 12 o'clock and 6 o'clock, for I am a bit anal like that. Then place 2 avocado quarters at, oh, I don't know, maybe 9 o'clock and 3 o'clock on each plate for a symmetrical presentation, if you like that kind of thing. Then crumble a piece of bacon over each of the four plates, season with salt and pepper, and drizzle each with 2 tablespoons of the refreshing dressing.

NOTE: If you are using corn kernels fresh off of the cob, you will need approximately 4 medium ears to end up with 2 cups of kernels. Cook the kernels in a large pot of boiling, salted water until they are golden, 1 to 2 minutes. Drain the corn in a colander, rinse it with cold water, and allow it to cool for 5 minutes before using. Or, you may do this a day in advance and simply store the cooked corn kernels in an airtight container in your refrigerator until you are ready to use them.

POOR GIRL GOURMET TIP: If you wanted to knock a couple dollars plus a bit of change off of the bill, you could substitute—dare I say it? Yes, yes, I do—one head of iceberg lettuce in place of the two heads of Boston or Bibb. There. It's out. It is crisp, refreshing, and you would usually find it shredded with these very same ingredients in a taco or similar snack, so why not? Tuck those two bucks back in your pocket now. Go on. Or put it toward a wedge of watermelon for Watermelon-Lime Granita (page 160). Very summery, indeed.

ESTIMATED COST FOR FOUR: $16.27. The Boston or Bibb lettuce is $2.00 per head, so $4.00 for this dish. The beans are 99¢ per can. The corn could come either from 4 fresh ears at 55¢ per ear or from a 1-pound bag of frozen corn, which can be yours for the low, low price of $1.39. We'll use $2.20 for our mathematics here. The time to make this is while avocados are on sale, which would save you some money and bring this back down into non-Splurge territory. However, the avocados cost $1.99 each, and the tomato should run you around $1.63. The eggs should be no more than 26¢ each, so that's $1.04. Four slices of fancy bacon is about a quarter of a pound costing $6.99, so that's $1.75. The dressing costs 68¢ for ½ cup.

OLIVE CAPER FISH CAKES WITH LEMON-DILL SAUCE

{ Serves 4, $15.00 to $20.00 }

You might have noticed that there isn't a whole lot of seafood in this here cookbook. Right. Like, none but this recipe. It's not that I don't enjoy seafood, it's that I am a bit concerned about the state of our oceans' fish stocks. Many varieties of fish are in danger of being wiped out if we continue consuming them at our current clip, and so we're making just one fish dish here and are using U.S.-farmed tilapia, as it is considered among the best options for seafood consumption by the Monterey Bay Aquarium, according to their seafood guide. In the Resources section of this book, you can find their Web site address for more information.

That said, I happen to love fish cakes, and olives, capers, and crushed red pepper flakes really can't get enough use at my house, so without further ado, we shall set about the making of our responsibly sourced fish cakes which, incidentally, pair well with the Red Potato and Green Bean Salad with Mustard-Dill Sauce (page 113).

1 pound tilapia fillets, approximately 5 (3- to 3½-ounce) fillets, any bones removed, cut into ½-inch cubes

4 ounces Castelvetrano or other good-quality green olives, pitted, finely chopped (see Note)

1 tablespoon capers, packed in water, drained, coarsely chopped (see Note)

1 medium shallot, finely chopped

¼ teaspoon crushed red pepper flakes

1 large egg, lightly beaten

½ cup mayonnaise

1 cup panko breadcrumbs, plus an additional ½ to ¾ cup for coating the fish cakes

Kosher salt

Freshly ground black pepper

½ to ¾ cup extra virgin olive oil, for frying

1 lemon, quartered, for serving

Dressing

1 cup mayonnaise

The zest and juice of 1 lemon

1 tablespoon finely chopped fresh dill

1 tablespoon capers, packed in water, drained, coarsely chopped

⅛ teaspoon crushed red pepper flakes

1 Line a 9 by 13-inch rimmed baking sheet with waxed paper.

2 Combine the tilapia, olives, capers, shallot, and crushed red pepper flakes in a large mixing bowl and stir well. Add the egg, mayonnaise, and 1 cup of breadcrumbs, and mix well. Season with salt and pepper.

3 On a dinner plate or large, shallow pan such as a pie dish, place another ½ cup of the panko breadcrumbs for coating. You may need to add an additional ¼ cup of the breadcrumbs after coating the first 4 fish cakes.

4 Using your hands, form the tilapia mixture into 2- to 3-inch-diameter patties, each roughly ¾ to 1 inch thick. Place each of the fish cakes onto the plate that contains the breadcrumbs for coating. I find that preparing 4 cakes at a time saves me the aggravation of having clumps of breadcrumbs stuck to my hands between each one, so once I have 4 cakes formed up and on the plate, I wash my hands, then coat each of the 4 fish cakes evenly with the breadcrumbs. Transfer those 4 cakes to the waxed paper–lined baking sheet, wash the old hands again, suss out whether or not you need to add the additional ¼ cup of breadcrumbs to the plate for this next batch of 4—adding them, of course, if you do—and then form up the remaining 4, repeating the breadcrumb coating process. Refrigerate the coated fish cakes for 30 minutes before frying.

5 While the fish cakes are firming up in the refrigerator, whisk together the mayonnaise, lemon zest, lemon juice, dill, capers, and crushed red pepper flakes in a small mixing bowl. Cover the dressing and refrigerate it until it's time to serve the whole lot forth.

6 Preheat the oven to 375°F.

7 In a large, nonstick sauté pan or well-seasoned cast-iron skillet, heat ½ cup of the olive oil over medium-high heat until the oil shimmers, 3 to 5 minutes.

8 Working in batches, fry the fish cakes until they are golden brown on both sides, 2 to 3 minutes per side. Once they are browned, transfer them to a baking dish, or, as I do, remove the waxed paper from the area where they were sitting, and place them directly on the baking sheet. Once you have fried all of the fish cakes to golden brown, remove the waxed paper in its entirety from the baking sheet, place those last fish cakes on the baking sheet, and into the oven they go.

9 Bake the fish cakes until they are cooked through, 12 to 15 minutes. Remove from the oven and let them sit for 1 to 2 minutes before serving them forth. Present each of your dining companions 2 fish cakes, a

wedge of lemon, and the dressing on the side, or drizzled over the cakes, this is up to you, and serve them forth.

NOTE: I did find that Whole Foods 365 Everyday Value Ripe Green Pitted Olives, which come in a 6-ounce can, were a good alternative to the Castelvetranos, particularly if you don't have a good source for olives nearby. They cost $1.99 for 6 ounces, and the remaining 2 ounces not called for in the

recipe can easily be snacked upon while the fish cakes chill, so let's just go ahead and say that they would add 24¢ to the total, shall we?

And if you aren't familiar with capers, they are the pickled flower buds of a perennial bush of the same name that grows wild in the Mediterranean, particularly in rocky coastal regions, so it is understandable that capers are often paired with seafood.

ESTIMATED COST FOR FOUR: $18.41. The tilapia costs $9.99 per pound. We are using 1 pound, so we'll call that $10.00. The olives cost $6.99 per pound, so that adds $1.75 to the total. The capers cost $7.99 per pound, but they weigh so little, the 2 tablespoons we used between the cakes and the sauce cost us 25¢. The shallot costs approximately 25¢. The crushed red pepper flakes for the entire dish cost 9¢. The egg will run us 26¢. The mayonnaise for the cakes costs 50¢, the breadcrumbs for the entire dish cost 87¢ as the Whole Foods 365 Everyday Value brand type cost $1.99 for 4 cups. The mayonnaise for the sauce costs $1.00. The dill would be about half of a supermarket bunch costing $1.99, so that will add $1.00 to our bill. The lemons each cost 50¢, and the olive oil for frying costs $1.44 on the high end.

If you wanted to stretch this a bit further, you could serve the fish cakes on your favorite sandwich rolls with the Lemon-Dill Sauce, which would enable you to serve 8 people from this one recipe. Figuring that each roll would cost around 50¢, the cost per serving would then be $2.80, and the total for serving 8 would be $22.41, or 2 meals for four, each costing just over $11.20. And just like that, it's not a Splurge any longer.

LAMB SHANKS IN AN ORANGEY FIG SAUCE

{ **Serves 4, $25.00 to $30.00** }

When days grow shorter and the weather pushes us indoors, I crave slow-cooked meals. This frequently used to mean dishes like osso buco (braised veal shanks) and standing rib roast. However, there are plenty of so-called lesser cuts of meat that are just as flavorful as those fancy cuts. They allow you to enjoy the smell of slow-cooked provisions lilting through the house without causing you to eat pasta with butter all week long because you decimated your food budget. If you have a good butcher nearby, you should suss him or her out, for he or she might have a good price on shanks and the like.

This sauce is a little bit sweet, so if you don't share my unabashed love for sweet and savory combinations you can counter that by adding additional goat cheese crumbled over the top of the dish, spooning less sauce on your plate, or omitting the honey. You could also use different fruits in the sauce. Dried apricots would be pretty amazing, as would my beloved prunes. JR and I love these shanks served with Risotto Formaggio di Capra (page 123) and Caramelized Onions (page 110). It also goes well with Roasted Carrots with Thyme (page 92), or Butternut Squash Risotto (page 126).

4 lamb shanks, approximately ¾ pound each

Kosher salt

Freshly ground black pepper

2 seedless clementines (see Note)

¼ cup extra virgin olive oil

1 medium yellow onion, coarsely chopped

5 cloves roasted garlic (page xvii)

1 tablespoon dried thyme

1 tablespoon Dijon mustard

1 tablespoon honey

2 cups red wine

2 cups chicken stock

6 dried figs, quartered

¼ cup raisins

1 bay leaf

1 tablespoon unsalted butter

1 Remove the shanks from the refrigerator approximately an hour before you intend to start cooking to allow them to come up to room temperature. This allows the meat to cook more evenly as there isn't a cold interior that requires additional time to come up to the proper cooking temperature. Generously salt and pepper the shanks.

2 Cut the clementines into ¼-inch circles. Wheels of clementine, as it were. As you are cutting these into ¼-inch pieces, you may find seeds. If so, just remove them. You don't want to be crunching on seeds at dinner.

3 Over medium-high heat, heat the oil in a Dutch oven or other large, heavy pot with a tight-fitting lid. Working in batches, add the lamb shanks to the oil and brown well on both sides, 3 to 5 minutes per side. Once the shanks are browned, transfer them from the pan to a plate where they will stay until you have prepared the cooking liquid—which later becomes the sauce—at which time you can return them to the pan.

4 Decrease the heat to medium. Add the onion and garlic. Sauté until the onion is translucent, 3 to 5 minutes. Add the thyme, mustard, and honey, and stir to combine, cooking for 1 minute to meld the flavors. Pour in the red wine and cook at a simmer for 1 minute. Add the stock, give it a good stir, and simmer for 1 minute. Return the shanks to the pan, and scatter the clementine pieces, fig pieces, and raisins around the shanks. Toss the bay leaf in as well. The liquid should come approximately halfway up the side of the shanks. Bring to a gentle simmer, cover, and cook, flipping the shanks over a few times during the process to ensure that they are evenly cooked, until the meat falls off the bone—testing with a fork to see if it does. This will take 2 to 2¼ hours.

5 Remove the lamb shanks from the pan, and tent with aluminum foil to keep them warm. Bring the liquid in the pan to a boil and boil until it is reduced by half, 8 to 10 minutes. Remove the pan from the heat and stir in the butter until it is completely melted and combined with the sauce. Remove the bay leaf and serve the shanks and sauce forth.

NOTE: As a purely informational tidbit and because I know you will be wondering, the rinds of the clementines are completely edible, even the bit where the flower meets the fruit is softened enough to eat. I know this, for I tried. All in the name of science. Or love of food. Whichever.

ESTIMATED COST FOR FOUR: $26.23. The lamb shanks are $5.99 per pound. At ¾ pound each, the total cost will be around $18.00. The onion is around 33¢. The olive oil is 48¢. The garlic costs 27¢. The thyme will go into the math at 18¢. The Dijon mustard is 1 tablespoon out of 19 for $2.99, so that's 16¢. The honey is 2 tablespoons at 25¢ each, therefore it costs us 50¢. The 2 cups of red wine should be the least expensive drinkable wine you feel comfortable using. Two cups is approximately two-thirds of a 750ml bottle, and we wouldn't spend more than $5.00 on that, now, would we? So the wine costs $3.34. The chicken stock is half of 4 cups at $2.19 for the Whole Foods store brand chicken stock, so that's $1.10. The figs are approximately 3 ounces from a 10-ounce package that costs $2.99, and they cost us 90¢. The clementines cost $5.99 for 5 pounds. Two clementines weigh around 6 ounces, which adds 45¢ to the tally. The raisins cost $1.99 for 24 tablespoons, so 4 tablespoons costs us 33¢. The bay leaf will add another dime or so to the bill, and the 1 tablespoon of butter is 9¢ at 32 tablespoons for $2.79.

BEEF SHORT RIBS IN MUSHROOM GRAVY

{ **Serves 4, $20.00 to $25.00** }

Here at my house, we love a good, slow-cooked beef short rib. Even in the freewheeling, shopping fool phase of my life, short ribs were oftentimes preferred over a standing rib roast. In fact, any time that JR has been working outside on a raw, blustery day, I try to get a pot of short ribs going—served with Buttery Mashed Potatoes with Roasted Garlic (page 121), there is no surer way to warm the bones.

4 (¾-pound) bone-in beef short ribs (see Note)

Kosher salt

Freshly ground black pepper

¼ cup extra virgin olive oil

1 medium yellow onion, finely chopped

1 medium carrot, peeled, trimmed, finely chopped

1 celery stalk, finely chopped

1 (10-ounce) package white mushrooms, rinsed, trimmed, sliced ¼ inch thick

1 teaspoon dried thyme, or 1 tablespoon fresh

1 tablespoon Dijon mustard

2 tablespoons Worcestershire sauce

2 tablespoons unbleached all-purpose flour

4 cups beef broth

1 Season the short ribs with salt and pepper.

2 Heat the olive oil in a large Dutch oven or other large, heavy pot with a tight-fitting lid over medium-high heat. Working in batches if necessary, add the short ribs and brown on all sides, 3 to 4 minutes per side. Transfer the browned short ribs to a plate while cooking the remaining ribs.

3 Once the whole lot of ribs is browned, decrease the heat to medium and add the onion, carrot, and celery. Cook, stirring frequently, until the vegetables are soft, the onion is translucent, and they are beginning to meld together, for this is our soffritto, 10 to 12 minutes. Add the mushrooms and thyme, cooking until the mushrooms are softened, 3 to 5 minutes.

4 Add the mustard and Worcestershire sauce, and stir to combine. Add the flour and give it a good stir to distribute the flour throughout. Cook for 2 to 3 minutes, until the flour is no longer raw, meaning that you do not see any white, powdery flour in the bottom of your pot.

5 Now that your flour is cooked, add the beef broth, scraping up any browned bits from the bottom of the pan. Return the short ribs to the pan, bring to a gentle simmer, cover, and cook, flipping the short ribs over every 40 minutes to ensure even cooking, until the beef is falling off of the bone and is able to be cut without a knife, 2 to 2 ½ hours, stirring occasionally. Be sure to mind the vigor of the simmer throughout the cooking time, as you do not want mushrooms encrusted on the bottom of the pan when the cooking time comes to an end. Add salt and pepper to taste, and serve it forth, ideally propping up each short rib in a dramatic flourish over Buttery Mashed Potatoes with Roasted Garlic (page 121), and spooning mushrooms and gravy all around as though you are forming a mushroom gravy moat.

NOTE: Short ribs are a fatty cut of meat, and cooking them on the bone means that there will be a fair bit of fat rendered into the dish.

If you are concerned about this, a solution for removing the fat is to prepare the dish the day before you intend to serve it, refrigerate it, and then skim the fat off. At which point, you are free to reheat it whenever you please. Within reason, of course. You don't want to wait a week. Short ribs are a dish that does not suffer in the least for sitting a day or two. However, if the temptation of a bone-warming dish is just too much to bear waiting 24 hours to enjoy, yet fat-skimming *is* something that appeals to you, you can substitute boneless beef short ribs. They are slightly more expensive per pound, though they do help reduce the amount of fat in the dish, and, because there is no bone, you only require ½ pound per person, so roughly 2 pounds to serve four adults.

ESTIMATED COST FOR FOUR: $24.45. Now, ideally, you want to buy short ribs when they are on sale, which can save you as much as $2.00 per pound, as has been my experience. But because it is my way, we will factor in the ribs at the regular price, and that cost is $5.99 per pound. You are aiming for 3 pounds, but as the cows do not grow uniform weight ribs, nor do butchers cut uniform size ribs, we'll add a little extra to the tally and call it $18.00. Oh, and so worth it. The olive oil is 48¢. The onion is 33¢; the carrot, 14¢; the celery, 20¢. The package of mushrooms was $1.99. The flour was right around 1½¢, so we'll be generous and call it 2¢. The thyme was 18¢, or free from your garden or pot of thyme, the Dijon was 16¢, the Worcestershire was 56¢, and the beef broth was the Whole Foods 365 Everyday Value brand that costs $2.39.

VEAL STEW

{ **Serves 4, $20.00 to $25.00** }

As has been previously noted, I am a carnivore, though I do want to know that the animals are treated humanely while they are alive. For this reason, I recommend you spend the extra money on humanely raised veal—those that are not kept trapped in cages and that have unlimited access to their feed.

That appeal now made, this is an easy dish to prepare for company and then reheat when they arrive. The flavors only improve for the sitting, and even if you can't suffer the wait that comes with preparing a dish for consumption on another day, it is incredibly scrumptious immediately upon completion. And even more scrumptious with Basic Polenta (page 118) or Buttery Mashed Potatoes (page 121).

¼ cup plus 2 tablespoons unbleached
   all-purpose flour

1 ½ pounds veal stew meat, cut into
   1-inch pieces

¼ cup extra virgin olive oil

1 medium yellow onion, finely chopped

2 medium carrots, peeled, trimmed, finely
   chopped, plus 1 pound carrots, peeled,
   trimmed, cut crosswise into 1-inch pieces

2 celery stalks, finely chopped

1 teaspoon dried thyme, or 1 tablespoon
   fresh

2 cups beef broth

1 (28-ounce) can fire-roasted whole
   tomatoes such as Muir Glen, or regular
   unroasted whole tomatoes

Kosher salt

Freshly ground black pepper

1 Place ¼ cup of the flour in a medium mixing bowl, and, working in batches, add the veal, tossing to coat with the flour.

2 Heat the olive oil in a large Dutch oven or other large, heavy pot with a tight-fitting lid over medium-high heat. Working in batches, add the veal and brown it on all sides, 1 to 2 minutes per side. Transfer the veal to a plate as you cook the remaining batches.

3 Once the veal is browned, decrease the heat to medium and add the onion, finely chopped carrots, and celery. Cook, stirring frequently, until the vegetables are soft, the onion is translucent, and they are beginning to meld together, in a soffritto-like fashion, 10 to 15 minutes. Add the thyme and the remaining 2 tablespoons of flour, and

continue stirring for 2 to 3 minutes, until the flour is cooked, meaning that the raw flour taste has been cooked out of it. If you still see white, powdery flour, it is not yet done.

4 Add the beef broth, scraping up any browned bits from the bottom of the pan. Add the whole tomatoes and use your stirring spoon to cut them in half. Add the veal and any accumulated juices, then add the 1-inch carrots and stir well. Bring to a gentle simmer, cover, and cook until the veal is tender, 55 to 60 minutes, stirring occasionally to prevent the stew from sticking to the bottom of your pan and starting to burn. That would be unpleasant. Add salt and pepper to taste, and serve it forth.

POOR GIRL GOURMET TIP: This recipe is a wonderful do-ahead dish, so it is a likely candidate for impressing your friends at the very next potluck you attend.

ESTIMATED COST FOR FOUR: $21.75. Or thereabouts. The veal costs $9.99 per pound, and we are using approximately $15 worth. The flour costs 6¢ to coat the veal; the olive oil is 48¢; the onion, 33¢, the carrots, 28¢, and the celery, approximately 40¢. The thyme is 18¢, the additional flour is approximately 3¢. One half of a 4-cup container of beef broth is $1.20. The tomatoes are $2.99, though even when we do splurge, we should still buy them on sale. Hey, a buck is a buck. The carrots cost 80¢ per pound at 5 pounds for $3.99.

value wines

First, A Few Wine Words

VARIETAL: the type of grape used in making a particular wine

BLEND: a wine that is produced from the blending of two or more varietals.

VINEYARD: the actual physical property—the farm—upon which the grapes are grown

VINTAGE: the year in which a particular bottle of wine was produced. Growing conditions vary from year to year, which is why some vintages are considered better than others—those better vintages tend to have optimal growing conditions, namely, good weather.

MOUTHFEEL: the consistency or viscosity of the wine in the mouth

NOSE: the smell of the wine

I was a bartender throughout college and for a few years beyond to supplement my then-meager income, so one might expect that I've been tasting wines for years and years. Alas, this is not the case. The gin joints I worked in were all local-type bars. Wonderful people and uproariously funny stories abound, but wine was not a priority, even, in many cases, to the wine drinkers who frequented those bars.

Early in my television career, a director of photography—the guy who makes the pictures pretty—bestowed upon each of my coworkers and me a bottle of French wine as a holiday gift. I saved it for months, waiting for the proper occasion to drink something so fancily outfitted—its label in gilded script carrying the name of the vineyard, varietal, and vintage all in indecipherable French. At the time, vineyard, vintage, and varietal were also foreign words. JR and I were dating then, and on the appointed special-enough day, we poured ourselves each a glass and were mesmerized. "How can we get another one?" I asked, a touch of panic peppered with longing in my tone, as the last of the wine disappeared.

JR made a pilgrimage—empty bottle in hand—to a local wine shop with a good reputation and expertise in French wines. They didn't have that precise bottle, but they did have something similar. JR carried it back to my apartment, where we reveled in yet another bottle full of character, flavors, and smells we couldn't quite place.

Over the years, JR and I have been fortunate enough to visit wineries in Italy and France—you'll notice a heavy leaning toward Italian wines here—and, in my obsessive reading, and, of course, tasting, of various wines, we have come to have a slightly better vocabulary with which to identify the flavors we find pleasing in wines than we did during those first attempts. Make no mistake, I am always learning, and it is important to note that everyone's palate differs to some degree, so if you sample some of the wines listed here—and I hope you do—you may find you don't agree with my descriptions. That's okay. So long as you find flavors and character you like, our mission is complete. Wine, in my opinion, is about enjoyment, not about snobbery, one-upmanship, or the perfect arsenal of terminology.

These wines are known as value wines, in this case, wines that retail for $15 or under—we do have a $15-or-less theme going here, so I thought we should stick with $15 as our limit for wines as well, though prices may fluctuate from region to region and depending upon the value of world currencies, but you knew that already.

In the interest of trying new flavors, these wines are from lesser-known varietals. I'll wager that you're probably quite adept at locating a Cabernet Sauvignon, Merlot, Chardonnay, Pinot Grigio, or even a Chianti, for a decent price, but, if like me, you find the lower-priced bottlings of those varietals to be a wee bit too generic, tasting simply of "wine," but not possessing their own unique personality, then I think the wines reviewed herein will pique your interest.

It would take a lifetime, I'm fairly well convinced, to make a comprehensive list of value wines, such is the state of the market that indigenous varietals are being reintroduced—or simply appreciated once more—in their home countries each year. Typically, those wines aren't in as high demand as their better-known counterparts, and so they sell for a more wallet-friendly price. This doesn't mean they aren't good wines, it just means that not as many people are in on the secret. But now you are. My hope is that you'll try at least some of these wines and will continue to sample other lesser-known wines that aren't on these pages, knowing that a single chapter in this cookbook couldn't possibly be a complete list of value wines but is a good place from which to start.

In order to give you an idea of what each varietal or blend tastes like, I've listed the name of a representative bottle that I have drunk—ahem, tasted—in each varietal or blend description. Just as JR and I weren't able to find that exact bottle of French wine—our very first foray into wine appreciation—it's entirely likely that you may not be able to find the exact bottle of wine from those listed here in your area. In that case, I recommend you be open to suggestions from your local wine merchant, as he or she can guide you to a wine that is similar in style. If you're just starting to delve into wine exploration, that wine merchant will prove an invaluable resource in your efforts, and will usually be quite happy to share his or her knowledge with you.

bubbles

Moscato d'Asti

Not cloying in the least, this low-alcohol (5.5%), semibubbly wine from the Piedmont region in the northeast of Italy is a perfect aperitif or wine for brunch. Many times, I will serve this light, sweet, effervescent wine when guests first arrive in the warmer weather, as it is refreshing and floral, and always a crowd pleaser. The Tenute Cisa Asinari dei Marchesi di Gresy Moscato d'Asti La Serra 2006 ($12.99/750ml) is a bit of a mouthful in name, but worth seeking out for its toasty, honey and peach flavor, the pale golden color of the wine punctuated by a cluster of tiny bubbles clutching onto the bottom of the glass. This wine makes me think spring, and as such, I would have it with lighter fare, or with dessert, such as Cornmeal Crust Peach Crostata (page 166).

Prosecco

I've long been a fan of Prosecco, Italy's sparkling white wine, and would often serve a cocktail of limoncello and Prosecco to dinner guests as they'd arrive at my house. I have hosted a few Prosecco and pizza parties—homemade pizza, of course—and it's surprising how well bubbly goes with pizza. It has the added allure of bringing sparkling wines into a more "ordinary" realm. I, for one, think the world would be a better place if we didn't always reserve the bubbly for special occasions. And with the affordable prices at which most Prosecco may be acquired, you needn't delay.

There are two fermentations in the creation of sparkling wines. The first one occurs after the harvest. In early, or farm-style, Prosecco production, the grapes were harvested late, so they were laden with sugar, and they would ferment in open vats until winter, when the cold stopped the fermentation process. Then, in the springtime, the warmth would spark a second fermentation, which resulted in carbon dioxide bubbles in the wine. This resulted in a very sweet sparkling wine. In the modern era of Prosecco, and of all sparkling wines, the second fermentation is controlled rather than left to the spring thaw. Champagne, which refers only to the sparkling wines produced in the Champagne region of France, employs a method of introducing that second, bubble-producing fermentation into wines already in the bottle, rather than prior to bottling. This is known as *mèthode Champenoise*. Wines outside of the Champagne region may employ *mèthode Champenoise*, and many sparkling wines do, but only those from Champagne, France, may be called

Champagne. In the case of Prosecco, producers employ *Metodo Italiano*, which introduces the second fermentation in the tank, so prior to bottling. *Metodo Italiano* is a less expensive process than *mèthode Champenoise*. As you can imagine, introducing the second fermentation into individual bottles is a very time-consuming process, whereas introducing it to a vat holding a large quantity of wine prior to bottling involves far less labor, hence, the savings are passed on to the consumer. And we consumers are then able to have sparkling wine anytime we like.

One Prosecco that JR and I sampled is from a large producer, Mionetto, and it was quite pleasant, not astringent at all, and a pleasure to look at as well. In the glass, it was like a snowy dusting on top of a skating pond—as though you happen to have a cross-section view, safely, of course—so white were the bubbles in contrast to the nearly-silver wine. The Mionetto Prosecco Brut ($14.99/750ml) smelled of rose petals and pear, it was dry with hints of pear flavor, and it was a wine I could drink all night—not a wine that is good only for an aperitif and then leaves you thinking, "Okay, I need to move on, this is too tart." No, not at all.

Cava is another budget sparkling wine and is produced in Spain. It employs the *mèthode Champenoise* to achieve its bubbles, but remains a value wine despite this more intensive process. Like Prosecco, Cava lacks the sophistication of true Champagne, though it also is generally more affordable than Champagne. In the interest of full honesty, and knowing that I do not have access to all value Cavas in the world, I was unable to find a Cava I would strongly

recommend in the course of tasting for this book, and so, I will not.

Sparkling Shiraz

The lack of popularity of Sparkling Shiraz outside of Australia is evidenced by the incredible dearth of information available on it. I consulted all of the wine reference books in my house, yet I found only one reference to it, that one being disparaging, citing it as one of the reasons why Australian Shiraz had developed a bad rap. The other reasons for the bad rap of Aussie Shiraz were its use to make cheap whites and fortified wines. Poor fortified wines, they don't deserve that abuse, but that's a topic for another chapter in an entirely different book. In any case, Sparkling Shiraz is made using the *mèthode Champenoise*.

One thing that piqued my curiosity about Sparkling Shiraz was that Australians are rather enamored of it, and Americans are not. I sense that this could be tied up in what we might call the Lambrusco Fiasco of the 1970s and 1980s—inexpensive sparkling red wine with a large marketing budget that undermined what a good sparkling red could actually be. Lambrusco seems still to battle this perception of, well, badness, and as it turns out, so, too, does Sparkling Shiraz. As a side note, I like Lambrusco, just not the fiasco-style Lambrusco.

Sparkling Shiraz is, of course, made from the Shiraz grape, which is widely planted in Australia. One bottle I sampled was Paringa's Individual Vineyard Sparkling Shiraz 2004 ($10.99/750ml). It met all of the value bubbly criteria, fun, sparkling, and acceptable in price. I found that the bubbles were better experienced drinking from Champagne flutes, but decided that the wine and I would be better served by using a regular red wineglass. Once poured into a red wineglass, the bubbles quickly evaporated, but I was then better able to get the full aroma of the wine—hints of honey, cracked black pepper, and berries.

The wine was sweet, a bit syrupy—which isn't a bad thing in this case—tasted slightly of honey and very much of blueberry, but wasn't terribly layered or complex. But did I not say that I was embracing a fun wine? Yes. I did. And this wine is fun. It benefits greatly from being paired with food; JR and I did eat some Gorgonzola dolce with it and found it to be a near-perfect partner, complementing the sweetness of the wine as it did. I also thought it would pair well with the Cinnamon Roasted Chicken (page 71) or the Harvest Salad with Honey-Balsamic Dressing (page 30).

Australians enjoy Sparkling Shiraz with their Christmas turkey, so poultry is a good match. Sparkling Shiraz would also pair nicely with foods that traditionally match with Lambrusco—cured meats and rich cheeses, a salty yin to the sweet yang of the Sparkling Shiraz. Paringa's importer's Web site recommends trying the wine with bacon and eggs. Still with the salty, they are, so it seems as though we're all liking the idea of contrast-to-complement for this wine.

whites

Albariño/Chardonnay blend

Imagine that? I go beating on value Chardonnay in the introduction to this chapter and then immediately throw a blend that includes Chardonnay into this list? Well, it is with good reason. As far as white wines go, I prefer wines that are light and refreshing as opposed to heavy—like an oaky Chardonnay. That said, this wine, The Spanish Quarter Chardonnay Albariño ($9.99/750ml), is decidedly light and refreshing. Albariño is a Spanish grape, grown in the northwestern province of Galicia, just over the border from the growing region of Portugal's Vinho Verde—to be discussed further along in this chapter. It is considered a very high-quality grape, and because it produces little juice, it can command high prices. However, this bottle does not, and for that fact, we can all live our lives a little more refreshed on a hot summer day. The wine smells distinctly of tropical fruit; pineapple and bananas are what I picked up, and it also tastes of tropical fruit, as well as peach. Like a subtle fruity summer drink without the kick of a high-proof liquor. I served this to JR's entire family on a hot July day, and all who partook thoroughly enjoyed it—a perfect aperitif wine, I would say.

Inzolia (also known as Insolia and Ansonica)

When I bought this bottle, I was told that it was a rock star. I'm inclined to think it's more like a crooner—à la Frank Sinatra, smooth and sophisticated. Whether rock star or crooner, it is a superstar in my opinion—Baglio del Sole Inzolia Sicilia 2007 ($12.99/750ml) is by far one of the most interesting whites I sampled for this chapter. At first, I smelled a toasty fire smell, as though the neighbors were having a fire pit and the smoke was wafting toward me, but, no, it was the wine. Then there were toasted almond notes and a herbaceous smell—similar to the overall smell of my garden. The wine is thick, succulent, and coats the mouth, all while being very well balanced and juicy. Each sip made me want more, and this Inzolia is not as tart as many of the other whites featured here. The wine is a rich gold in the glass, like the star that would be on its dressing room door. If only it had a dressing room door.

Inzolia, which is native to Sicily, has traditionally been one of the primary grapes in Marsala, just as Catarratto has. Inzolia did make its way up the coast of Italy to Tuscany, where it is known as Ansonica. Making a break from use in Marsala—I like to make my grapes anthropomorphic whenever possible, as though the grape ran away from Marsala making—Inzolia is now being used to great success in varietal wines. Like this one. Seriously good.

Grillo/Catarratto blend

Both Grillo and Catarratto are grapes indigenous to Sicily, and are more commonly used in the aforementioned famous sweet wine of that island, Marsala. In this dry-style wine—dry simply means that the wine is not sweet—from Salvatore Ajello, the Majus Grillo Catarratto Sicilia 2007 ($12.99/750ml), the grapes come together to form a high-

alcohol (14%) wine redolent of tropical fruit. Despite the high alcohol content, the wine is smooth, with tropical fruit notes on the nose, banana and tropical fruit to taste, and a delightful light metallic gold color to admire in your glass. When I think island whites, I think seafood, so I would try this with the Olive Caper Fish Cakes with Lemon-Dill Sauce (page 183), though it would also be interesting with Honey-Balsamic Chicken Thighs (page 65).

Fernão Pires/Moscatel/Arinto blend

Fernão Pires is the most abundantly planted grape in the Portuguese region of Ribatejo. Cooperativa de Pegõe's Adega de Pegões 2008 ($8.99/750ml) is an incredibly clear— almost water-like—wine in the glass. The bottle is tinted a bit blue, which makes the wine appear a deeper yellow, so don't be confused if you do seek this wine out and it doesn't appear clear in the bottle. It has a very floral smell—orange blossoms and springtime in the Mediterranean come to mind—and is well balanced, pleasantly acidic, but not biting, with a subtle grapefruit flavor. It gets my vote for a good quaffing wine, and at that price, it's inexpensive enough to stock up—your friends will love it at your next barbecue—and it would be perfect with simply prepared seafood. Sustainably raised seafood, of course.

Fiano

Fiano is an ancient grape—even mentioned in writings by Pliny the Elder around A.D. 77—grown primarily in the Italian region of Campania, though it may now be found growing in Basilicata, Puglia, and Sicily. One

bottle I sampled was from Sicilian winemakers Mandrarossa ($9.99/750ml), winners of numerous awards for their efforts. The wine smells of green apple, pear, and citrus, and is extremely pale—the lightest shade of straw—in the glass. It is smooth, slightly sweet with a hint of honey in flavor, and a rich, syrupy mouthfeel. It is high in alcohol, 13.5%, as is frequently the case with wines grown in warmer climates, and does have a bit of a bite, or heat, from the alcohol, though that didn't detract from the wine itself. It would go nicely with Honey Mustard–Marinated Pork Chops with Peach Salsa (page 176), or Cinnamon Roasted Chicken (page 71).

Torrontes

Torrontes is a grape varietal that is grown solely in Argentina, though recent studies reveal that it is genetically the same as Malvasia, a white grape grown in Mediterranean countries. There is speculation that Torrontes was, in fact, introduced to Argentina by Spanish missionaries, and quite a while ago—as in when Spanish missionaries first arrived in Argentina—as Argentines consider Torrontes their national white grape, indicating that their collective memory must not recall a time before Torrontes. Torrontes, as is the case with many Argentine wines, provides a great value and can routinely be found for $10 to $12 per bottle, and at a consistent level of quality at that price.

I found Finca el Origen Torrontes 2007 ($10.99/750ml) to be a very crisp and pleasant wine, and while it had tropical fruit on the nose, I only detected pineapple—and just mildly—in my tasting of the wine. The typical aroma profile of Torrontes includes passion fruit and lychee, which I have to admit I did not identify, but I did pick up a bit of honey aroma in addition to my general "tropical fruit" assessment.

If you're looking for a change of pace from Pinot Grigio or if you want to get away from oaky Chardonnay, I recommend you give Torrontes a try.

Verdicchio dei Castelli di Jesi

Verdicchio has been grown in the Italian region known as Le Marche since at least the fourteenth century. The growing area of Castelli di Jesi is so named because the hill towns surrounding the larger town of Jesi are fortified, like castles (*castelli* in Italian). Verdicchio is an important grape in Le Marche, as is the red varietal Montepulciano d'Abruzzo. The Colle del Sole Verdicchio dei Castelli di Jesi Classico Superiore 2008 ($12.99/750ml)—yes, that is quite the mouthful—that I sampled had a floral nose with hints of tropical fruit and green apple. From certain angles, the wine looked like a transparent moonstone in the glass, so pale is its hue. I found it to be a pleasantly herbal wine that was light and refreshing. The Castelli di Jesi region is located near the ocean, and, as such, its wine would be appropriately paired with seafood, though I think it would be worth trying with Roasted Chicken Legs with Olives (page 73) to contrast with the buttery yet briny flavor of those olives.

Vermentino di Sardegna

Sella and Mosca is one of the most venerated wineries on the island of Sardinia. Their Vermentino di Sardegna La Cala 2007 ($12.99/750ml) is very fragrantly floral, with a hint of sea breeze—I'm not joking, I thought it smelled of the beach—not tanning lotion, mind you, the actual beach. It is a straw-colored pale gold in the glass, and slightly sparkling—only very slightly—to taste. It's a soft wine with light herbal notes, and a bit of minerality as well. Vermentino, the grape, is thought to have originated in Spain, though there is no grape variety in modern Spain that bears similarity in name. Wherever its origin, Vermentino is most often planted in warm, coastal areas, and that should provide you a hint as to what you might like to pair it with: seafood and lighter fare, such as the Olive Caper Fish Cakes with Lemon-Dill Sauce (page 183), and the Southwestern-Style Cobb Salad (page 181).

Vernaccia di San Gimignano

I have been fortunate enough to visit San Gimignano, and, as it was my first experience in a medieval hill town—fortified walls and soaring towers all overlooking rolling hills and patchwork fields—I am completely enamored of its charms. However, its famous wine, Vernaccia di San Gimignano—enjoyed in its home city even as medieval families were planning their towers—stands on its own, deserving of my, and hopefully your, adoration as well. The bottle quaffed for the purposes of this book was Palagetto Vernaccia di San Gimignano 2007 ($13.99/750ml), a syrupy yet refreshing wine with a tingly, thick mouthfeel, its tangy, but sweet flavors reminding me of lightly bubbly honey. I would have this with chicken or pork—it would be smashing with the Honey Mustard–Marinated Pork Chops with Peach Salsa (page 176) or the Honey Mustard and Cider–Marinated Pork Spareribs (page 81)— a little bit of a stretch from the porchetta so popular around central Tuscany, but still in keeping with that spirit.

Vinho Verde

It is with some reservation that I suggest Vinho Verde, but its sheer value has guaranteed its inclusion on this list. Vinho Verde was oft referred to in its homeland of Portugal as "the poor man's Champagne," and, as that nickname implies, it has historically been a slightly frizzante, or bubbly, wine. Not to the same degree as Champagne, Prosecco, or Cava, but just enough that the bubbles do register. Over time, some producers have ventured away from this style, which then gives you some options for a less fizzy wine experience. I do recommend trying Quinta da Aveleda's Vinho Verde 2007 ($7.99/750ml) as a reference point for a slightly bubbly style. There is a slight layer of fizz on the top of the wine when you first pour it into your glass, similar to the bit of foam that appears on water lapping up on the beach. It quickly dissipates, leaving the pale, silvery-gold wine in the glass. It is not a complex wine, but is pleasant, has good acidity, and tastes of citrus, making it a great value for hot summer nights, and a good quaffing wine.

a word on rosé

Rosé has long gotten a bad rap. Apologies to you who enjoy a White Zinfandel more often than now and again, but it is your beloved White Zin that has poisoned the vat for rosé. Where rosé is dry and possessing of structure, White Zin is sweet, and—yeah—sweet. Rosé is made from red grapes, as is White Zin, but White Zin's fermentation stops before all of the sugars are converted to alcohol, hence its cloying nature. I did mention that this chapter would contain my opinions on wine, didn't I? Yes, well some of those opinions are strong.

The skin of grapes is what gives wine its color. In the production of rosé, the skins are left in contact with the fermenting juice for only a short time and then drained off, resulting in a lighter color than a red wine, which is fermented in contact with skins for a longer period, resulting in a deeper color. Rosé is produced in winemaking countries around the world, though the rosé tradition is most strongly associated with the south of France. Each of the world's rosé-producing regions uses different grapes for rosé, hence, there is a wide variety in color—ranging from a light apricot shade to bright purple—and flavor. But always there is structure, and, in my humble opinion, refreshment. Once the summer rolls around, I want only rosé to drink. Except during the day when I have water until I can't stand water for even a second longer and open a bottle of rosé. I usually make it safely to dinnertime before this water rage ensues. And that is convenient, for rosé is a fine accompaniment to a wide variety of dishes—it pairs equally as well with fish as it does with lamb and, yes, that's right, even steak.

In my opinion, it's not necessary to pay more than $15 for an enjoyable rosé experience, and there are plenty to choose from. Just about all wine-producing regions of the world produce rosé—ranging from Argentine Malbec, to Australian Shiraz, to Washington State blends. I sampled a Garnacha rosé from Campo de Borja called ZaZa ($10.99/750ml)—a lively and fruity wine smelling and tasting quite distinctly of strawberries, though those strawberries were possibly candied—as well as a French blend, Domaine de Fontsainte Gris de Gris 2008 ($14.99/750ml), also made from Grenache (*Garnacha* in Spanish), though with the addition of four additional varietals; Mourvèdre, Syrah, Cinsault, and Carignan, which rendered it a much more sophisticated take on rosé, a richer, more copper-pink color in the glass, and a much more balanced wine in general. Castello d'Ama's Rosato 2008 ($12.99/750ml)—*rosato* is Italian for rosé—had a musky, floral note on the nose, and tasted of pure strawberry, the actual fruit, sans candying. So more nuanced than the strawberry of the Za Za. Its pink hue was also less bright than the Za Za, and I would say that it falls between the Za Za and the Gris di Gris in sophistication—oddly, this happens to progress in the same fashion as do the prices of these bottles relative to one another. Imagine that? It doesn't always work that way, though, as I have had lovely and balanced rosés at the lower end of the cost spectrum. In any event, you should

experiment with rosé—if you aren't already a convert, I think you'll be pleasantly surprised.

Why Pay Attention to Who Imports the Wine?

Once you find an importer whose taste you like—these are actual humans with actual taste buds, after all—it's likely that other wines they import will also suit your fancy. It's a good idea to ask your local wine merchant which importers provide good-quality value wines in your region, and, if you find a wine you are absolutely wild about, you can find the importer information on the label on the back of the wine bottle. In most cases, they will have a Web site so you can find out additional information about the wine you're newly enamored of, as well as information on other wines they sell, making it easier for you to find other wines to hold dear.

reds

Cannonau/Garnacha/Grenache

The island of Sardinia produces a wine called Cannonau di Sardegna, the grape being the same as the Garnacha of Spain. The Catalans of Spain ruled Sardinia for nearly 400 years from the 1300s to the 1700s, so it's no surprise that their influence would be felt throughout the island, and wine production is not exempt. You are familiar, now, with Garnacha/Grenache, from our discussion about rosé. The Sella and Mosca Cannonau di Sardegna Riserva 2005 ($14.99/750) is a wine meant for food—it's a bit tannic, with a mushroomy aroma, mild berry and prune-like flavor, a pleasant tartness, and a deep garnet with almost a copper tint in the glass. I would—and did—chill it slightly—for remember, red wine is not meant to be drunk at 80°F (that is not what is meant by "room temperature") and enjoy a glass or two with a slice of Tomato Tart (page 50).

Dolcetto d'Alba

Dolcetto is one of the most important grapes grown in the Italian region of Piedmont, trailing behind its more famous—and far more expensive—counterpart, Nebbiolo. Now, I love me a good Barolo or Barbaresco, but those wines, made from Nebbiolo, are not budget friendly, nor should they be, given their well-deserved reputations. Dolcetto d'Alba imparts some of the same earthiness Nebbiolo-based wines provide, but at a fraction of the cost. Renato Ratti Dolcetto d'Alba Colombe 2005 ($12.99/750ml) is produced in La Morra, a tiny hill town in the Alba region. The wine *is* earthy smelling, with peppery notes, a deep ruby red in the glass. It requires a bit of air to smooth out, so don't be afraid to get all fancy and decant this wine. For that small effort, you'll be rewarded with an extremely rich, tart, berry flavor, with just a hint of tang in the finish. To my mind, this is a winter warmer, perfect with Untraditional Bolognese Sauce (page 58), Ribollita (page 16), sausage, and strong cheeses.

Prieto Picudo/Tempranillo blend

Tempranillo is Spain's most important red grape, and you may, then, be familiar with it from Rioja wines. Rioja, of course, is a well-established growing zone with prices, generally, to match. Tempranillo prefers a northern climate, though heat helps to develop thick skins resulting in a deeper color in the finished wine. For this reason, the terrain of northern Spain, with the cooling effect of mountains to counter high heat in the afternoon, is ideal. Tempranillo is known as Tinta Roriz in neighboring Portugal, and can be found in Port blends there.

Enter Prieto Picudo, a varietal typically used to produce rosé wines and with shockingly little information available as to its history, though Jancis Robinson's infinitely useful book, *Vines, Grapes, and Wines*, did inform me that in 1981, it was the twentieth most-planted varietal in Spain, is comparable to Tempranillo, and is often blended with it.

And that blend works to great effect in the Dehesa de Rubiales Alaia 2006 ($11.99/750ml). The majority of juice comes from the Spanish Grape of Mystery, Prieto Picudo, at 50%. Tempranillo comprises 45%

of the blend, with the remaining 5% Merlot. This wine is ruby red in the glass with earthy, barnyard aromas, smoky tobacco notes, and what I determined to be truffles—the expensive fungi, not the chocolates—with berries in the nose. The berries come through in the tasting of this very smooth yet high-alcohol (14%) wine. If I were having Garlicky Tomatoes and Olives with Whole-Wheat Spaghetti (page 46), I would be opening up a bottle of this wine.

Malbec

The Malbec grape originated in the Bordeaux region of France, where it is known as Cot. It is a rough and rustic grape with a thick skin in its native France, but upon being planted in Argentina, it began to evolve and become more finessed, resulting in smoother, more sophisticated wines. The change in the grape's characteristics between France and Argentina has been attributed to the high altitude of the vineyards in Argentina. The vineyards of Finca el Origen, the producers of a bottle I sampled, are between 1,050 and 1,200 meters (roughly 3,400 to 3,900 feet) above sea level in the upper Uco Valley of Mendoza province. The Andes mountain range marks the western edge of their viticultural zone. It sounds like a fantastic place to visit, drink wine, and admire the mountains.

This is a boozy wine, this Finca el Origen Reserva Malbec 2007 ($10.99/750ml). It is a deep garnet red in the glass, and smells toasty, earthy, and of leather. For you wine connoisseurs out there, after a spin around the glass, the abundant legs present themselves alerting you to the 14.5% alcohol contained within. You want to share this bottle—with a few people—unless your goal is to become drunk. Then go ahead, keep it to yourself.

For those of you non-wine geeks, *legs* is a term that applies to the clear streaks that trail down the glass after you've given the wine a vigorous swirl. More legs means more alcohol. And this wine has legs like a centipede. Only centipedes are gross and make me scream, and this wine is excellent, and I am now screaming it from the mountaintop that is this chapter on value wines.

This Malbec tastes of black cherry, a little bit of the oak from the barrel aging in the form of vanilla, but very subdued vanilla. The wine has a rich, smooth mouthfeel and would be excellent with steak and rich dishes.

Montepulciano d'Abruzzo

This is a warm-climate grape that ripens late in the season—toward the end of September into October. Regulations in this area of Italy—Le Marche, on the Adriatic coast—are such that yields can be small or large, contingent upon the producer's desire. Conventional wisdom is that smaller yields, with a focus on harvesting only the best fruit, result in better-quality wines. The bottle of Montepulciano d'Abruzzo from Capestrano ($9.99/750ml) was a deep, plum-colored purple in the glass and smelled of prunes and tobacco. The prune theme carried over in my tasting; the wine was well rounded, not terribly tannic, and one I would seek out for an everyday wine, particularly to accompany foods that are rich or tomato-based, such as the Untraditional Bolognese Sauce (page 58), Mom's Meatballs and Not My Nana's Red Sauce (page 61), or Pasta Carbonara (page 38), as well as cured meats and strongly flavored cheeses.

The skins of the Montepulciano grape are so rich in chemical compounds that produce its characteristic deep, opaque purple in the glass that the rosé version of Montepulciano, called Cerasuolo—look for it while the weather is warm and your glass demands rosé—requires little contact with the skins in its transformation from grape juice to wine to be rendered a lovely shade of pink.

Rosso Piceno: Sangiovese/ Montepulciano d'Abruzzo blend

Rosso Piceno is a blend of Montepulciano d'Abruzzo and Sangiovese. Sangiovese is the varietal used for classic Tuscan wines such as Chianti, Nobile di Montepulciano (which is no relation to the *grape* Montepulciano d'Abruzzo), and Brunello di Montalcino. I sampled Colle del Sole's Rosso Piceno Superiore ($12.99/750ml). In it, I smelled cherries and blackberries as well as a hint of fireplace aroma—a good wine with which to relax in front of said fireplace, I'm thinking. The wine itself was tangy with berry flavor, buttery, and smooth right from the first pour—not always the case for a wine that's 13.5% alcohol. Like the Montepulciano d'Abruzzo, this blend would also work with those very same rich and tomato-based dishes. Perhaps you and yours should do a tasting to compare the 100% Montepulciano d'Abruzzo with the blend of Rosso Piceno. It's always a bit easier to determine flavors when comparing them in contrast to another wine, and it's a good excuse to gather willing tasters around your table.

Monastrell

Monastrell is grown in the Spanish province of Yecla, which is in the southeastern part of the country, not far from France's western border. Fortunate, then, that Monastrell is a warm weather–loving grape, ripening late in the year—usually in October.

Bodegas Castaño's Monastrell 2007 ($9.99/750ml) is earthy, smelling of blueberry and jam, and tasting of blackberries, reminding me somewhat of fig jam, and with a pleasant tanginess in the finish. The wine is a deep ruby red, and is quite a lovely wine for this price. I would have it with the Lamb Shanks in an Orangey Fig Sauce (page 186).

Negroamaro

One of my favorite everyday wines is Rocca Bella Negroamaro 2007 ($9.99/750ml)—a fruity, eminently drinkable red from Puglia. I happen to purchase this wine from my local neighborhood general-type store. The owner of said store knows quite a bit about wine and stocks his wine section accordingly. I can stop in there if I need the local newspaper, some milk, or a lightbulb, yet still find good-value wines. I tell you this so that you, too, will be open to finding value wines in unexpected places.

So here's the deal with my everyday Negroamaro: It's a deep ruby red in the glass, not terribly complex on the nose; it is slightly sweet, tastes of black cherry, and has a smooth finish. And at just about ten dollars a bottle, it's a great deal. It is imported by Monsieur Touton Selections, a company known not for high marks on the 100-point scale from the wine press, but for its solid value wines. This one certainly fits that billing. And my glass. And my budget.

Another importer whose wines I seem to gravitate toward is Dalla Terra. Their LiVeli Passamante Negroamaro ($10.99/750ml)

is earthy smelling with hints of barnyard and caramel on the nose. I personally like barnyard, seeing as I happen to have something of a barnyard at my house. I suggest you be open to barnyard before out and out dismissing it. The LiVeli Negroamaro is well balanced, with a deep, rich purple color—a teeth stainer for certain—with cherry flavor and a hint of strawberry in the finish.

Negroamaro is grown predominantly in the southern portion of Puglia, which is the heel of the Italian boot, along with Primitivo and Malvasia Nera. It has been a site for viticulture since as early as 2000 B.C. (I'll let you do the math on that, okay?). Negroamaro is the base of nearly all of the red wines of southern Puglia, and you may have already enjoyed it as part of the blend in another value wine, Salice Salentino Rosso. It tends to be a bit robust, but both of these bottlings are smooth and accessible—perfect for everyday sloshers, as I like to say. *Slosher* seems like a good word, wouldn't you agree?

Salice Salentino: Negroamaro/ Malvasia Nera blend

Salice Salentino is a blend of Negroamaro and Malvasia Nera grapes. I thoroughly enjoyed the bottle of Cantele Salice Salentino Riserva 2003 ($12.99/750ml) sampled in the name of making these recommendations. This wine is smooth, with a nose of leather and berries. It would almost be a shame to do this, as this wine should be drunk, but if you had leftovers, the intense prune flavors along with peppery spice notes make this an ideal wine to use for the Prunes in Red Wine with Cinnamon Mascarpone (page 173). However, I would feel much better about it if you drank this with a grilled steak or sausage and the Quick White Beans with Bacon (page 120). Or with a flavorful stinky cheese. Yes, this wine is good enough for those special-occasion cheese splurges we discussed previously.

Nero d'Avola

Nero d'Avola is a varietal native to Sicily. It is often compared to Shiraz: It is big and bold, and may be aged. A bottling I am particularly enamored of is Ajello Majus Nero d'Avola 2006 ($11.99/750ml). You might remember that Ajello's Grillo/Catarratto blend also rocked my world. Salvatore Ajello is a third-generation winemaker, working the vineyards that his grandfather first planted. He has a high regard for nature's role in creating great wines and sees the winemaker as a steward of what the harvest provides. Ajello's Nero d'Avola is a great value that will have you smiling all the way to the bottom of the leather-scented, berry-flavored bottle. It's a perfect match for meat: roast lamb, grilled steak, Untraditional Bolognese Sauce (page

58) and House-Made Egg Pasta (page 53) or a pungent, flavorful cheese. It has a pleasant bite in the finish, though it is very smooth and not at all tannic or imbalanced, as many young, high-alcohol-content wines can be.

Primitivo

Primitivo is a very ancient grape, and is the same grape as Zinfandel in California. The California Zinfandel likely found its way from Europe to California with settlers who had brought vines with them from the Austro-Hungarian rootstock during the 1820s. During the 1970s, scientists discovered similarities between Zinfandel and Primitivo, which they later confirmed were the same grape. The Primitivo of Italy likely arrived from Croatia, where it is known as Crljenak Kastelanski. I think one day I'll take a look at Crljenak Kastelanski to see how terroir affects wine making—despite the fact that I am unable to pronounce said grape name—but for now, our history lesson on Primitivo is complete.

The Primitivo I sampled is Castello Monaci's Piluna Primitivo 2006 ($10.99/750ml). It smells of blackberries, toast, and butter, and I also I thought I detected a sweet sulfur smell, as though someone had lit a sugary match and quickly put it out. Many an aroma arose from the glass, including honey, baked bread, and caramel. The wine was very pleasant tasting, and despite so many scents in the nose, blackberry is the primary flavor when tasting it. An extremely pleasant and drinkable wine, with soft tannins and a lush mouthfeel.

Tannat

Tannat is a highly tannic varietal, with one theory on the origin of its name being that it is derived from "tannin." Makes sense to me: tannin, Tannat. In its native France, it is blended with less tannic varietals and then aged in oak to counter those inherent tannins. But in the high altitude of Argentina's Cafayate Valley—some 6,000 feet above sea level—the cool nighttime temperatures help to contain the natural tannins of this grape while emphasizing its natural deep violet color. Tannat is known as Uruguay's national wine, so it makes sense that it would eventually gain popularity in neighboring Argentina, though it seems just a speck on the Argentine red wine map, where Cabernet Sauvignon, Merlot, and Malbec rule.

With the reduced tannins afforded by the high-altitude growing conditions, the don Rodolfo Vina Cornejo Costas Tannat 2006 ($10.99/750ml) I sampled is a lovely, deep purple-colored red wine with pepper, buttered toast, and a floral tobacco scent on the nose. It was incredibly smooth, thanks to that reining in of the tannins, and that even with its 13.5% alcohol content. In my first taste, I detected raspberry and black cherry. Also in that first taste, I thought, "Wow, smooth." (Have I mentioned "smooth"?)

The don Rodolfo estate is one of just a few in the Cafayate Valley, and those few vintners produce 4% of all of Argentina's wine. The high altitude protects the vines from pollution and disease, and irrigation is provided to a large degree by melting snow. The Tannat is harvested by hand and aged in stainless steel vats before being bottled and then aged in the bottle for an additional four months. This is an outstanding, rich, and smooth wine that is beautiful to look at as well. When your friends wonder aloud how the winemakers at don Rodolfo got the wine to be such a dark purple without the mouth-drying effect of assertive tannins, you can tell them. That's just how it is in the Cafayate Valley at 6,000 feet above the sea.

Touriga Nacional

Alrighty there, party people (or person), heads up. Portuguese wine is coming into its own. Though I am sure there are some who will say that Portuguese wine has already arrived. While I have had some slightly dicey experiences with the lowest end of Portuguese wine—and this, in my adulthood, I might add—I have had some amazingly good, and amazingly inexpensive, Portuguese wines.

Touriga Nacional is the most important red table grape in Portugal, where it is particularly important to the production of Port. Its fruit is small, with low yields, and the smallness of the grapes bestows upon its wine a dark, prune color in the glass. The Quinta do Carniero Pactus Touriga Nacional Estremadura ($14.99/750ml) that I sampled was not quite as purple as other Touriga Nacionals I have tried, but it was still rather opaque and deeply purple-red, just the same. Like the Dolcetto d'Alba, it wouldn't hurt to decant this wine, or allow it a bit of time in the glass to allow air to get at it to give it a chance to open up. It smelled of a tannery—and you should know that I find leather smell in wine appealing—cherry, spice, and prunes, and tasted of cherry. It was quite smooth and well balanced, particularly given its high alcohol content (14%). I would serve this with the Beef Short Ribs in Mushroom Gravy (page 188) or the Blue Cheese Wedge Salad with Grilled Sirloin Tips (page 26), but *not* with the Ginger Soy Sirloin Tip Stir-Fry with Mushrooms (page 87), as that sauce would fight the wine.

Though this next bottle is a blend, the majority of which is Castas Baga, a very widely planted grape in the region of Bairrada, I'm including it here so you'll know to be on the lookout for Portuguese blends that include Touriga Nacional. I have found Touriga Nacional blends that are outstanding values, generally in the $10 to $12 range.

The wine in question is Caves Sao João Frei João 2003 ($9.99/750ml). The wine is tannic, but pleasantly so. There is tobacco and honey on the nose, and the wine itself is full of fruit, with cherry in the finish. It's a balanced, earthy wine that got a big "wow" from me, and then a big "wow" from JR when we tasted it. It is so pleasant, and so affordable, that I think it may usurp the Roccabella Negroamaro as my everyday wine. Or at least alternate with the Negroamaro. So long as it isn't rosé season, that is.

As you can see from this list—a list that just scratches the surface of affordable and interesting wines—there are a great many from which to choose. Be on the lookout also for special deals your local wine merchant offers up—sometimes referred to as "bin end" sales. Essentially, these are overstocks sold at a discount to wine retailers in order to make room for new wines—if it helps, think of them as fashion, or like car model years—we must make room for the new to arrive. The wine retailer therefore passes on the savings to you, and through them, your taste buds and your purse strings can often benefit as well.

Saluté!

menu suggestions

Just so that you have them all in one handy location, here are some recommendations for what to eat with what in order to stay under that $15 limit. Except, of course, when it comes to the Splurges, for they are already over said limit. But, then, you knew that already.

Tomato Tart (page 50)	$8.51		Honey-Balsamic Chicken Thighs (page 65)	$4.96
Simple Green Salad: 5 ounces greens,			Israeli Couscous with Chickpeas	
olive oil, balsamic vinegar	$5.44		and Almonds (page 112)	$6.24
	TOTAL $13.95		Roasted Carrots with Thyme (page 92)	$2.14
				TOTAL $13.34

Untraditional Bolognese Sauce (page 58)	$5.85		Chicken in Cider Gravy (page 67)	$10.92
1 pound of House-Made Egg Pasta			Buttery Mashed Potatoes (page 121)	$ 2.49
(page 53)	$1.50			TOTAL $13.41
	TOTAL $7.35			

1 pound of House-Made Egg Pasta			Chicken in Cider Gravy (page 67)	$10.92
(page 53)	$1.50		Smashed Sugar-Roasted Sweet Potatoes	
8 tablespoons of Harvey Marrs'			(page 116)	$ 3.33
Homemade Butter (page 147)	$1.50			TOTAL $14.25
½ cup grated Pecorino Romano	$0.50			
	TOTAL $3.50		Chicken in Cider Gravy (page 67)	$10.92
			Basic Polenta (page 118)	$ 3.35
				TOTAL $14.27

Honey-Balsamic Chicken Thighs (page 65)	$4.96			
Basic Polenta with Gorgonzola (page 118)	$3.73		Perfect Roasted Chicken with Spicy	
Roasted Beets with Caramelized Beet Greens			Orange Sauce (page 69)	$7.91
and Orange-Walnut Pesto (page 101)	$6.05		Smashed Sugar-Roasted Sweet Potatoes	
	TOTAL $14.74		(page 116)	$3.33
			Roasted Carrots with Thyme (page 92)	$2.14
				TOTAL $13.38

Honey-Balsamic Chicken Thighs (page 65)	$4.96			
Butternut Squash Risotto (page 126)	$7.26			
	TOTAL $12.22		Perfect Roasted Chicken with Spicy	
			Orange Sauce (page 69)	$7.91
			Roasted Beets with Caramelized Beet Greens	
Honey-Balsamic Chicken Thighs (page 65)	$4.96		and Orange-Walnut Pesto (page 101)	$6.05
Buttery Mashed Potatoes (page 121)	$2.49			TOTAL $13.96
Caramelized Onions (page 110)	$2.76			
	TOTAL $10.21			

Perfect Roasted Chicken with Spicy
Orange Sauce (page 69) $7.91
1 cup steamed white rice $1.60
1 pound steamed broccoli $3.99
                          TOTAL **$13.50**

Perfect Roasted Chicken (no sauce)
(page 69) $6.76
Buttery Mashed Potatoes (page 121) $2.49
Mushrooms in Cream Sauce (page 90) $5.44
                          TOTAL **$14.69**

Perfect Roasted Chicken (no sauce)
(page 69) $6.76
Buttery Mashed Potatoes (page 121) $2.49
Caramelized Onions (page 110) $2.76
                          TOTAL **$12.01**

Perfect Roasted Chicken (no sauce)
(page 69) $6.76
Buttery Mashed Potatoes (page 121) $2.49
Roasted Carrots with Thyme (page 92) $2.14
                          TOTAL **$11.39**

Perfect Roasted Chicken (no sauce)
(page 69) $6.76
Roasted Cauliflower (page 108) $3.97
Roasted Garlic Collard Greens (page 94) $3.15
                          TOTAL **$13.88**

Perfect Roasted Chicken (no sauce)
(page 69) $6.76
Pan-Sautéed Corn and Tomatoes (page 98) $5.80
                          TOTAL **$12.56**

Perfect Roasted Chicken (no sauce)
(page 69) $6.76
Zucchini with Pecorino Romano (page 100) $2.99
                          TOTAL **$9.75**

Perfect Roasted Chicken (no sauce)
(page 69) $6.76
Red Potato and Green Bean Salad
with Basil Pesto (page 113) $7.56
                          TOTAL **$14.32**

Cinnamon Roasted Chicken (page 71) $8.31
Israeli Couscous with Chickpeas and
Almonds (page 112) $6.24
                          TOTAL **$14.55**

Cinnamon Roasted Chicken (page 71) $8.31
Basic Polenta (page 118) $3.35
Roasted Carrots with Thyme (page 92) $2.14
                          TOTAL **$13.80**

Roasted Chicken Legs with Olives
(page 73) $6.67
Basic Polenta (page 118) $3.35
Roasted Garlic Collard Greens (page 94) $3.15
                          TOTAL **$13.17**

Roasted Chicken Legs with Olives
(page 73) $6.67
Buttery Mashed Potatoes (page 121) $2.49
Roasted Cauliflower (page 108) $3.97
                          TOTAL **$13.13**

Braised Pork Shoulder (page 77) $7.97
Basic Polenta (page 118) $3.85
Roasted Carrots with Thyme (page 92) $2.14
                          TOTAL **$13.96**

Braised Pork Shoulder (page 77) $7.97
Basic Polenta (page 118) $3.85
Roasted Garlic Collard Greens (page 94) $3.15
                          TOTAL **$14.97**

Braised Pork Shoulder (page 77) $7.97
Smashed Sugar-Roasted Sweet Potatoes
(page 116) $3.33
Caramelized Onions (page 108) $2.76
                          TOTAL **$14.06**

Braised Pork Shoulder (page 77) $7.97
Cider-Braised Fennel (page 104) $3.98
                          TOTAL **$11.95**

Pulled pork sandwich (page 77) $8.53
Honey-Mustard Coleslaw (page 96) $4.30
                          TOTAL **$12.83**

Honey Mustard and Cider–Marinated		Sweet Italian Sausage with Apple	
Pork Spareribs (page 81)	$7.56	and Fennel Seed (page 85)	$8.00
Buttery Mashed Potatoes (page 121)	$2.49	Cider-Braised Fennel (page 104)	$3.98
Roasted Carrots with Thyme (page 92)	$2.14	**TOTAL $11.98**	
TOTAL $12.19			

Honey Mustard and Cider–Marinated		1 pound sausage, grilled	$4.99
Pork Spareribs (page 81)	$7.56	Quick White Beans with Bacon (page 120)	$4.05
Buttery Mashed Potatoes (page 121)	$2.49	Pan-Sautéed Cabbage with Roasted	
Cider-Braised Fennel (page 104)	$3.98	Garlic (page 106)	$2.68
TOTAL $14.03		**TOTAL $11.72**	

Honey Mustard and Cider–Marinated		1 pound sausage, grilled	$4.99
Pork Spareribs (page 81)	$7.56	Quick White Beans with Bacon (page 120)	$4.05
Smashed Sugar-Roasted Sweet Potatoes		Roasted Garlic Collard Greens (page 94)	$3.15
(page 116)	$3.33	**TOTAL $12.19**	
Caramelized Onions (page 110)	$3.12		
TOTAL $14.01			

		4 (¾-pound) chicken legs, grilled	$4.50
		Tangy Barbecue Sauce (page 79)	$1.53
		Pan-Sautéed Corn and Tomatoes (page 98)	$5.80
		TOTAL $11.83	

Sweet Italian Sausage with Apple and		4 (¾-pound) chicken legs, grilled	$4.50
Fennel Seed (page 85)	$8.00	Red Potato and Green Bean Salad	
Pan-Sautéed Cabbage with Roasted		with Basil Pesto (page 113)	$7.56
Garlic (page 106)	$2.68	**TOTAL $12.06**	
TOTAL $10.68			

splurges

Honey Mustard–Marinated Pork Chops		Lamb Shanks in an Orangey Fig Sauce	
with Peach Salsa (page 176)	$19.35	(page 186)	$26.23
Smashed Sugar-Roasted Sweet Potatoes		Risotto Formaggio di Capra (page 123)	$ 7.76
(page 116)	$ 3.33	Caramelized Onions (page 110)	$ 2.76
Roasted Garlic Collard Greens (page 94)	$ 3.15	**TOTAL $36.75**	
TOTAL $25.83			

Almond-Crusted Chicken Breasts with		Lamb Shanks in an Orangey Fig Sauce	
Cherry–Red Wine Reduction Sauce		(page 186)	$26.23
(page 178)	$21.90	Risotto Formaggio di Capra (page 123)	$ 7.76
Risotto Bianco (page 123)	$ 7.16	Roasted Carrots with Thyme (page 92)	$ 2.14
TOTAL $29.06		**TOTAL $36.13**	

Olive Caper Fish Cakes with Lemon-Dill		Lamb Shanks in an Orangey Fig Sauce	
Sauce (page 183)	$18.41	(page 186)	$26.23
Red Potato and Green Bean Salad		Butternut Squash Risotto (page 126)	$ 7.26
with Mustard-Dill Dressing (page 113)	$ 6.54	**TOTAL $33.49**	
TOTAL $24.95			

Beef Short Ribs in Mushroom Gravy
(page 188) $24.45
Buttery Mashed Potatoes with
Roasted Garlic (page 121) $ 3.03
                                     TOTAL   **$27.48**

Beef Short Ribs in Mushroom Gravy
(page 188) $24.45
Risotto Bianco (page 123) $ 7.16
                                     TOTAL   **$31.61**

Veal Stew (page 190) $21.75
Buttery Mashed Potatoes (page 121) $ 2.49
                                     TOTAL   **$24.24**

Veal Stew (page 190) $21.75
Basic Polenta (page 118) $ 3.35
                                     TOTAL   **$25.10**

Veal Stew (page 190) $21.75
Risotto Bianco (page 123) $ 7.16
                                     TOTAL   **$28.91**

Now, what are you doing just sitting there? Let's get cooking!

resources

CANNING EQUIPMENT

For those of you with one nearby, you are likely already quite aware that your local tractor supply company or hardware store has all you need for canning. For those of you without a tractor supply—so, most anyone in a city—here are some resources for acquiring canning gear:

Ball's Fresh Preserving: www.freshpreserving .com

Sur La Table. I happen to love their fancy canning jars for gift giving. And also for hoarding pretty jars of preserves at home. www.surlatable.com

CANNING REFERENCE:

The National Center for Home Food Preservation is funded in part by the USDA, and has a handy Web site where you can find answers to all of your canning and preserving questions: www.uga.edu/nchfp/index.html

FARMERS MARKETS

For locations of farmers markets throughout the United States, visit:

www.localharvest.org/farmers-markets/ or http://apps.ams.usda.gov/FarmersMarkets/

FLOUR

I do not want bromate or bleach in my flour, so I purchase King Arthur Flour, which is unbleached and unbromated. In addition to that, they sell yeast in bulk, which is quite handy and cost effective if you intend to bake yeast breads on a regular basis. And why wouldn't you? Surely you love kneading as much as I do if you're reading about flour here in the Resources list, right? To order directly from King Arthur Flour, visit their Web site: www.kingarthurflour.com

GARDENING KNOWLEDGE AND ASSISTANCE

While this is a lifelong pursuit, you can get a jump start by contacting a Master Gardeners in your area for guidance and answers to gardening questions. Master Gardeners are trained by the USDA in the science of gardening, and in exchange for that training, they volunteer to assist gardeners in learning to grow their own food. There are more than 90,000 Master Gardeners throughout the United States. To find one near you, visit this Web site: www.extension.org/pages/ Extension_Master_Gardener

HAZELNUTS (ALSO KNOWN AS FILBERTS):

I have been able to locate whole hazelnuts at Whole Foods with great regularity, but if you are not able to get to Whole Foods and your local grocer does not carry whole hazelnuts, you can mail-order hazelnuts from either of these sources:

http://www.fastachi.com
http://www.nutsonline.com

MONTEREY BAY AQUARIUM SEAFOOD WATCH
To find out what seafood is okay to eat in order not to deplete the oceans' stock, visit their Web site:

http://www.montereybayaquarium.org/cr/ cr_seafoodwatch/download.aspx

POLENTA (GRITS)
I like the texture of Bob's Red Mill stone-ground cornmeal (also known as grits, as it says on the packaging). Bob's Red Mill also offers a plethora of gluten-free products.

Bob's Red Mill Whole Grain Store
5000 SE International Way
Milwaukie, OR 97222
503.607.6455 phone
800.349.2173 mail order
www.bobsredmill.com

SEEDS
While you can purchase both seed starts—baby plants that have been started for you—and seeds at your local nursery, both Seeds of Change and Seed Savers Exchange are excellent sources of seeds for interesting and rare varieties:

www.seedsofchange.com
www.seedsavers.org

SLOW FOOD USA
Slow Food USA promotes the ideals of Slow Food International—that food should be good, clean, and fair. Which means that food should taste good—hey, we're all about that, aren't we?; that it should be clean—good for our bodies as well as the planet; and that it should be fair—that the people who grow and produce our food should be treated well and compensated properly. To learn more, visit www.slowfoodusa.org.

WINE
I purchase wine from these shops in my area. I highly recommend that you seek out a knowledgeable wine merchant in your area, or contact these folks to inquire about shipping (which, of course, may defeat some of the frugal points we've been making, but this is up to you):

Gasbarro's Wines
361 Atwells Avenue,
Providence, RI 02903
401.421.4170 phone
www.gasbarros.com

Town Wine and Spirits
179 Newport Avenue
East Providence, RI 02916
401.434.4563 phone
www.townwineandspirits.com

Bin Ends Wine
236 Wood Road
Braintree, MA 02185
781.817.1212 phone
Email: info@binendswine.com
www.binendswine.com

WINE IMPORTERS
Wine importers can vary from region to region, so, as previously mentioned, if you enjoy a bottle of wine from a particular importer, you are likely to enjoy other bottles they import. Therefore, it is helpful to make note of those wines-you-like importers' names for your next wine shopping trip.

bibliography

Belfrage, Nicolas, *Barolo to Valpolicella: The Wines of Northern Italy*, Mitchell Beazley Classic Wine Library, 2004

Belfrage, Nicolas, *Brunello to Zibibbo: The Wines of Tuscany, Central and Southern Italy*, Mitchell Beasley Classic Wine Library, 2003

Cernilli, Daniele, and Sabellico, Marco, *The New Italy: A Complete Guide to Contemporary Wine*, Wine Appreciation Guild, 2001

Clarke, Oz, *Oz Clarke's Encyclopedia of Wine*, Simon and Schuster, 1993

Del Conte, Anna, *The Gastronomy of Italy*, Prentice Hall Press, 1987

Fisher, M.F.K., *The Art of Eating (50th Anniversary Edition)*, John Wiley and Sons, Inc., 2004

Gibbs Ostmann, Barbara, and Baker, Jane L., *The Recipe Writer's Handbook (Revised and Expanded)*, John Wiley and Sons, Inc., 2001

MacDonough, Giles, *Portuguese Table Wines: The New Generation of Wines and Wine Makers*, Grub Street London, 2001

Mangnelli, Victtorio, and Petrini, Carlo, *A Wine Atlas of the Langhe: The Great Barolo and Barbaresco Vineyards*, Slow Food Editore, 2003

Piggot, Stuart, *Planet Wine: A Grape by Grape Visual Guide to the Contemporary Wine World*, Mitchell Beazley Drink, 2004

Robinson, Jancis, *Wines, Grapes, and Vines*, Alfred A. Knopf, 1986

Rombauer Becker, Marion; Becker, Ethan; and Rombauer, Irma S., *The Joy of Cooking*, Scribner, 1997

Seibert Pappas, Lou, *Ice Creams and Sorbets: Cool Recipes*, Chronicle Books, 2005

Touring Club of Italy, The, *The Italian Wine Guide: Where to Go and What to See, Eat, and Drink*, 2000

Tyler Herbst, Sharon, and Herbst, Ron, *The New Food Lover's Companion, Fourth Edition*, Barron's Educational Series, Inc., 2007

Spice Trade. (2009), In *Encyclopædia Britannica*, Retrieved August 02, 2009, from Encyclopædia Britannica Online: http://www.britannica.com/EBchecked/topic/559803/spice-trade

a million thanks

Writing a book has long been a goal of mine, perhaps since that first "The Story of Amy" paperback with string binding I crafted in third grade. When I was in my late twenties, I thought I'd write a semiautobiographical novel about my career path called *The Malcontents*. Fortunately for me, it turned out that I wasn't so malcontented after all, and have found joy in creating and sharing my love of food. And in keeping with the self-focused theme, I've now written a semi-autobiographical cookbook. So to those who were here for every last bite, I need to offer up a bit of thanks as well.

To my immediate family, the McCoys. My mother, for instilling a love of cooking and for keeping processed snacks and TV dinners out of our lives for as long as was humanly possible—which technically speaking, was up until second grade (note: McCoy children might have *experimented* with those elongated yellow, frosting-stuffed convenience store cakes, but we quickly learned why the other kids were offering up the trade for our homemade chocolate chip cookies). My father, who has always supported my dreams, as he himself is a dreamer and knows their power. My sister, Seth, for her sage advice at times it was needed. My brother, Nate, for his constant questioning—it is to him that you all are indebted for as much clarity as I can muster. My brother, Ben, for his generous support, superb Master-of-English-language-usage proofreading, and balance of humor and intellect, therefore keeping me balanced throughout. And my sister-in-law Erin, for her support and quest to make all of these Poor Girl Gourmet recipes in a four-week period.

To my in-laws, the Richardsons, who have long suffered my forty-five side dishes at Thanksgiving, and with whom a good time is never far from arising. Joy, Bill, Will, Buffy, Trip, MaryBeth, Kristin, Ian, Kellie, and Eli have all been vocal cheerleaders throughout.

To my dear friends who are too numerous to list, and who have helped immeasurably in getting me to this point. Among them, Kellie, Tammy, Alison, and Jacqueline, who have always believed in me, even when, perhaps, I have not. Celia and Mark, for their wisdom and guidance as I navigate this new course. In addition to Celia, LMK, Andrea, and Mary, for the years of listening to my scheming and venting (perhaps *The Malcontents* isn't such a horrible idea after all); it has been invaluable. To John and Judy, whom I ply with my latest creations, whether they want them or not, and whose gardens I envy greatly. To Mike and Anne, who have supported me in every endeavor I undertake. To Karen and Peter, who, since my long-ago bartending days have given me a vote of confidence that one day I would get this done. And one of whom, I'm sure, has to pay up because I did write a book. To my friends Mark, Frank, and Greg at Gasbarro's for their generosity in sharing their knowledge of wine, and their willingness to humor me as I drone on about it, among the other things I tend to drone on about. Oh, the monster that has been created. To the folks at Grub Street in Boston, where I took a wonderful food writing class, and whose mention of my blog in their newsletter led directly to this book. Special thanks to Amy Farrell and her wonderful grandfather, Harvey Marrs, for so kindly sharing their family lore and fantastic recipes.

To my agent, Eve Bridburg, who saw some sliver of potential in my blog, encouraged me to pursue it, and then guided me through a completely foreign experience. Without your belief in and support of this project, I would not be writing these words. To my editor, Lane Butler, who saw that same promise, understood my vision from the very start, and helped me to execute it. I couldn't be more thrilled. Thank you also to the wonderful team at Andrews McMeel: publisher Kirsty Melville, Tammie Barker, Amy Worley, Holly Camerlinck, and Deborah Golden—their help and expertise has been invaluable.

To all of the people who read the Poor Girl Gourmet blog, post comments, and spread the word to your friends, thank you so much for all of your support. You make my little corner of the Internet seem as though it's the neighborhood joint—a place to hang out and chat—just what I would have wanted had I opened a restaurant or coffee shop instead.

To my husband JR, without whom none of this would be possible. You are my strongest supporter, advocate, and the most amazing friend and husband I could ask for.

Lastly, to my Nana Wilby and Nana McCoy. Nana Wilby for her joie de vivre, laugh (that I was fortunate enough to inherit), and for instilling in me forever a love of Italian food. To my Nana McCoy, who, in all her Britishness, gifted me with a love of words and turns of phrase, as well as a deep and abiding love of ice cream.

about the author

Amy McCoy was a successful freelance broadcast and cable producer for thirteen-plus years, working on graphic packages and on-air promotions for clients such as A&E, The CBS Evening News, Discovery Channel, ESPN, and History. During the economic slow-down at the end of 2008, she launched the Poor Girl Gourmet blog (http:// poorgirlgourmet.blogspot.com) to share her recipes, tips, and techniques to eat high-quality food while keeping a tight budget. She is the leader of Slow Food Rhode Island, and her writing has been featured on the Slow Food USA blog.

Amy has long been obsessed with food and wine, going so far as to study cheese in a course at Boston University, where she earned a certificate in cheese studies. Yes, there is such a thing. Amy relies on techniques learned from her mother, grandmothers, and years of home cooking in her ongoing quest to create memorable meals on a budget.

Amy and her husband, JR, were married in the medieval hill town of Montepulciano, Italy, home of the wine Nobile di Montepulciano, and neighbor to Pienza, famous for its sheep's milk cheese, Pecorino di Pienza. In the days before and after their ceremony, they drove back and forth, forth and back, collecting wine and cheese for themselves and their guests. They live on a circa-1850 gentleman's farm in southeastern Massachusetts with their Golden Retriever, Miele, an assortment of chickens, and an awful lot of bees.

index